AWS SysOps Cookbook
Second Edition

Practical recipes to build, automate, and manage your
AWS-based cloud environments

Eric Z. Beard
Rowan Udell
Lucas Chan

BIRMINGHAM - MUMBAI

AWS SysOps Cookbook
Second Edition

Commissioning Editor: Karan Sadawana
Acquisition Editor: Heramb Bhavsar
Content Development Editor: Alokita Amanna
Technical Editor: Dinesh Pawar
Copy Editor: Safis Editing
Language Support Editor: Rahul Dsouza
Project Coordinator: Vaidehi Sawant
Proofreader: Safis Editing
Indexer: Rekha Nair
Production Designer: Deepika Naik

First published: April 2017
Second edition: September 2019

Production reference: 1260919

Published by Packt Publishing Ltd.
Livery Place
35 Livery Street
Birmingham
B3 2PB, UK.

ISBN 978-1-83855-018-9

www.packt.com

This book is dedicated to the Horde, an extended team of partner solutions architects at AWS. They go above and beyond to work with our emerging partners to help them grow and succeed on AWS. I count everyone in the group among my mentors. They come from a wide array of technical backgrounds and bring an impressive amount of brainpower and creativity to the job. It's a humbling group to work with, and I do my best to try and learn from all of them.

– *Eric Z. Beard*

Packt.com

Subscribe to our online digital library for full access to over 7,000 books and videos, as well as industry leading tools to help you plan your personal development and advance your career. For more information, please visit our website.

Why subscribe?

- Spend less time learning and more time coding with practical eBooks and Videos from over 4,000 industry professionals

- Improve your learning with Skill Plans built especially for you

- Get a free eBook or video every month

- Fully searchable for easy access to vital information

- Copy and paste, print, and bookmark content

Did you know that Packt offers eBook versions of every book published, with PDF and ePub files available? You can upgrade to the eBook version at www.packt.com and as a print book customer, you are entitled to a discount on the eBook copy. Get in touch with us at customercare@packtpub.com for more details.

At www.packt.com, you can also read a collection of free technical articles, sign up for a range of free newsletters, and receive exclusive discounts and offers on Packt books and eBooks.

Contributors

About the authors

Eric Z. Beard, a former United States Marine, has nearly two decades of experience in technology, leading diverse DevOps and solutions architecture teams. Eric is currently a manager at Amazon Web Services in Seattle, Washington, and holds nine AWS certifications.

> *First I have to thank my wife, Kate, for being so patient with me while I worked on this book over many nights and weekends. Without her support, I can't imagine how I'd be successful in any of my endeavors. I would also like to thank Rowan Udell and Lucas Chan, authors of the first edition of the book. They gave me a great foundation to work from, and much of the content they created is still in this edition, mostly intact with minor edits to reflect changes made by AWS since that printing. And a big shout out to the people on the service teams at AWS who work so hard to keep innovating on behalf of customers.*

Rowan Udell has been working in development and operations for 15 years. His travels have seen him work in start-ups and enterprises in the finance, education, and web industries in both Australia and Canada. He currently works as a Technical Director at Versent, an AWS Premier Consulting Partner, working with teams building cloud-native products on AWS. He specializes in serverless applications and architectures on AWS, and contributes actively in the AWS and serverless communities.

Lucas Chan has been working in tech since 1995 in a variety of development, systems admin, and DevOps roles. He is currently a senior consultant and engineer at Versent and was a technical director at Stax. He's been running production workloads on AWS for over 10 years. He's also a member of the APAC AWS warriors program and holds all five of the available AWS certifications.

About the reviewers

Ian Scofield, a former United States Army Officer, has a background in technology and communications. He is a Solutions Architect Manager at AWS and works with his team to build internal applications. He lives in Austin, Texas with his wife, an adorable labradoodle, and a grumpy cat.

Gajanan Chandgadkar has more than 13 years' IT experience. He has spent over 6 years in the USA, assisting large enterprises in architecting, migrating, and deploying applications in AWS. He's been running production workloads on AWS for over 6 years. He is an AWS certified solutions architect professional and a certified DevOps professional with 7+ certifications in trending technologies. Gajanan is also a technology enthusiast who has an extended interest and experience in a variety of topics, including application development, container technology, and continuous delivery.

Currently, he is working with a product company as a DevOps expert, having worked with the Wipro Limited in the past.

Packt is searching for authors like you

If you're interested in becoming an author for Packt, please visit `authors.packtpub.com` and apply today. We have worked with thousands of developers and tech professionals, just like you, to help them share their insight with the global tech community. You can make a general application, apply for a specific hot topic that we are recruiting an author for, or submit your own idea.

Table of Contents

Preface

The AWS platform is developing at a rapid rate and is being increasingly adopted across all industries and sectors. As the saying goes, friends don't let friends build data centers. No matter how you look at it, the model of pay-as-you-go computing, networking, and storage is here to stay. It's also becoming increasingly hard to argue against standing on the shoulders of giants, especially when you look at the rate at which features and enhancements are being added to the AWS platform compared to what you'd typically get out of other cloud providers or a so-called private cloud.

We work with many technical professionals who are highly knowledgeable in their domain, but who are often completely new to the AWS platform. Alternatively, they may be familiar with AWS, but are new to automation and infrastructure code practices.

We wanted to write a book for these people.

This book is intended to kick start your journey on AWS by providing recipes, patterns, and best practices across the areas we are often asked to help with on our consulting engagements. All the recipes and recommendations contained in this book are based on our personal experiences and observations from our time helping customers on the AWS platform.

CloudFormation is the AWS-native method for automating the (repeatable and reliable) deployment of AWS resources, and we use it extensively throughout this book. The recipes that follow will help you get well acquainted with CloudFormation and you'll soon be on your way to customizing and building your own templates. With so much power at your fingertips, there's a lot of potential for finding yourself in a rabbit hole. This book aims to steer you in the right direction and help you adopt the platform in a sustainable and maintainable way.

Who this book is for

This book is for anyone with a technical background who is interested in using AWS, either for moving existing workloads or deploying entirely new applications. Those who want to learn CloudFormation will also find this book useful.

What this book covers

Chapter 1, *AWS Fundamentals*, provides an overview of infrastructure as code, CloudFormation, and the AWS CLI tools.

Chapter 2, *Account Setup and Management*, includes everything you need to know to manage your accounts and get started with AWS organizations.

Chapter 3, *AWS Storage and Content Delivery*, shows how to back up your data and serve file objects to your users.

Chapter 4, *AWS Compute*, dives deep into how to run VMs (EC2 instances) on AWS, how to autoscale them, and how to create and manage load balancers.

Chapter 5, *Monitoring the Infrastructure*, provides an overview of how to audit your account and monitor your infrastructure.

Chapter 6, *Managing AWS Databases*, shows how to create, manage, and scale databases on the AWS platform.

Chapter 7, *AWS Networking Essentials*, introduces private networks, routing, and DNS.

Chapter 8, *AWS Account Security and Identity*, offers advice and practical solutions for managing identities and role-based access.

Chapter 9, *Managing Costs*, provides an overview of how to estimate your spend on the AWS platform as well as how to reduce your costs by purchasing reserved instance capacity.

Chapter 10, *Advanced AWS CloudFormation*, explains how to pursue plans that will enable you to customize the behavior of CloudFormation, and apply your scripts over various regions and accounts.

Chapter 11, *AWS Well-Architected Framework*, introduces the AWS Well-Architected Framework, which was created by AWS following years spent working with clients, to enable them to build secure, highly performant, and reliable systems.

Chapter 12, *Working with Business Applications*, enables you to gain proficiency with these services so that you can supplant costly on-premises assets with cloud-based options.

Appendix, *AWS Partner Solutions*, presents a few recipes covering products offered by members of the **AWS Partner Network (APN)**.

To get the most out of this book

The recipes in this book show you how to deploy a wide variety of resources on AWS, so you'll need at least one AWS account with full administrative access. You'll also need a text editor to edit YAML/JSON CloudFormation templates and the AWS CLI tools, which are supported on common operating systems (macOS/Linux/Windows).

Download the example code files

You can download the example code files for this book from your account at `www.packt.com`. If you purchased this book elsewhere, you can visit `www.packtpub.com/support` and register to have the files emailed directly to you.

You can download the code files by following these steps:

1. Log in or register at `www.packt.com`.
2. Select the **Support** tab.
3. Click on **Code Downloads**.
4. Enter the name of the book in the **Search** box and follow the onscreen instructions.

Once the file is downloaded, please make sure that you unzip or extract the folder using the latest version of:

- WinRAR/7-Zip for Windows
- Zipeg/iZip/UnRarX for Mac
- 7-Zip/PeaZip for Linux

The code bundle for the book is also hosted on GitHub at `https://github.com/PacktPublishing/AWS-SysOps-Cookbook-Second-Edition`. In case there's an update to the code, it will be updated on the existing GitHub repository.

We also have other code bundles from our rich catalog of books and videos available at `https://github.com/PacktPublishing/`. Check them out!

Download the color images

We also provide a PDF file that has color images of the screenshots/diagrams used in this book. You can download it here: `http://www.packtpub.com/sites/default/files/downloads/9781838550189_ColorImages.pdf`.

Conventions used

There are a number of text conventions used throughout this book.

`CodeInText`: Indicates code words in text, database table names, folder names, filenames, file extensions, pathnames, dummy URLs, user input, and Twitter handles. Here is an example: "Next, we define `Resources` parameters."

A block of code is set as follows:

```
Resources:
  ExampleEC2Instance:
    Type: AWS:EC2::Instance
```

Any command-line input or output is written as follows:

```
pip install --upgrade awscli
```

Bold: Indicates a new term, an important word, or words that you see on screen. For example, words in menus or dialog boxes appear in the text like this. Here is an example: "Expand the **Create individual IAM users** section and click **Manage Users**."

 Warnings or important notes appear like this.

 Tips and tricks appear like this.

Sections

In this book, you will find several headings that appear frequently (*Getting ready*, *How to do it...*, *How it works...*, *There's more...*, and *See also*).

To give clear instructions on how to complete a recipe, use these sections as follows.

Getting ready

This section tells you what to expect in the recipe and describes how to set up any software or any preliminary settings required for the recipe.

How to do it...

This section contains the steps required to follow the recipe.

How it works...

This section usually consists of a detailed explanation of what happened in the previous section.

There's more...

This section consists of additional information about the recipe in order to make you more knowledgeable about the recipe.

See also

This section provides helpful links to other useful information for the recipe.

Get in touch

Feedback from our readers is always welcome.

General feedback: If you have questions about any aspect of this book, mention the book title in the subject of your message and email us at `customercare@packtpub.com`.

Errata: Although we have taken every care to ensure the accuracy of our content, mistakes do happen. If you have found a mistake in this book, we would be grateful if you would report this to us. Please visit `www.packtpub.com/support/errata`, selecting your book, clicking on the Errata Submission Form link, and entering the details.

Piracy: If you come across any illegal copies of our works in any form on the internet, we would be grateful if you would provide us with the location address or website name. Please contact us at `copyright@packt.com` with a link to the material.

If you are interested in becoming an author: If there is a topic that you have expertise in, and you are interested in either writing or contributing to a book, please visit `authors.packtpub.com`.

Reviews

Please leave a review. Once you have read and used this book, why not leave a review on the site that you purchased it from? Potential readers can then see and use your unbiased opinion to make purchase decisions, we at Packt can understand what you think about our products, and our authors can see your feedback on their book. Thank you!

For more information about Packt, please visit `packt.com`.

1
AWS Fundamentals

Amazon Web Services (**AWS**) was the pioneer in cloud computing, launching its offering over a decade ago, and it continues to rapidly introduce new services and features based on customer demand. AWS was developed by Amazon.com when the company decided to turn its expertise in building large-scale, reliable, and cost-efficient internet systems into a product that could be used by customers to host their own sites and services.

At the time of writing, AWS has 136 services listed on its web console, ranging from foundational services such as **Identity and Access Management** (**IAM**) and **Elastic Compute Cloud** (**EC2**) to high-level machine learning services such as **Rekognition**. The breadth and depth of the services that are available make it possible to implement almost any idea quickly and efficiently – your imagination is the only true limit to what you can do. But all of those services mean that you – as a developer, systems administrator, or solutions architect – have a lot to learn!

Luckily, we are here to help, and if you stick with us throughout the next 12 chapters, you will have a solid foundation for establishing yourself as an AWS expert.

In this chapter, we will cover the following topics:

- Signing up for an AWS account
- Understanding AWS's global infrastructure
- Using the web console
- Learning the basics of AWS CloudFormation
- Using the AWS CLI

Signing up for an AWS account

To follow along with the recipes in this book, you will need to set up an AWS account. Follow all of these steps to learn how to create an account that you will securely access with an IAM user and a **Multi-Factor Authentication** (**MFA**) device.

How to do it...

Follow these steps to create an AWS account:

1. Create an account at `https://aws.amazon.com/` by clicking on the **Sign Up** button and entering your details:

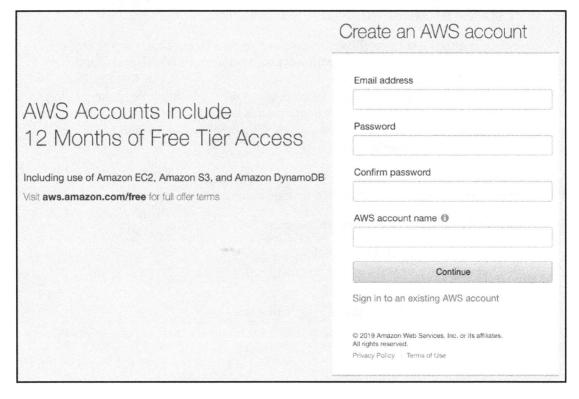

AWS Accounts Include
12 Months of Free Tier Access

Including use of Amazon EC2, Amazon S3, and Amazon DynamoDB

Visit **aws.amazon.com/free** for full offer terms

Create an AWS account

Email address

Password

Confirm password

AWS account name ℹ

Continue

Sign in to an existing AWS account

© 2019 Amazon Web Services, Inc. or its affiliates. All rights reserved.
Privacy Policy   Terms of Use

Creating an AWS account

Even though we will be taking advantage of the free tier wherever possible, you will need a valid credit card to complete the signup process. Go to `https://aws.amazon.com/free/` for more information. Note that the free tier only applies for the first year of your account's lifetime.

2. Before we get started using that shiny new account, let's go over some best practices regarding basic account security. The very first thing you should do as the owner of an AWS account is enable MFA on the root login:

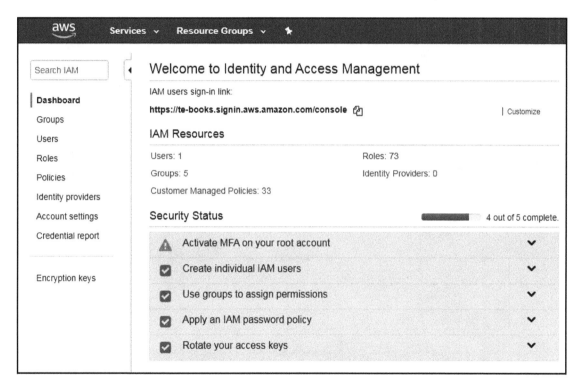

Identity and Access Management

Protect your logins with MFA. Check out this article by Okta on why MFA is a good idea:
`https://www.okta.com/identity-101/why-mfa-is-everywhere/`.

3. As you can see, when you first visit the IAM console, AWS recommends that you **Activate MFA** as the next step to improve your security status. Expand the **Activate MFA** section and click through it to get to your security credentials screen:

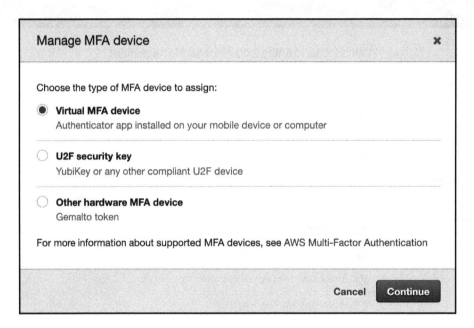

Managing the MFA device

4. Choose the type of MFA device you prefer and complete the setup. If you choose to use a virtual device, note how the app on your phone saves your data. Some apps, such as Google Authenticator, don't back up your data to the cloud, so, if you lose your phone, you will no longer be able to log in to your account. Try apps such as Authy or LastPass Authenticator if you want your MFA device to be synced with an online account.

MFA is an essential extra layer of security that you should apply to all of your online accounts, not just AWS. Now that you have protected your root login with MFA, it's time to take your account security to the next level by creating an IAM account for routine access. Let's get started:

Never use the root login account for routine access. Secure the root credentials and the MFA device so that a very limited group of people have access to them, for use only when absolutely necessary. This will reduce the chances of a bad actor compromising your account.

1. Expand the **Create individual IAM users** section and click **Manage Users**:

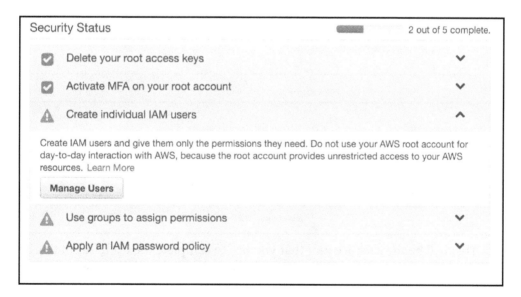

Manage Users

2. Add a new user account:

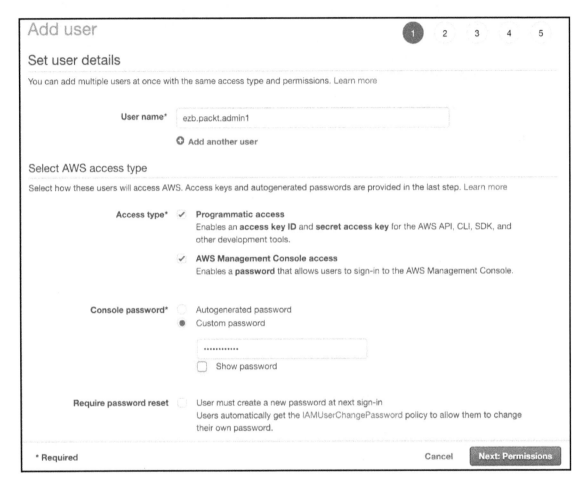

Adding a new user account

This will be the user account that you use to complete the exercises in this book. On the next screen, you will be asked to create a group for this user.

3. Create a group called `Admins` and select **AdministratorAccess**:

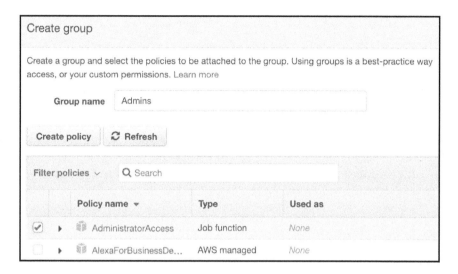

Creating a group

Once you have finished creating the new IAM user, make sure that you save these credentials so that you can access the CLI later.

4. One last thing we will do before logging out of the root is apply a password policy to the account so that all the users are required to have strong passwords:

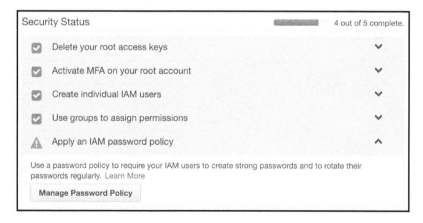

Password policy

5. Once you have done this and see five green checkboxes under **Security Status**, log out of the root user and log back in as your newly created user.

How it works...

When you create an IAM user within your AWS account, you are addressing authentication, which answers the question, *Who is this user?* By itself, a user has no rights to accomplish anything in your account. Access management, or authorization, determines what the principal identities within your account can do. Authorization answers the question, *What is this user allowed to do?* In AWS, you create policies that define what those principals are allowed to do. Policies are attached to users, roles, and groups.

There's more...

Keep in mind that changes that are made to users, groups, and roles need to be consistent eventually. This means that those changes might not be immediately available across your entire account. AWS recommends that you do not include IAM changes in latency-sensitive code.

See also

- Check out the *AWS Organizations* and *AWS Control Tower* recipes in Chapter 2, *Account Setup and Management*, for an in-depth look at setting up multiple accounts for your company's cloud-based applications

Understanding AWS's global infrastructure

One of the primary benefits of building your applications on the AWS cloud is that you can deploy globally in minutes. The global infrastructure is divided up into segments called regions. Each region is completely isolated from other regions, meaning that a region has its own independent installations of AWS services, and customer data will never flow out of that region unless an application is designed to export it over the internet. At the time of writing, there are 20 regions around the world.

Regions and availability zones

A region is further subdivided into **availability zones** (**AZ**), of which there are currently 60. A typical region has three availability zones, which are closely placed clusters of data centers with link speeds high enough that all resources within an availability zone are essentially treated as a single local network. AWS carefully plans the location of data centers within an AZ so that the separate AZs within a region have unique geographic profiles – for example, flood plains are taken into consideration so that, if a rare natural disaster occurs, only one of the AZs within the region will be affected. However, AZs are still close enough together that the network connection between them is very fast.

The design of this global infrastructure allows customers to create highly fault-tolerant and performant applications. An example of the resilience that can be created by using multiple availability zones is Amazon S3, which achieves an incredible 11 x 9s of durability for objects stored by customers. That's 99.999999999%, which means that, in theory, if you stored 10 million objects in S3, you would expect to lose only 1 object every 10,000 years!

AWS is steadily adding more regions throughout the world to give customers more options regarding where their applications are deployed. Some countries have strict compliance regulations that require data to be stored in a region within a country, so be sure to research those regulations before making your choice.

See `https://aws.amazon.com/about-aws/global-infrastructure/` for the most up to date list of regions and availability zones.

Global resources

It's important to understand that there are some AWS services that are considered global, meaning that those services are configured once per account and apply to all regions. In the web console, look at the upper right-hand corner of the screen to see which region you are currently viewing:

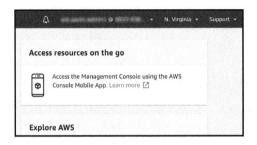

As you can see, I am currently in the Northern Virginia region

Now, select the IAM service, and note that you are no longer referencing a single region. When you create users, groups, and roles in IAM, those entities apply to all AWS regions. It isn't necessary to recreate your IAM resources each time you deploy to a new region:

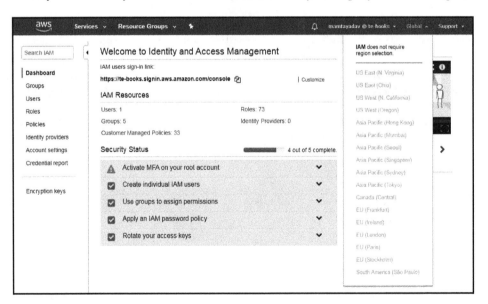

Global resources

Other examples of global services are Amazon Route 53, Amazon CloudFront, and AWS WAF.

Using the web console

You have already had some exposure to the AWS administration console at `https://console.aws.amazon.com`. For some users, the web interface is all they ever need to create and administer their cloud resources. Later in this chapter, we will introduce CloudFormation and the **command-line interface** (**CLI**) as worthy options for using a web browser. As good practice for production accounts, we highly recommend automating all of your resource changes with a templating system such as CloudFormation.

However, for routine discovery and education, the web console is an excellent tool, so we will highlight some of its features here. Keep in mind that the UI evolves over time, so the screenshots you see in this section may not exactly match what you see when you log in:

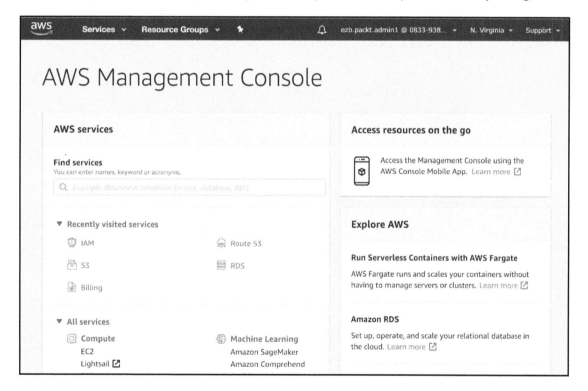

AWS Management Console

The menu bar

Let's start by dissecting that top menu bar and see what it has to offer.

AWS logo

The AWS logo takes you back to the top-level page of the console. It actually ends up being very useful when you decide you want to open a new console window without leaving the page you are currently viewing – just middle-click it or right-click and open the page in a new tab:

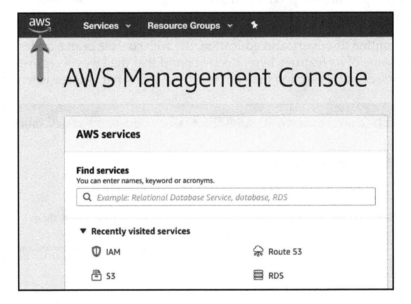

The AWS logo

Services

Expand the **Services** dropdown to see a screen with all the AWS services listed, and a recent history of the services you visited on the left. The search box will end up being the fastest way for you to find the service you are looking for:

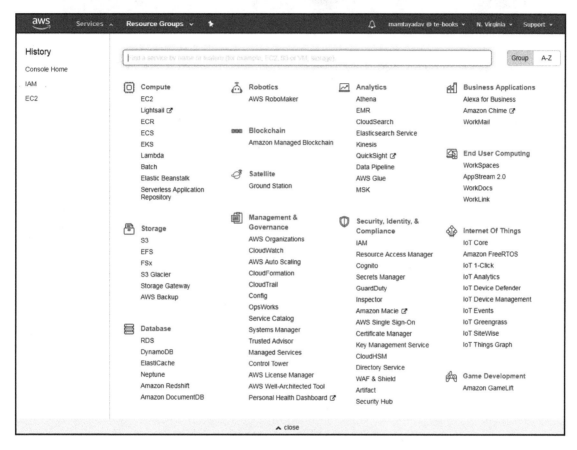

Clicking the Services link replaces the page's contents with an exhaustive list of services

Resource Groups

Resource Groups are a way to manage groups of resources – a topic that we will explore in detail in Chapter 9, *Managing Costs*:

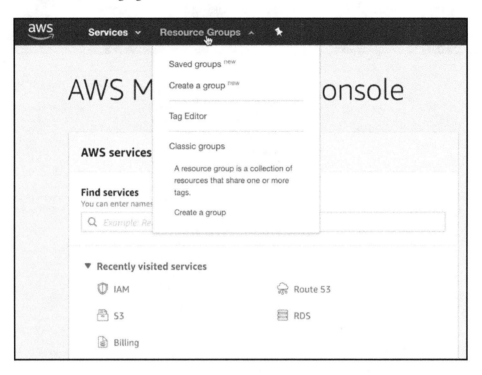

Resource Groups

Pins

Click the pin icon to view a list of service widgets that can be added to the menu bar:

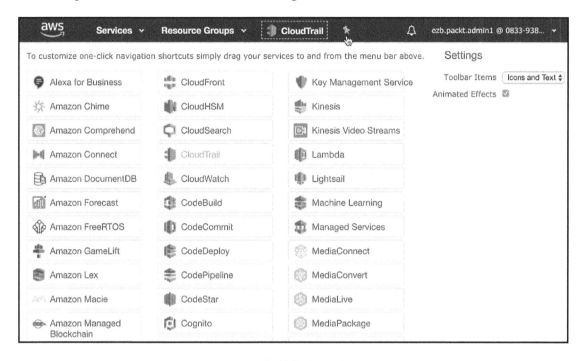

As you can see, I have pinned CloudTrail to give me quick access to that service

Alerts

The bell icon shows alerts and notifications that are relevant to your account:

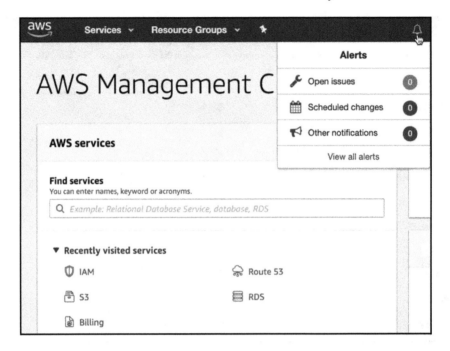

Keep an eye on the alerts for important notifications from AWS

Click **View all alerts** to see an event log of all the operational issues that may have affected your account recently.

Account

Click on your username to see links to the various screens related to your AWS account:

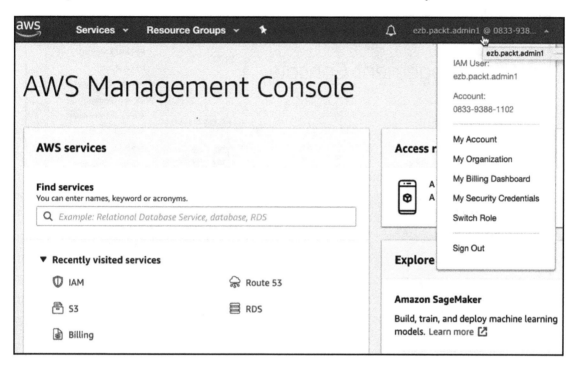

The username link

You already spent some time on the **My Security Credentials** screen when you created your account and set up security for the root login and your first IAM user. We will go into more detail about **My Organization**, **My Billing Dashboard**, and **Switch Role** in Chapter 2, *Account Setup and Management* and Chapter 9, *Managing Costs*.

Region and support

Click on the region selector to see all the regions that are available to you in your account:

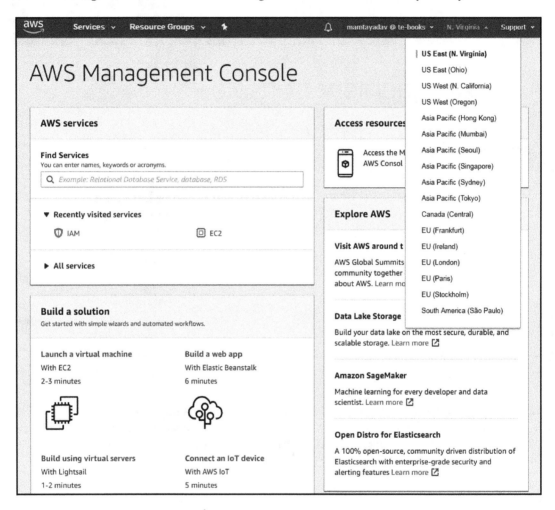

AWS regions available in your account

Remember that selecting a new region takes you to a completely isolated AWS environment, so any regional resources you had set up in the previous region will no longer be visible. If you ever find yourself in a panic because it looks like one of your resources, such as an RDS database or an EC2 instance, seems to have disappeared, it's probably because you are in the wrong region.

Finally, we have the **Support** link, which exposes several support resources.

Speaking of support, we should mention another best practice recommendation: all production accounts should have, at a minimum, Business support enabled. A support contract gives you rapid access to help when you need it. Don't skimp on this critical resource!

Learning the basics of AWS CloudFormation

We'll use CloudFormation extensively throughout this book, so it's important that you have an understanding of what it is and how it fits into the AWS ecosystem. There should be enough information here to get you started, but, where necessary, we'll refer you to the AWS documentation.

What is CloudFormation?

The CloudFormation service allows you to provision and manage a collection of AWS resources in an automated and repeatable fashion. In AWS terminology, these collections are referred to as stacks. Note, however, that a stack can be as large or as small as you like. It might consist of a single S3 bucket, or it might contain everything needed to host your three-tier web app.

In this chapter, we'll show you how to define the resources to be included in your CloudFormation stack. We'll talk a bit more about the composition of these stacks and why and when it's preferable to divvy up resources between a number of stacks. Finally, we'll share a few of the tips and tricks we've learned over the years building countless CloudFormation stacks.

Why is CloudFormation important?

By now, the benefits of automation should be starting to become apparent to you. But don't fall into the trap of thinking CloudFormation will only be useful for large collections of resources. Even performing the simplest task of, say, creating an S3 bucket, can get very repetitive if you need to do it in every region.

We work with a lot of customers who have very tight controls and governance around their infrastructure, especially in the network layer (think VPCs, NACLs, and security groups). Being able to express their cloud footprint in YAML (or JSON), store it in a source code repository, and funnel it through a high-visibility pipeline gives these customers confidence that their infrastructure changes are peer-reviewed and will work as expected in production. Discipline and commitment to IaC SDLC practices are, of course, a big factor in this, but CloudFormation helps bring us out of the era of following 20-page run-sheets for manual changes, navigating untracked or unexplained configuration drift, and unexpected downtime that's caused by fat fingers.

Infrastructure as Code (IaC)

AWS CloudFormation is an **Infrastructure as Code** (**IaC**) service. IaC has emerged as a critical strategy for companies that are making the transformation to a DevOps culture. DevOps and IaC go hand in hand. The practice of storing your infrastructure as code encourages a sharing of responsibilities that facilitates collaboration.

There are many benefits to IaC, some of which are as follows:

- Modeling your infrastructure as code gives you a single source of truth to define the resources that are deployed in your account.
- Once there are no manual steps to create your resources, you can fully automate deployment. You can deploy changes to an existing environment or create a brand new environment from scratch automatically by launching stacks based on your CloudFormation templates.
- Treating your infrastructure as code allows you to apply all the best practices of modern software development to your templates. Use code editors, distributed version control, code reviews, and easy rollbacks as part of your process.

The layer cake

Now is a good time to start thinking about your AWS deployments in terms of layers. Your layers will sit on top of one another, and you will have well-defined relationships between them.

Here's a bottom-up example of what your layer cake might look like:

- VPC with CloudTrail
- Subnets, routes, and NACLs
- NAT gateways, VPN or bastion hosts, and associated security groups
- App stack 1: Security groups and S3 buckets
- App stack 2: Cross-zone RDS and read replica
- App stack 3: App and web server autoscaling groups and ELBs
- App stack 4: CloudFront and WAF config

In this example, you may have many occurrences of the app stack layers inside your VPC, assuming that you have enough IP addresses in your subnets! This is often the case with VPCs living inside development environments. So, immediately, you have the benefit of multi-tenancy capability with application isolation.

One advantage of this approach is that, while you are developing your CloudFormation template, if you mess up the configuration of your app server, you don't have to wind back all the work CloudFormation did on your behalf. You can just scrap that particular layer (and the layers that depend on it) and restart from there. This is not the case if you have everything contained in a single template.

We commonly work with customers for whom the ownership and management of each layer in the cake reflect the structure of the technology divisions within a company. The traditional infrastructure, network, and cybersecurity folk are often really interested in creating a safe place for digital teams to deploy their apps, so they like to heavily govern the foundational layers of the cake.

Even if you are a single-person infrastructure coder working in a small team, you will benefit from this approach. For example, you'll find that it dramatically reduces your exposure to things such as AWS limits, timeouts, and circular dependencies.

CloudFormation templates

This is where we start to get our hands dirty. CloudFormation template files are the codified representations of your stack and are expressed in either YAML or JSON. When you wish to create a CloudFormation stack, you push a template file to CloudFormation through its API, web console, command-line tools, or some other method (such as the SDK).

Templates can be replayed over and over again by CloudFormation, thus creating many instances of your stack.

YAML versus JSON

Up until recently, JSON was your only option. We actually encourage you to adopt YAML, and we'll be using it for all of the examples that are shown in this book. Some of the reasons for this are as follows:

- It's just nicer to look at. It's less syntax-heavy, and should you choose to go down the path of generating your CloudFormation templates, pretty much every language has a YAML library of some kind.
- The size of your templates will be much smaller. This is more practical from a developer's point of view, but it also means that you're less likely to run into the CloudFormation size limit on template files (50 KB).
- The string-substitution features are easier to use and interpret.
- Your EC2 `UserData` (the script that runs when your EC2 instance boots) will be much easier to implement and maintain.

A closer look at CloudFormation templates

CloudFormation templates consist of a number of parts, but these are the four we're going to concentrate on:

- Parameters
- Resources
- Outputs
- Mappings

Here's a short YAML example:

```
AWSTemplateFormatVersion: '2010-09-09'
Parameters:
  EC2KeyName:
    Type: String
    Description: EC2 Key Pair to launch with
Mappings:
  RegionMap:
    us-east-1:
      AMIID: ami-9be6f38c
    ap-southeast-2:
      AMIID: ami-28cff44b
```

We declare a parameter and mappings to start the template. Mappings will be covered in
Chapter 10, *Advanced AWS CloudFormation*. Next, we define Resources:

```
Resources:
  ExampleEC2Instance:
    Type: AWS:EC2::Instance
    Properties:
      InstanceType: t2.nano
      UserData:
        Fn::Base64:
          Fn::Sub': |
            #!/bin/bash -ex
            /opt/aws/bin/cfn-signal '${ExampleWaitHandle}'
      ImageId:
        Fn::FindInMap: [ RegionMap, Ref: 'AWS::Region', AMIID ]
      KeyName:
        Ref: EC2KeyName
```

Then, in the final section of the template, we define WaitHandle, WaitCondition, and
Outputs:

```
ExampleWaitHandle:
  Type: AWS::CloudFormation::WaitConditionHandle
  Properties:
ExampleWaitCondition:
  Type: AWS::CloudFormation::WaitCondition
  DependsOn: ExampleEC2Instance
  Properties:
    Handle:
      Ref: ExampleWaitHandle
    Timeout: 600
Outputs:
  ExampleOutput:
    Value:
      Fn::GetAtt: ExampleWaitCondition.Data
    Description: The data signaled with the WaitCondition
```

Outputs give you a way to see things such as auto-generated names, and, in this case, the
data from the wait condition.

Parameters

CloudFormation parameters are the input values you define when creating or updating a stack, similar to how you provide parameters to any command-line tools you might use. They allow you to customize your stack without making changes to your template. Common examples of what parameters might be used for are the following:

- **EC2 AMI ID**: You may wish to redeploy your stack with a new AMI that has the latest security patches installed.
- **Subnet IDs**: You could have a list of subnets that an autoscaling group should deploy servers in. These subnet IDs will be different between your dev, test, and production environments.
- **Endpoint targets and credentials**: These include things such as API hostnames, usernames, and passwords.

You'll find that there are a number of parameter types. In brief, they are as follows:

- `String`
- `Number`
- `List`
- `CommaDelimitedList`

In addition to these, AWS provides some AWS-specific parameter types. These can be particularly handy when you are executing your template via the CloudFormation web console. For example, a parameter of the `AWS::EC2::AvailabilityZone::` type causes the web console to display a dropdown list of valid AZs for this parameter. In the `ap-southeast-2` region, the list would look like this:

- `ap-southeast-2a`
- `ap-southeast-2b`
- `ap-southeast-2c`

The list of AWS-specific parameter types is steadily growing and is so long that we can't list them here. We'll use many of them throughout this book, however, and they can easily be found in the AWS CloudFormation documentation.

When creating or updating a stack, you will need to provide values for all the parameters you've defined in your template. Where it makes sense, you can define default values for a parameter. For example, you might have a parameter called debug that tells your application to run in debug mode. Typically, you don't want this mode enabled by default, so you can set the default value for this parameter to false, disabled, or something else your application understands. Of course, this value can be overridden when you're creating or updating a stack.

You can – and should – provide a short, meaningful description for each parameter. These are displayed in the web console, next to each parameter field. When used properly, they provide hints and context to whoever is trying to run your CloudFormation template.

At this point, we need to introduce the built-in Ref function. When you need to reference a parameter value, you use this function to do so:

```
KeyName:
    Ref: EC2KeyName
```

While Ref isn't the only built-in function you'll need to know about, it's almost certainly going to be the one you'll use the most. We'll talk more about built-in functions later in this chapter.

Resources

Resources are your actual pieces of AWS infrastructure. These are your EC2 instances, S3 buckets, ELBs, and so on. Almost any resource type you can create by pointing and clicking on the AWS web console can also be created using CloudFormation.

It's not practical to list all the AWS resource types in this chapter. However, you will get familiar with the most common types as you work your way through the recipes in this book.

 AWS has a definitive list of resources types here: http://docs.aws.amazon.com/AWSCloudFormation/latest/UserGuide/aws-template-resource-type-ref.html.

There are a few important things to keep in mind about CloudFormation resources.

New or bleeding-edge AWS resources are often not immediately supported. CloudFormation support typically lags a few weeks (sometimes months) behind the release of new AWS features. This used to be quite frustrating for anyone who found that infrastructure automation was key. Fast-forward to today, and this situation is somewhat mitigated by the ability to use custom resources. These are discussed later on in this chapter.

Resources have a default return value. You can use `Ref` to fetch these return values for use elsewhere in your template. For example, the `AWS::EC2::VPC` resource type has a default return value, which is the ID of the VPC. It looks something like this:

```
vpc-11aa111a
```

Resources often contain additional return values. These additional values are fetched using the built-in `Fn::GetAtt` function. Continuing from the previous example, the `AWS::EC2::VPC` resource type also returns the following:

- `CidrBlock`
- `DefaultNetworkAcl`
- `DefaultSecurityGroup`
- `Ipv6CidrBlocks`
- `Outputs`

Just like AWS resources, CloudFormation stacks can also have return values, called outputs. These values are entirely user-defined. If you don't specify any outputs, then nothing is returned when your stack is completed.

Outputs can come in handy when you are using a CI/CD tool to create your CloudFormation stacks. For example, you might like to output the public hostname of an ELB so that your CI/CD tool can turn it into a clickable link within the job output.

You'll also use them when you are linking pieces of your layer cake together. You may want to reference an S3 bucket or security group that's was created in another stack. This is much easier to do with the new cross-stack references feature, which we'll discuss later in this chapter. You can expect to see the `Ref` and `Fn::GetAtt` functions a lot in the output section of any CloudFormation template.

Dependencies and ordering

When executing your template, CloudFormation will automatically work out which resources depend on each other and order their creation accordingly. Additionally, resource creation is parallelized as much as possible so that your stack execution finishes in the timeliest manner possible.

Let's look at an example where an app server depends on a DB server. To connect to the database, the app server needs to know its IP address or hostname. This situation would actually require you to create the DB server first so that you can use `Ref` to fetch its IP and provide it to your app server. CloudFormation has no way of knowing about the coupling between these two resources, so it will go ahead and create them in any order it pleases (or in parallel, if possible).

To fix this situation, we use the `DependsOn` attribute to tell CloudFormation that our app server depends on our DB server. In fact, `DependsOn` can actually take a list of strings if a resource happens to depend on multiple resources before it can be created. So, if our app server were to also depend on, say, a Memcached server, then we would use `DependsOn` to declare both dependencies.

If necessary, you can take this further. Let's say that, after your DB server boots, it will automatically start the database, set up a schema, and import a large amount of data. It may be necessary to wait for this process to complete before we create an app server that attempts to connect to a DB expecting a complete schema and dataset. In this scenario, we want a way to signal to CloudFormation that the DB server has completed its initialization so that it can go ahead and create resources that depend on it. This is where `WaitCondition` and `WaitConditionHandle` come in.

First, you create an `AWS::CloudFormation::WaitConditionHandle` type, which you can later reference via `Ref`.

Next, you create an `AWS::CloudFormation::WaitCondition` type. In our case, we want the waiting period to start as soon as the DB server is created, so we specify that this `WaitCondition` resource `DependsOn` our DB server.

After the DB server has finished importing data and is ready to accept connections, it calls the callback URL provided by the `WaitConditionHandle` resource to signal to CloudFormation that it can stop waiting and start executing the rest of the CloudFormation stack. The URL is supplied to the DB server via `UserData`, again using `Ref`. Typically, `curl`, `wget`, or some equivalent is used to call the URL.

A `WaitCondition` resource can have a `Timeout` period too. This is a value that's specified in seconds. In our example, we might supply a value of `900` because we know that it should never take more than 15 minutes to boot our DB and import the data.

Here's an example of what `DependsOn`, `WaitConditionHandle`, and `WaitCondition` look like when combined:

```
ExampleWaitHandle:
  Type: AWS::CloudFormation::WaitConditionHandle
  Properties:
ExampleWaitCondition:
  Type: AWS::CloudFormation::WaitCondition
  DependsOn: ExampleEC2Instance
  Properties:
    Handle:
      Ref: ExampleWaitHandle
    Timeout: 600
```

Functions

CloudFormation provides some built-in functions to make composing your templates a lot easier. We've already looked at `Ref` and `Fn::GetAtt`. Let's look at some others you are likely to encounter.

Fn::Join

Use `Fn::Join` to concatenate a list of strings using a specified delimiter, for example:

```
"Fn::Join": [ ".", [ 1, 2, 3, 4 ] ]
```

This would yield the following value:

```
"1.2.3.4"
```

Fn::Sub

Use `Fn::Sub` to perform string substitution. Consider the following code:

```
DSN: "Fn::Sub"
  - mysql://${db_user}:${db_pass}@${db_host}:3306/wordpress
  - { db_user: lchan, db_pass: ch33s3, db_host: localhost }
```

This would yield the following value:

```
mysql://lchan:ch33s3@localhost:3306/wordpress
```

When you combine these functions with `Ref` and `Fn::GetAtt`, you can start doing some really powerful stuff, as we'll see in the recipes throughout this book.

Other available built-in functions include the following:

- `Fn::Base64`
- `Fn::FindInMap`
- `Fn::GetAZs`
- `Fn::ImportValue`
- `Fn::Select`

> Documentation on all of these functions is available at `http://docs.aws.amazon.com/AWSCloudFormation/latest/UserGuide/intrinsic-function-reference.html`.

Conditionals

It's reasonably common to provide a similar but distinct set of resources based on which environment your stack is running in. In your development environment, for example, you may not wish to create an entire fleet of database servers, instead opting for just a single database server. You can achieve this by using conditionals, such as the following ones:

- `Fn::And`
- `Fn::Equals`
- `Fn::If`
- `Fn::Not`
- `Fn::Or`

Permissions and service roles

One important thing to remember about CloudFormation is that it's more or less just making API calls on your behalf. This means that CloudFormation will assume the very same permissions or role you use to execute your template. If you don't have permission to create a new hosted zone on Route 53, for example, any template you try to run that contains a new Route 53-hosted zone will fail.

On the flip side, this has created a somewhat tricky situation where anyone developing CloudFormation typically has a very elevated level of privileges, and those privileges are somewhat unnecessarily granted to CloudFormation each time a template is executed.

If my CloudFormation template contains only one resource, which is a Route 53-hosted zone, it doesn't make sense for that template to be executed with full admin privileges to my AWS account. It makes much more sense to give CloudFormation a very slim set of permissions to execute the template with, thus limiting the blast radius if a bad template were to be executed (that is, a bad copy-and-paste operation resulting in deleted resources).

Thankfully, you can use service roles to define an IAM role and tell CloudFormation to use that role when your stack is being executed, giving you a much safer space to play in.

Cross-stack references

When using the layered cake approach, it's very common to want to use outputs from one stack as inputs in another stack. For example, you may create a VPC in one stack and require its VPC ID when creating resources in another.

For a long time, you needed to provide some glue around stack creation in order to pass the output between stacks. Cross-stack references provide a more native way of doing this.

You can now export one or more outputs from your stack. This makes those outputs available to other stacks. Note that the name of this value needs to be unique, so it's probably a good idea to include the CloudFormation stack name in the name you're exporting to achieve this.

Once a value has been exported, it becomes available to be imported in another stack using the `Fn::ImportValue` function – very handy!

Make sure, however, that during the time an exported value is being referenced, you are not able to delete or modify it. Additionally, you won't be able to delete the stack containing the exported value. Once something is referencing an exported value, it's there to stay until there are no stacks referencing it at all.

Updating resources

One of the principles of IaC is that all the changes should be represented as code for review and testing. This is especially important where CloudFormation is concerned.

After creating a stack for you, the CloudFormation service is effectively hands-off. If you make a change to any of the resources created by CloudFormation (in the web console, command line, or by some other method), you're effectively causing configuration drift; CloudFormation no longer knows the exact state of the resources in your stack.

The correct approach is to make these changes in your CloudFormation template and perform an update operation on your stack. This ensures that CloudFormation always knows the state of your stack and allows you to be confident that your infrastructure code is a complete and accurate representation of your running environments.

Changesets

When performing a stack update, it can be unclear exactly what changes are going to be made to your stack. Depending on which resource you are changing, you may find that it will need to be deleted and recreated in order to implement your change. This, of course, is completely undesired behavior if the resource in question contains data you'd like to keep. Keep in mind that RDS databases can be a particular pain point.

To mitigate this situation, CloudFormation allows you to create and review a changeset prior to executing the update. The changeset shows you which operations CloudFormation intends to perform on your resources. If the changeset looks good, you can choose to proceed. If you don't like what you see, you can delete the changeset and choose another course of action – perhaps choosing to create and switch to an entirely new stack to avoid a service outage.

Other things to know

There are a few other things you should keep in the back of your mind as you start building out your own CloudFormation stacks. Let's take a look.

Name collisions

Often, if you omit the name attribute from a resource, CloudFormation will generate a name for you. This can result in weird-looking resource names, but it will increase the replayability of your template. Using `AWS::S3::Bucket` as an example, if you specify the `BucketName` parameter but don't ensure its uniqueness, CloudFormation will fail to execute your template the second time around because the bucket will already exist. Omitting `BucketName` fixes this. Alternatively, you may opt to generate your own unique name each time the template is run. There's probably no right or wrong approach here, so just do what works for you.

Rollback

When creating a CloudFormation stack, you are given the option of disabling rollback. Before you go ahead and set this to `true`, keep in mind that this setting persists beyond stack creation. We've ended up in precarious situations where updating an existing stack has failed (for some reason) but rollback has been disabled. This is a fun situation for no one.

Limits

The limits that are the most likely to concern you are as follows:

- The maximum size allowed for your CloudFormation template is 50 KB. This is quite generous, and if you hit this limit, you almost certainly need to think about breaking up your template into a series of smaller ones. If you absolutely need to exceed the 50 KB limit, then the most common approach is to upload your template to S3 and then provide an S3 URL to CloudFormation to execute.
- The maximum number of parameters you can specify is 60. If you need more than this then, again, consider whether or not you need to add more layers to your cake. Otherwise, lists or mappings might get you out of trouble here.
- Outputs are also limited to 60. If you've hit this limit, it's probably time to resort to a series of smaller templates.
- Resources are limited to 200. The same rules apply here as they do for the previous limit.
- By default, you're limited to a total of 200 CloudFormation stacks. You can have this limit increased simply by contacting AWS.

Use nested stacks to reduce the complexity of any one CloudFormation template, and to avoid hitting the limits we've described here.

Circular dependencies

Something to keep in the back of your mind is that you may run into a circular dependency scenario, where multiple resources depend on each other for creation. A common example is where two security groups reference each other in order to allow access between themselves.

A workaround for this particular scenario is to use the `AWS::EC2::SecurityGroupEgress` and `AWS::EC2::SecurityGroupIngress` types instead of the ingress and egress rule types for `AWS::EC2::SecurityGroup`.

Credentials

Under no circumstances do you want to have credentials hardcoded in your templates or committed to your source code repository. Doing this doesn't just increase the chance that your credentials will be stolen – it also reduces the portability of your templates. If your credentials are hardcoded and you need to change them, that obviously requires you to edit your CloudFormation template.

Instead, you should add credentials as parameters in your template. Be sure to use the `NoEcho` parameter when you do this so that CloudFormation masks the value anywhere the parameters are displayed.

Stack policies

If there are resources in your stack you'd like to protect from accidental deletion or modification, applying a stack policy will help you achieve this. By default, all resources can be deleted or modified. When you apply a stack policy, all the resources are protected unless you explicitly allow them to be deleted or modified in the policy. Note that stack policies do not apply during stack creation – they only take effect when you attempt to update a stack.

Using the command-line interface (CLI)

The AWS **command-line interface** (**CLI**) tool is an important piece of the AWS administrator's toolkit.

The CLI tool is often one of the quickest and easiest ways to interact with the API. As a text-based tool, it scales much easier than using the web console. Unlike the console, it can be automated, for example, via scripts. The AWS **application programming interface** (**API**) represents all the functionality that's available to you as an AWS administrator. It is also easier to keep track of through your command-line history. Like all good CLI tools, simple individual commands can be chained (or piped) together to perform complex tasks.

 The CLI tool is open source software, and is maintained on GitHub (`https://github.com/aws/aws-cli`). For more detailed documentation, refer to the AWS CLI home page at `https://aws.amazon.com/cli`.

Installation

The CLI tool requires Python 2.6.5 or greater.

The easiest way to install it is to use the Python package manager, `pip`:

```
pip install awscli
```

This will make the `aws` command available on your system.

Upgrade

AWS frequently releases new services and functionality. To use these new features, you will need to upgrade the CLI tool.

To upgrade the CLI tool, run the following `pip` command periodically:

```
pip install --upgrade awscli
```

Configuration

Authentication between the CLI tool and the AWS API is done via two pieces of information:

- Access key ID
- Secret access key

As its name suggests, you should keep your secret access key a secret! Be careful where you store or send it.

Once you have created a user, you can configure the tool so that you can use it for authentication purposes.

While you can configure the CLI tool with access keys directly, this should be avoided. Instead, you should use profiles to store your credentials. Using profiles gives you a more consistent and manageable centralized location to secure your secret keys.

Default profile

Without any additional configuration or options, your CLI tool commands will use the default profile.

To set up the default profile, you can use the following command:

```
aws configure
```

This will prompt you for an access key ID, secret access key, region, and output format.

Named profiles

In addition to the default profile, you can configure other, named profiles. This is useful for switching between users with different levels of access (for example, read-only and administrator) or even between users in different accounts:

```
aws configure --profile <profile-name>
```

Once you have responded to these prompts, you can reference the named profile by passing the --profile <profile-name> option with your command.

Environment variables

You can also configure the CLI via the use of environment variables:

```
export AWS_PROFILE=<profile-name>
```

While you should prefer to use profiles over setting your access ID and secret keys directly, sometimes you may have to do so. If you must set your keys directly, do so via environment variables so that you don't need to pass your keys around or hardcode them:

```
export AWS_ACCESS_KEY_ID=<access-key-id>
export AWS_SECRET_ACCESS_KEY=<secret-access-key>
```

Instance roles

When running the CLI tool on an EC2 instance, you can leverage the instance's IAM role to make calls. This means that you don't need to configure credentials or set environment variables (manually).

Behind the scenes, the instance will retrieve and set its own AWS environment variables that allow API calls. You need to ensure that the instance has the appropriate permissions.

 The AWS CLI tool comes preinstalled on AWS Linux-based instances.

Usage

All CLI tool commands are service-based. By using service commands and subcommands, you can make calls directly to the AWS API.

Commands

Each command represents an AWS service. While most services have one command associated with them, some services have multiple commands (for example, S3 has s3 and s3api).

Run `aws help` to see all the commands/services that are available – they will have probably changed by the time this book is printed!

Subcommands

Each command has a selection of subcommands to perform service-specific actions.

Run `aws <command> help` to see all the available subcommands.

Options

Subcommands take options and start with `--`.

You can view all the options and their purposes by running `aws <command> <subcommand> help`.

While most are optional (hence the name), those that are *not* surrounded by square brackets (`[]`) are required. You will get an error message (with the appropriate details) if you don't include them.

The built-in documentation is the best place to start looking for answers. There are usually examples after all of the options have been described. Otherwise, there are plenty of examples available online.

Some options are available for all or most commands, so they are particularly useful to know.

Output

The CLI tool can be configured to output in JSON, table, or text format. To control the output type, use the `--output` option.

To set a default output type for all your commands, set the `output` parameter for your profile.

JSON

JavaScript Object Notation (JSON) (http://json.org/) is a standard machine- and human-readable information interchange format. Here's what the AZs in the us-east-1 (North Virginia) region look like, represented as JSON:

```
aws ec2 describe-availability-zones --output json
{
    "AvailabilityZones": [
        {
            "State": "available",
            "ZoneName": "us-east-1a",
            "Messages": [],
            "RegionName": "us-east-1"
        },
        {
            "State": "available",
            "ZoneName": "us-east-1b",
            "Messages": [],
            "RegionName": "us-east-1"
        },
        ...
    ]
}
```

 Note that a portion of the output was elided for space.

Table

The table format displays a text/ASCII table of results. This can be useful for generating printable reports:

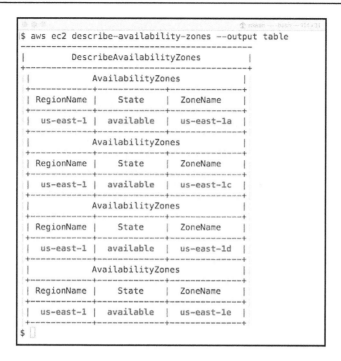

Table format

Text

The text output format only displays the resulting key/value response. No additional formatting or display characters are added:

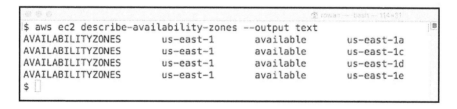

Text format

The text format is the default and is suitable for most routine CLI tasks.

Querying

The CLI tool supports transforming the response from the API with the `--query` option. This option takes a JMESPath query as a parameter and returns the query result.

 JMESPath is a query language for JSON. For more information, visit http://jmespath.org/.

As the query is processed as part of the command, it takes place on the server, not the client. By offloading work to the server, you can reduce the size of the resulting payload and improve response times.

JMESPath can be used to transform the response that you receive:

```
$ aws ec2 describe-availability-zones \
  --output json \
  --query "AvailabilityZones[].ZoneName"
[
"us-east-1a",
"us-east-1c",
"us-east-1d",
"us-east-1e"
]
```

It can also be used to filter the data that is received:

```
$ aws ec2 describe-availability-zones
  --output json
  --query "AvailabilityZones[?ZoneName == 'us-east-1a'].State"
[
"available"
]
```

Using the `--query` option can open up a number of possibilities to give you flexible options for solving problems with the AWS CLI.

Generating a CLI skeleton

When performing complex tasks with the CLI tool, it may be easier to pass a JSON object of options. This kind of interaction may signify that you should use one of the AWS **software development kits (SDKs)**.

Input

To generate a sample JSON object that will be accepted, run any command with the `--generate-cli-skeleton` option:

```
$ aws ec2 describe-availability-zones --generate-cli-skeleton
{
"DryRun": true,
"ZoneNames": [
""
    ],
"Filters": [
        {
"Name": "",
"Values": [
""

            ]
        }
    ]
}
```

You can then copy, edit, and use this object to define your command options without passing lots of individual options. It works best for commands with arrays of options or a variable number of options.

Output

You can also get a preview of the output of a command by calling the command with the `--generate-cli-skeleton output` option. This can speed up the process of combining CLI commands as you can see a response without actually calling the API:

```
$ aws ec2 describe-availability-zones --generate-cli-skeleton output
{
   "AvailabilityZones": [
     {
       "ZoneName": "ZoneName",
       "State": "State",
       "RegionName": "RegionName",
       "Messages": [
         {
            "Message": "Message"
         } ]
     } ]
}
```

Pagination

The results that are returned by the CLI tool are limited to 1,000 resources by default.

This is not normally an issue, but at a certain scale, you may run into pagination issues. A common example is a list of files in an S3 bucket.

 If you are absolutely sure you should be seeing a particular resource in the response but cannot, check your pagination. The resource may be included in the matching resources, just not in the part of the response that was returned to you.

The following options allow you to control the number and starting point of the results that are returned to you from the API:

- --page-size: This limits how many resources will be displayed to you, but does not actually limit the number that's returned. The default number of items (that is, 1,000) will still be processed and returned to you.
- --max-items: This sets an upper limit on how many items will actually be returned in the response. You may receive fewer items, but you will not receive more than this number.
- --starting-token: This changes where the response starts. Use this to display subsequent results, beyond the first page:

  ```
  aws s3api list-objects --bucket bucket-name --max-items 100 --
  starting-token [TOKEN]
  ```

Use a token that's been returned by a previous CLI command to continue where you left off.

Autocomplete

You can enable tab completion of commands, subcommands, and options by configuring the completer included with the CLI tool.

On macOS, Linux, and Windows systems with a bash shell, you can load the completer with the following command:

```
complete -C 'which aws_completer'aws
```

By default, the `aws_completer` program is installed in `/usr/local/bin`. If your tool is installed to a non-standard location, you will need to find it and change the `which aws_completer` command to the relevant path.

There's more...

At the time of writing, AWS is previewing a new tool called `aws-shell`. You can check it out at `https://github.com/awslabs/aws-shell`. When using `aws-shell`, you can use all the same commands offered by the CLI, but without the `aws` prefix. It also offers robust auto-completion, including the ability to autocomplete resources such as EC2 instance names.

See also

- `Chapter 10`, *Advanced CloudFormation,* will dive into more complex scenarios and features, such as custom resources

2
Account Setup and Management

We work with a lot of companies that maintain a large, ever-growing number of AWS accounts. Keeping a handle on all these accounts is typically quite difficult to do – even for the most seasoned **Amazon Web Services** (**AWS**) users.

With the release of AWS Organizations and, more recently, AWS Control Tower, you have the ability to centrally manage your AWS accounts, arrange them into logical groupings and hierarchies, and apply controls to them in ways that help you create a secure and compliant environment.

In this chapter, we will cover the following recipes:

- Setting up an automated landing zone with AWS Control Tower
- Setting up a master account with AWS Organizations
- Creating a member account
- Inviting an account
- Managing your accounts
- Adding a Service Control Policy (SCP)
- Setting up consolidated billing

Setting up an automated landing zone with AWS Control Tower

AWS Control Tower is a service that helps you set up an automated landing zone using best practices for account management that have been learned from years of working with a variety of customers who have complex multi-account environments. Control Tower is the successor to AWS Landing Zone and relies heavily on AWS Organizations, which will be covered in detail later in this chapter.

In this recipe, you will create a new account to serve as the Control Tower master, and within that account, you will launch your Control Tower environment, which will spawn two additional core accounts: **Log Archive** and **Audit**. Then, you will use the AWS Service Catalog to create a new provisioned account. Within a provisioned account, you will attempt to create resources that fail to comply with the guardrails established on the organizational unit and see that you are quickly alerted to the problem.

How to do it...

Follow these steps to set up your core accounts:

1. Create a new account using the recipe in `Chapter 1`, *AWS Fundamentals*. Pay special attention to the security recommendations, since this will be the master account for your new multi-account AWS environment. Give users strong passwords, and always configure multi-factor authentication!

2. Log in to the new master account as a user with full administrative privileges and navigate to the **Control Tower** console. Click the **Get Started** button to set up a new environment.

3. Configure the email addresses for each of the subordinate accounts that will be created for you by **Control Tower**:

Shared accounts

As a best practice for a well-architected multi-account environment, AWS Control Tower will set up accounts that offer isolated environments for specialized roles in your organization. Enter a unique email address for the owner of each of these accounts.

Log archive account

The log archive account is a repository of immutable logs of API activities and resource configurations from all accounts. The log archive account email must be unique and not already used for an existing AWS account.

log-archive@example.com

Audit account

The audit account is a restricted account for your security and compliance teams to gain read and write access to all accounts. The audit account email must be unique and not already used for an existing account.

audit@example.com

Setting up the AWS Control Tower Shared account

See the *How it works* section that follows for a full description of each account.

Some email providers have a nifty feature that is not very well documented: the ability to easily create email aliases by including a plus sign in the address. Gmail, for example, allows you to use addresses such as you@gmail.com and you+controltower-master@gmail.com as synonyms. If you aren't using Gmail, check with your company's system administrator to see if your email server supports this functionality. It can make setting up various AWS accounts much simpler since they will be associated with a single inbox. If you don't have that feature available, another option is to set up distribution lists instead of fully functional email accounts.

4. Select your desired region.
5. Check the box to grant Control Tower the administrative privileges it needs to administer accounts on your behalf.

6. Launch your Control Tower installation and go to the **Dashboard**, where you can watch the progress as it creates resources and accounts for you in the background. While the setup is in progress, you will receive a few emails, so keep an eye on your inbox so that you can verify your email address and confirm the subscription to **Simple Notification Service** (**SNS**) notifications related to the new accounts:

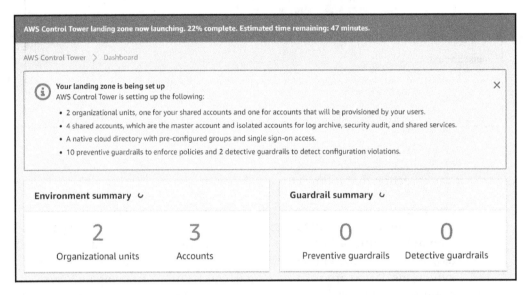

AWS Control Tower Launching

7. When the landing zone is fully launched, take some time to explore the **Dashboard** and inspect the various components, including **Organizational units**, **Accounts**, **Preventive guardrails**, **Detective guardrails**, **Recommended actions**, and **Non-compliant resources**.

8. You should have received an email with the following subject line: **Invitation to join AWS Single Sign-On**. Click **Accept Invitation** to create credentials for the master **Single-Sign-On** (**SSO**) user. Keep in mind that this is not the same identity that you used to create the master account, even if it does share the same email address! You will use these credentials later in this recipe.

9. On the side navigation bar, click **Guardrails** and scroll down to the bottom. Click **Disallow public read access to S3 buckets**. Note that this is a detective guardrail, meaning that provisioned accounts will not be prevented from creating public buckets, but you will receive a notification if a bucket is marked as public. We will test this guardrail in subsequent steps.

10. Scroll down to **Organizational units enabled** and click **Enable guardrail on OU**. Choose the custom OU and enable it. It may take a few minutes to appear in the list of enabled OUs. You should see an email with the subject line **Config Rules Compliance Change** to alert you to the configuration change that was made to the Custom OU:

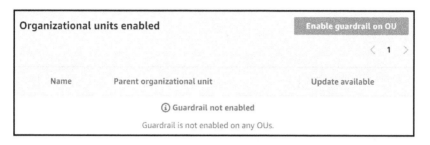

Organizational units enabled

11. Log out of your account and then log back in with the SSO credentials you created in *Step 8*.

12. Once logged in, you will land on a screen titled **Your applications**. Click the orange cube to see a list of accounts that you can access with this user:

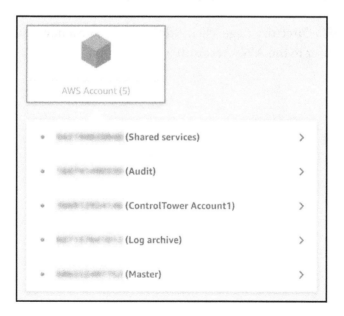

SSO accounts

13. Click your **Master** account and log in to the management console as an administrator.

14. On the side navigation bar, select **Users and access**, and then click **View in AWS Single Sign-On**:

Control Tower Users and access

15. On the SSO Directory page, click **Add User**. Create a new user account.

16. Add the user to the **AWSAccountFactory** group:

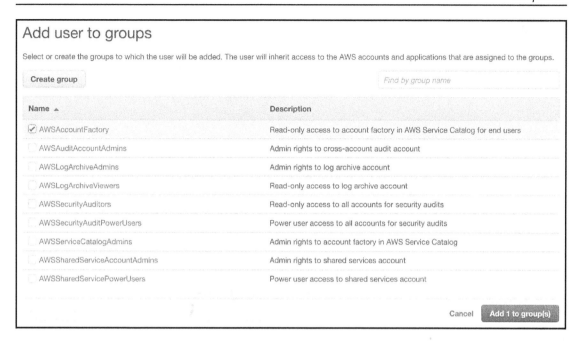

Add user to groups screen

17. Complete the user creation process. Log out of the console, and also log out of SSO. Then, log back in as the new user you just created. This is important because we need to be logged in as a user who has rights to provision accounts, and we want to simulate a real-world scenario: a user provisioning an account and then creating non-compliant resources.

18. Go to the **Service Catalog** service dashboard.

19. In the **Service Catalog,** choose **AWS Control Tower Account Factory**. Click **Launch Product**.

20. Fill in the parameters, tag options, and notifications for the new account. Launch the product and wait for your new account to be fully provisioned. When the process has finished, you can use AWS SSO to sign in to the new account.

21. Once you're logged in to the new account, create an S3 bucket and give it public access. (Note that this is bad practice and you should never create public buckets! Don't put any files into this bucket!) Use the following bucket policy to open the contents of the bucket to the world:

```
{
    "Version": "2012-10-17",
    "Statement": [
        {
            "Action": "s3:",
            "Effect": "Allow",
            "Resource": "arn:aws:s3:::my-noncompliant-bucket-name/",
            "Principal": "*"
        }
    ]
}
```

The following screenshot shows what the bucket policy screen will look like:

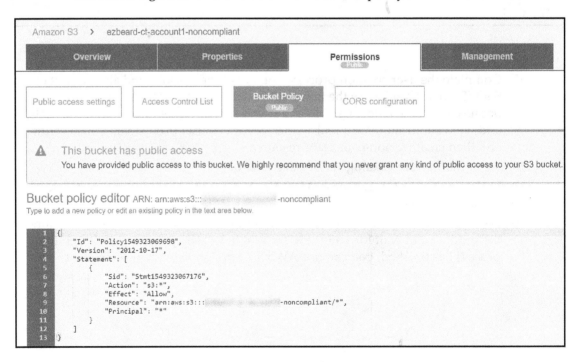

Bucket policy

The S3 console makes it very obvious when you have created a public bucket since it is considered bad practice!

22. Log out of the console and out of the SSO. Then, log back in as the administrator. If the guardrail on the **Custom** OU has had time to propagate, you should be able to go back to the guardrail screen and see the warning under **Noncompliant resources**:

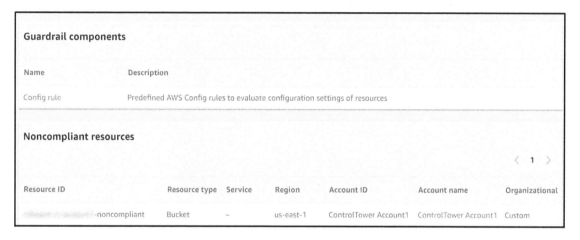

Guardrail components

At this point, you have created the basis for a secure, enterprise-ready account foundation on AWS. If you do not plan to continue using these accounts, be sure to go to each account and clean up the resources, as you may incur some future charges.

How it works...

AWS Control Tower is a service that helps you organize multi-account environments by creating a set of guardrails, which are sets of governance rules that specify the default operational and security posture of accounts that are created in this environment. It uses AWS SSO to manage a directory of users, whether this is a self-managed directory or your on-premises Active Directory installation. AWS Organizations and AWS Service Catalog are used to provide an **Account Factory** to your users so that they can create accounts that automatically comply with your company's best practices.

Accounts

It's important to understand the role of each of the accounts that are created by Control Tower when you launch a new environment. In the following diagram, you can see that we start with a master account. Within that account are AWS Organization's **Organizational Units (OU)**, called **Core** and **Custom**. Under the **Core OU**, Control Tower creates a **Log Archive Account** and an **Audit Account**. Later, you and your users will make use of AWS Service Catalog to create **Provisioned Accounts** under the **Custom OU**:

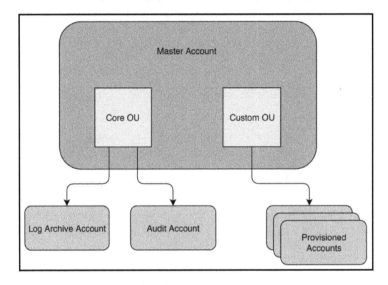

Control Tower accounts

Each of the blocks in the preceding diagram represents an account:

- **The Master Account**: This account is where all of the coordination happens for your multi-account environment. Take extra precautions with regard to user access in this account, and be careful with any actions you take here because you can affect all of the child accounts.
- **The Log Archive Account**: The logging account keeps a copy of the AWS CloudTrail and AWS Config logs as a secure backup to the copy that is kept in each provisioned account for operational purposes. It is good practice to store these logs in an account that is only accessible to auditors. That prevents a bad actor from covering up their tracks in an account where the logs are not shipped to a different location.

- **The Audit Account**: This account is to be used by auditors and comes equipped with cross-account roles into the other accounts. Auditors and security staff should log in to this account and then use those cross-account roles to switch context into the affected accounts while they are conducting investigations or implementing emergency security measures.
- **Provisioned Accounts**: These accounts are the whole reason we have gone to the trouble of creating our environment with Control Tower. This is where your application lives. You may have a single provisioned account to host your resources, but it's more likely that you will have a long list of accounts that are used for various purposes. It is good practice to create a separate account for production and development environments, for instance, to reduce the blast radius of changes that are made during the development process.

> In preview editions of Control Tower, a third core account was dedicated to shared services. This account was meant to host resources that need to be shared across all your provisioned accounts. A good example of something that should be provisioned in a shared services account is your domain registration. Use Route53 to register a domain, but then delegate the name servers to one of your provisioned accounts where the domain is configured. This makes it much easier to switch an application from one account to another.
>
> Since this account is no longer created for you, our recommendation is to provision an account under the Custom OU for shared services.

There's more...

AWS Control Tower uses guardrails to help you establish a compliant environment where all the subordinate accounts follow your company's best practices. Guardrails fall into one of two broad categories:

- Detective
- Preventative

Detective controls make use of AWS Config Rules to alert you to resources that are out of compliance within provisioned accounts. You can take manual action to correct the problems, or you can use AWS Lambda to automate your response.

Preventative controls use **Service Control Policies** (**SCP**) to make certain actions impossible within provisioned accounts, even to the root user! You must take great care with SCPs since they can have drastic effects on a large number of child accounts.

See also

- The *Setting up a master account with AWS Organizations* recipe in this chapter
- The *Adding a Service Control Policy (SCP)* recipe in this chapter

Setting up a master account with AWS Organizations

In the previous recipe, you used AWS Control Tower to automatically create your landing zone. AWS Control Tower relies on AWS Organizations to manage Organizational Units and Accounts, so it's very important to understand how it works. In this recipe, you will use AWS Organizations to create your own account structure from scratch, starting with a new master account.

All accounts that use AWS Organizations for billing and control purposes must have a master account. This account controls membership to the organization and pays the bills of all the members (someone's got to do it!).

How to do it...

To set up a master account, perform the following steps:

1. Go to the **My Organization** section of the account you want to become the master of. You must be logged in with your root credentials (that is, those you created the account with):

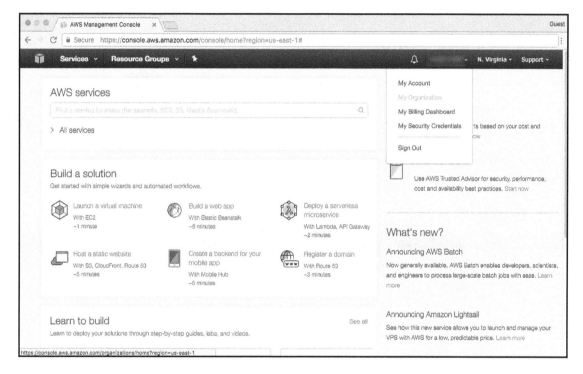

My Organization

2. In the **AWS Organizations** section of the AWS console, click on **Create organization**, as shown in the following screenshot:

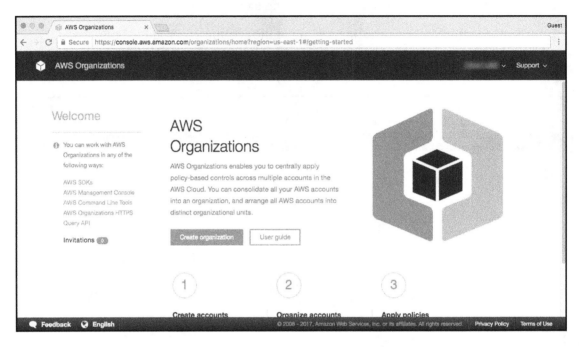

AWS Organizations

3. Unless you have a specific requirement, choose to **ENABLE ALL FEATURES** to get the full benefit of Organizations, as shown in the following screenshot:

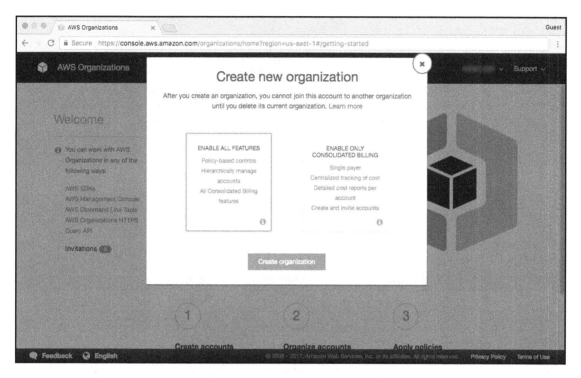

Create new organization screen

4. Now that your account has been converted, you can return to the **AWS Organizations** page to see a list of all your accounts:

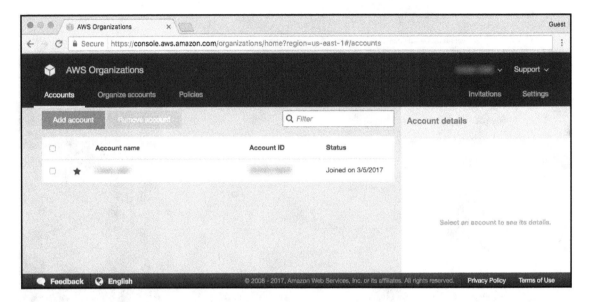

How it works...

While this is a very simple recipe, it's the first thing you must do before you can use any of the useful features in AWS Organizations.

The following is a high-level diagram showing the relationships between master accounts, members, and **organizational units (OUs)**:

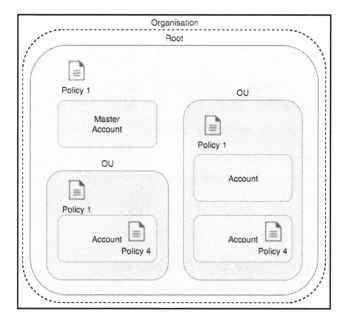

Organization units

We deliberately enable all the features of organizations. The consolidated billing option is available for backward compatibility; before Organizations, consolidated billing was your only option for linking accounts.

 Do not use your master account for day-to-day tasks. Since it is so important, it doesn't make sense to risk using it and/or having access keys for it. If your master account somehow became compromised, it would impact all of your member accounts. Just don't do it.

The master account will always have a star next to its name.

There's more...

All of AWS Organization's functionality is exposed via the API. This means you can use the AWS SDKs or the CLI tool to do the same things you would in the web console.

Using the CLI

You can easily create your master account with the CLI tool. The following command will turn your account into a master account, with all of AWS Organization's features enabled:

```
aws organizations create-organization
```

You can extend this command with the `--feature-set` flag to enable consolidated billing without the rest of the advanced features associated with AWS Organizations.

See also

- The *Inviting an account* recipe in this chapter
- The *Creating a member account* recipe in this chapter

Creating a member account

Once your organization is up and running, the most common use you will have for it is automating the account creation process. Accounts that are created inside an organization are referred to as **member accounts**.

All charges that are incurred by a member account will be billed to the master account.

Getting ready

Obviously, you will need an organization to perform this recipe. See the other recipes in this chapter to get started. In this recipe, we will use the CLI instead of the web console. It's good practice to flex your command-line skills now and then since the CLI is such a powerful tool for scripting and automation.

How to do it...

Perform the following steps to create a member account in your organization:

1. Run the CLI tool command to create a new account with the appropriate values:

```
aws organizations create-account \
        --email <member-account-owners@email.com> \
        --account-name <member-account-name> \
        --query 'CreateAccountStatus.Id'
```

2. This command will return a create-account-status request ID value that you can use to check the status:

```
aws organizations describe-create-account-status \
        --create-account-request-id <your-create-account-status-
id>
```

How it works...

The command to create a member account in your organization is extremely simple.

 The email address that's used cannot be associated with any other AWS accounts.

The account creation process takes some time, so it is done asynchronously. This means that you won't receive an immediate status for your create-account command. Instead, the command in this recipe will return a request ID.

This ID is then passed to another account to check the status of its creation. When the status is CREATED, you can start using the new account.

There's more...

While this functionality is definitely useful, the AWS Organizations service is relatively new. This means there are a few features you should be aware of. In this section, we will cover the following:

- Accessing the member account
- Service Control Policies
- Root credentials
- Deleting accounts

Accessing the member account

Once you've created your member account, it's time to put it to work!

An IAM role will be present in the new account; its default name is `OrganizationAccountAccessRole`. This is so you can assume the role (from your master account) and administer the member account. While this name is as good as any, it can be configured by passing the `--role-name` argument when creating the account.

To assume the role, you need to know its **Amazon Resource Name (ARN)**. Working out the ARN is a multi-step process:

1. List your member accounts by running the following command in your master account:

   ```
   aws organizations list-accounts
   ```

2. Find the account you created (by its name) and note the ID value in the record. Using that ID, generate the role's ARN by following this pattern:

   ```
   arn:aws:iam::<your-member-account-
   id>:role/OrganizationAccountAccessRole
   ```

3. If you have changed the created role's name, update the last part of the ARN accordingly.

See the recipes in `Chapter 8`, *AWS Account Security and Identity*, for information on how to best manage multiple accounts.

Service Control Policies

Service Control Policies (**SCPs**) are another major feature of AWS Organizations. You can apply them at multiple levels/resources, including accounts (both member accounts and invited accounts). Check the other recipes in this chapter for more details.

Root credentials

Some activities still require the root credentials of the account. An example activity would be closing (or deleting) an account (see the next section, *Deleting accounts*, for more details).

To do this, you will need to perform the password recovery process for the email that was associated with the account when the `create-account` request was sent.

Deleting accounts

At the time of writing, there is no way to delete an account that's been created in your organization via the API. You can still go into the member account and close it using the root credentials, but these don't exist by default. You will need to use the account credential recovery process to log in and close the account.

 While you can technically delete your organization via the API, you cannot do this if you have created any member accounts in your organization (since you can't delete them, your organization will never be empty).

See also

- The *Setting up a master account with AWS Organizations* recipe in this chapter
- The *Adding a Service Control Policy (SCP)* recipe in this chapter
- The *Cross-account user roles* recipe in `Chapter 8`, *AWS Account Security and Identity*

Inviting an account

While it makes sense to create new accounts in your organization, what do you do with all the other accounts you have now?

You can invite existing accounts into your organization, which means you can treat them just like a member account from an administrative point of view. This greatly simplifies the administrative overhead of your accounts, as there isn't a separate process for old and new accounts.

As this is generally performed once for each existing account, we will use the console.

All of AWS Organization's functionality is available via the SDKs and the AWS CLI tool. If you need to automate this process, you can.

Getting ready

You must have enabled AWS Organizations for one of your accounts (your master account) and have another account that has not been made part of an organization yet (that you will invite).

How to do it...

Perform the following steps to invite an account:

1. From the AWS Console of the master account, click on your username and select **My Organization** from the drop-down menu:

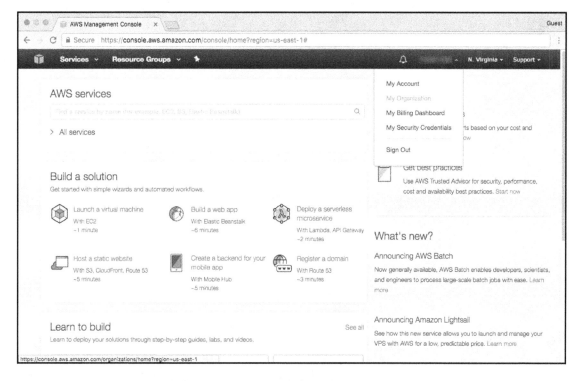

My Organization

2. You will be taken to the **AWS Organizations** console, where you will see your current account:

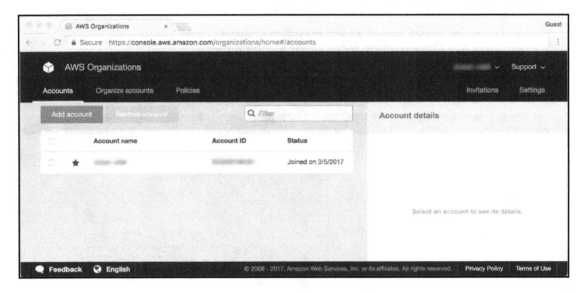

AWS Organizations

3. Click on the **Invitations** tab in the top-right corner of the console:

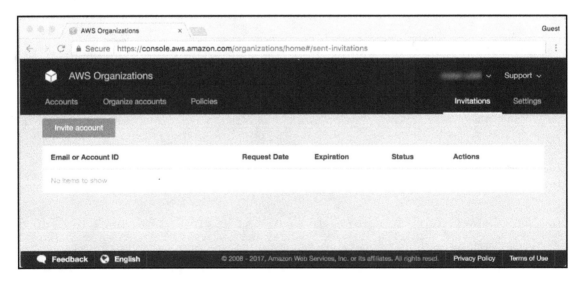

Invite account

4. Click on the **Invite account** button. Specify the account ID (or main email address) of the account to invite.

5. Once you click **Invite**, you will be taken to a list of invitations where you can view their status.

6. At this stage, the target/invited account will receive an email notifying it of the invite.

7. Log in to the invited account and go to the **My Organization** link under the user menu.

8. In the **AWS Organizations** console, you can see the pending invite on the left:

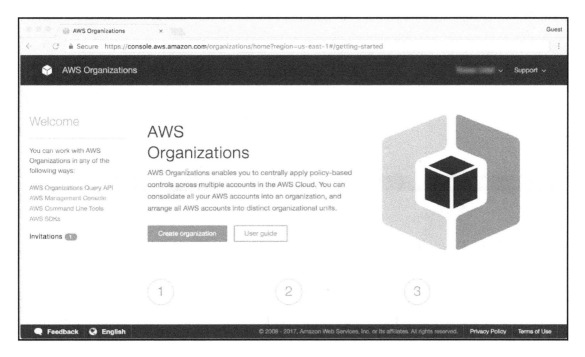

Pending invite

9. By clicking on the invite, you can see its details. Click **Accept**:

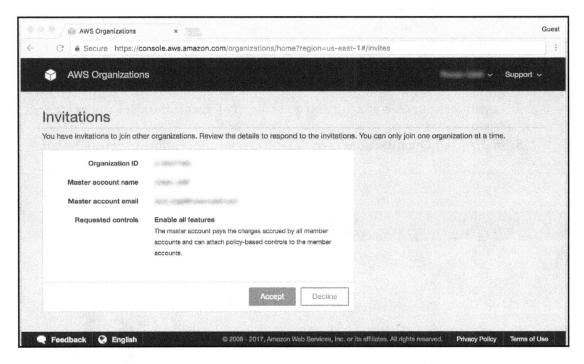

Invite details

10. When the invite includes all the necessary features, you will be asked to **confirm** your acceptance:

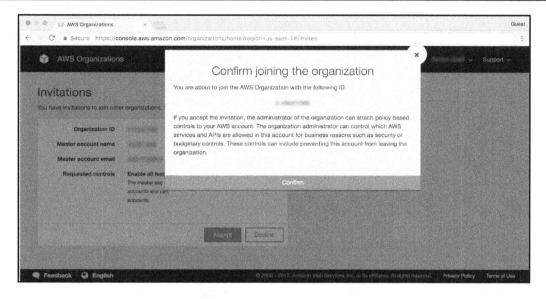

Confirm joining the organization

11. You can now see the details of the organization you have joined.
12. At this stage, the master account will be notified of the accepted invite.
13. Back in the master account, you can now see the new account alongside the master:

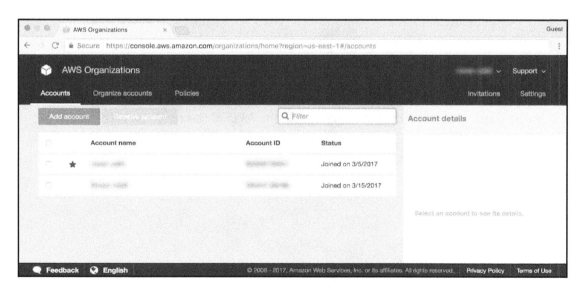

New Organizations account

How it works...

While there are many steps involved, the process of inviting an existing account is a relatively simple handshake process. This means that both sides must actively initiate/accept the invite for it to succeed – an invite cannot be forced.

After specifying the target account's account ID (or email address), the associated email address will be notified.

As part of the handshake process, the invited account must explicitly accept the invite.

 It is important to note that the default invite type (and what we have used in this recipe) uses the full feature set for AWS Organizations. As noted in the console, this means that the invited account could be prevented from leaving the organization if the relevant policies are configured.

After confirmation, both parties will receive an email detailing the membership. From now on, the bill for the invited account will be paid by the master account.

There's more...

Invited accounts are treated differently from accounts that are created via the organization's functionality. Below are two type of account that we will look into:

- Removing accounts
- Consolidated billing

Removing accounts

Unlike member accounts (which are created via the AWS Organizations API), invited accounts can be removed from an organization.

Consolidated billing

As an alternative to the full feature invite, it is possible to specify just consolidated billing mode for an organization. In this mode, no OUs or policies will be available; only the billing relationship will be shared between the accounts (that is, the master account will pay the bill of the member accounts).

 Any preexisting accounts that were configured to use consolidated billing will have been automatically migrated to AWS Organizations in consolidated billing mode.

See also

- The *Creating a member account* recipe in this chapter

Managing your accounts

There are a number of ways to group and arrange your AWS accounts. How you do this is completely up to you, but the following are a few examples to consider:

- **Business unit (BU) or location**: You may wish to allow each BU to work in isolation on its own products or services, on its own schedule, without impacting other parts of the business.
- **Cost center**: Grouping according to cost may help you track spending versus the allocated budget.
- **Environment type**: It may make sense to group your development, test, and production environments together in a way that helps you manage the controls across each environment.
- **Workload type or data classification**: Your company may want to isolate workload types from each other, or ensure that particular controls are applied to all the accounts containing a particular kind of data.

In the following fictitious example, we have isolated the **Sitwell Enterprises Account** from the rest of the organization by placing it in an OU called **Sudden Valley**. Perhaps they operate in a different geographical location and have different regulatory requirements around controls and access:

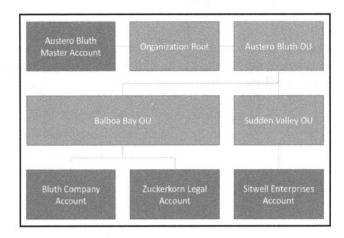

Organization hierarchy

Note that, while it's also technically possible for us to put the master account inside an OU, we avoid doing this to make the following obvious:

- It's the master account and it has control over the entire organization.
- The rules we set using the SCPs for the member accounts in our organization do not apply to the master account (because they can't).

You can learn more about SCPs in the *Adding a Service Control Policy (SCP)* recipe in this chapter.

Getting ready

Before we can proceed, you should have already done the following:

- Set up a master AWS account
- Created an organization
- Created member accounts in your organization, or manually added member accounts (by invitation) to your organization

How to do it...

We'll now cover the one-line commands you'll need in order to perform common tasks that are required to manage your OU. These commands can only be performed in your master account:

- Getting the root ID for your organization
- Creating an OU
- Getting the ID of an OU
- Adding an account to an OU
- Removing an account from an OU
- Deleting an OU

Getting the root ID for your organization

You can run this command to get the ID of the root for your organization. The root is created automatically for you when you create your organization in your master account:

```
aws organizations list-roots
```

The ID that's returned to you will look something like the following:

```
r-bmdw
```

Creating an OU

To create an OU, perform the following steps:

1. Determine where you'd like this OU to live. If it lives directly underneath the root, then your root ID will be the parent. Alternatively, if this OU is going to be a child of another OU, use the ID of the OU instead. Obviously, if this is the first OU you're creating, the root will be the parent.

2. Use the CLI to create your OU, as follows:

```
aws organizations create-organizational-unit \
  --parent-id <root-id or parent-ou-id> \
  --name <desired-ou-name>
```

Getting the ID of an OU

If you need to fetch the ID of an OU, you can use the CLI to do so; note that you'll need to know the parent of the OU. Here is how you'd get a list of all the OUs and their IDs in a root or OU:

```
aws organizations list-organizational-units-for-parent \
  --parent-id <root-id or parent-ou-id>
```

Adding an account to an OU

To add an account to an OU, perform the following steps:

1. When an account is initially added to your organization, it will be a child of the organization root. To add it to the OU you just created, you need to move it using the following CLI command:

```
aws organizations move-account \
  --account-id <twelve-digit-account-id> \
  --source-parent-id <root-id> \
  --destination-parent-id <new-parent-ou-id>
```

2. If you wish to move an account from one OU to another, simply use the same command but with the existing parent OU ID instead of the root ID.

Removing an account from an OU

To remove an account from an OU, perform the following steps:

1. If you wish to remove an account from an OU, you have two options. You can move it to another OU, or you can move it back to the root. If you decide you want to delete an OU, you'll need to make sure no accounts exist inside it first (we'll show you how to do this next).

2. Run the following command to move an account back to the root:

```
aws organizations move-account \
  --account-id <twelve-digit-account-id> \
  --source-parent-id <existing-parent-ou-id> \
  --destination-parent-id <root-id>
```

Deleting an OU

To delete an OU, you'll need to make sure it's empty by removing its child accounts (as we mentioned previously). You can then go ahead and delete the OU, as follows:

```
aws organizations delete-organizational-unit \
  --organizational-unit-id <ou-id>
```

How it works...

If done right, grouping your accounts together using OUs will help you simplify the way you manage and administer them. Try to use only just enough OUs to get the job done. The idea is to use OUs to make your life easier, not harder.

There's more...

Here are a few more things to keep in mind when managing your organization's accounts.

- **Organizational Control Policies (OCPs)** can be attached to your root, OU, or AWS accounts. At this time, only one kind of OCP is supported: SCP.
- Accounts can only belong to one OU or root.
- Similarly, OUs can only belong to one OU or root.
- It's best to avoid deploying resources in the master account because this account can't be controlled with SCPs. The master account should be treated as a management account for audit, control, and billing purposes only.

See also

- The *Adding a Service Control Policy (SCP)* recipe in this chapter

Adding a Service Control Policy (SCP)

Before we begin, we should talk about what SCPs are and how they apply to your organization.

An SCP consists of a policy document that defines (by way of filtering) the services and actions that can be used and performed within an OU or in an AWS account.

If you've previously configured an IAM policy, then you will have more than enough background knowledge to get started with SCPs. Apart from a couple of minor exceptions, they look exactly the same.

SCPs can be applied at different levels throughout an organization. The following are the levels, starting from the bottom and going up:

- **AWS account level**: An SCP that's applied to an AWS account takes effect on only that account. It's important to note that the SCP is very separate from the IAM policies that live inside the account. For example, an SCP might allow full access to S3 for an AWS account but the IAM policies inside the account may deny it (for certain roles and/or users).
- **OU level**: An SCP that's applied at the OU level will apply to all the AWS accounts that live inside the OU, as well as any child OUs (remember that an OU can be a member of an OU).
- **Root level**: If an SCP is applied at this level, it will apply to all the AWS accounts inside the organization.

Things can start to get really interesting when you have an SCP applied at multiple levels. The intersection of the policies at the root, OU, account, and IAM levels is evaluated and will determine whether or not an API call is allowed to be made. For example, someone belonging to an IAM role that has full administrator access to an account still won't be able to call any EC2 APIs if any of the SCPs above it (account, OU, or root) deny EC2 access.

In the following example, we have a top-level OU, **Austero Bluth**, with an **SCP** that allows access to all AWS resources for all OUs and accounts underneath it:

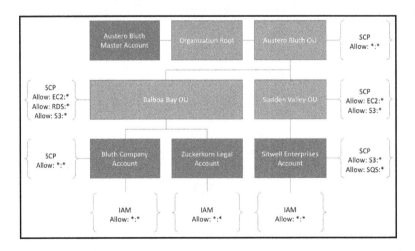

Organization hierarchy and policies

Austero Bluth has two child OUs; let's focus on **Sudden Valley**. It has an **SCP** that allows only **EC2** and **S3**. By using a whitelisting approach, anything except these two services will be denied. Remembering that SCPs act like a filter, any OU or AWS accounts living underneath the **Sudden Valley OU** will, at most, have access to **EC2** and **S3**.

The **Sitwell Enterprises Account** also has an **SCP** attached to it. This particular **SCP** allows **S3** and **SQS**. Note that the **SQS** statement will have no effect here because the **Sitwell** account is inside an OU that does not allow **SQS**. Also, note that this account has no access to **EC2**, despite the **Sudden Valley OU** allowing it; this is because **EC2** wasn't explicitly allowed in the **SCP** attached to the account.

At the **IAM** level, we have a role in the Sitwell AWS account that allows full administrator privileges. However, because the intersection of the SCPs governing this account will only allow **S3,** anyone using this role will be denied access if they attempt to use **EC2** or **SQS**, for example.

Let's also take a look at the **Bluth Company Account**. The **SCP** that is attached to it allows full AWS access; however, it lives inside an OU (**Balboa Bay**) that only allows **EC2**, **RDS**, and **S3**. There is an **IAM** role inside this account that also allows full admin access but, again, administrators in this account will be limited to **EC2**, **RDS**, and **S3**.

Getting ready

We're going to proceed step by step through creating an SCP and adding it to an OU.

You're going to need the ID of the OU in question; you can fetch it from the organization's web console or use the CLI. It will look something like this:

```
ou-bmdw-omzypry7
```

We'll be preparing a policy document as well. In this example, we're going to add an SCP to the Sudden Valley OU to allow access to EC2 and S3. Here's what our SCP looks like:

```
{
    "Version":"2012-10-17",
    "Statement":[
        {
            "Effect":"Allow",
            "Action":["EC2:*","S3:*"],
            "Resource":"*"
        }
    ]
}
```

How to do it...

Perform the following to create an SCP:

1. Open a new file in your text editor, add your JSON policy document, and save it.
2. Run the `create-policy` CLI command as follows. We're getting a little tricky with the `tr` command: here, we're using it to remove the carriage returns from the policy document, so pay close attention to the syntax in the example provided. Unfortunately, the organization's CLI doesn't allow us to provide the path to the policy document directly:

```
aws organizations create-policy \
  --content "$(tr -d '\n' < my-policy-file.json)" \
  --description "A policy description goes here" \
  --name "My policy" \
  --type SERVICE_CONTROL_POLICY
```

3. If the preceding CLI command works successfully, some JSON will be returned to you containing the ID of the policy we just added. It will look something like the following:

```
p-o9to04s7
```

4. You can now go ahead and attach this policy to the OU. Use the following CLI command to do this:

```
aws organizations attach-policy \
  --target-id <ou-or-aws-account-id> \
  --policy-id <policy-id>
```

5. Unfortunately, the preceding command does not output anything if it ran successfully. You can double-check your handiwork in the AWS web console or use the following CLI command to verify that it worked:

```
aws organizations list-targets-for-policy \
  --policy-id <policy-id>
```

How it works...

Again, the policies you add will act as filters at each level of your organizational structure. With this in mind, it might be a good time to point out that testing your policies on a single account before applying them organization-wide will save you a lot of heartache. Making sweeping changes to an SCP living at the top of your organization may create an unforeseen situation at the AWS account level at the bottom of the chain. A local admin in an AWS account is unable to override SCPs.

There's more...

There are a few more things to keep in mind about SCPs:

- At the time of writing, you can only have a single root inside an organization (it's created automatically for you when you create an organization).
- For obvious reasons, the master account is not affected by any SCPs that are attached to it. You may also notice that it's technically possible to place the master account in an OU; again, it will be unaffected by any SCPs that have been attached to that OU.
- Since the master account is unaffected by SCPs, it's a good idea to leave it as empty as possible and to not create any resources in it. Use child AWS accounts instead so that you can apply fine-grained controls to them.
- SCPs are required on each OU and account but shouldn't be considered the only form of access control for your AWS accounts. Apply IAM where appropriate.
- When we're creating our policy, we have to specify a `--type` parameter. At the time of publishing, AWS only supports one variant of OCP: `SERVICE_CONTROL_POLICY`.
- As much as possible, follow the principle of least privilege. You want to give your AWS accounts access to only the services they need. This helps you mitigate damage caused by misclicks, programming errors, or compromised accounts.
- In the long run, you may find it advantageous to not assign controls at the root level. Instead, you may be better off adding *all* accounts to an OU and applying your controls to the OU instead.

- Your policies can take a whitelisting or blacklisting approach. In this recipe, we've used a whitelist approach, but you may prefer to allow your OUs and accounts to use all services except those you explicitly disallow. You should choose one of these approaches and stick with it, as mixing the two will cause you lots of confusion down the road.
- Unlike IAM policies, you can't specify conditions in SCP documents and `Resource` must be `*`.

See also

- The *Federating with your AWS account* recipe in `Chapter 8`, *AWS Account Security and Identity*, for some discussion around IAM roles

Setting up consolidated billing

By setting up your accounts with AWS Organizations, you can consolidate your AWS bill so that you are not being charged separately for each of your child accounts. You get one bill for all the accounts and you can easily track the charges from a single place. By combining accounts, you will save money by sharing volume discounts and reserved instance pricing.

How to do it...

All you have to do to enable consolidated billing is create a master account in AWS Organizations (or via Control Tower, as described earlier in this chapter). The master account will be automatically configured to receive the bill for all subordinate accounts. For billing purposes, all accounts will be treated as one account, so you can maximize savings from any volume discount that you might have. Reserved instance pricing will aggregate your EC2 instances across accounts.

How it works...

The master account in an organization is responsible for paying the bill for all its accounts in the organization. If you are an administrator of the organization, you can see a consolidated billing report and view charges for each individual account. A separate bill is generated for each account, but it is for information purposes only. The only bill that needs to be paid is the bill that is associated with the master account.

Estimated charges are calculated several times per day, so that you can always get an idea of what your total monthly bill will be.

There's more...

The following are a few more things related to consolidated billing that you might want to keep in mind.

- Credits
- Support charges

Credits

If you have any AWS credits applied to any of your accounts, the credits will also apply to your organization as a whole.

 See the AWS documentation to find out exactly how credits are applied: https://docs.aws.amazon.com/awsaccountbilling/latest/aboutv2/useconsolidatedbilling-credits.html.

Support charges

Support contracts are still applied to each account individually. It is a highly recommended best practice to have, at a minimum, business support enabled on all production accounts. Each account in your organization needs to subscribe to the support agreement separately. The exception is an enterprise support contract, which can cover all of the accounts in your organization.

See also

- Chapter 9, *Managing Costs*

3
AWS Storage and Content Delivery

Storing data and delivering it to customers is at the heart of almost all applications, and AWS provides a myriad of services to help you accomplish these goals. Amazon **Simple Storage Service (S3)** is the foundation for storing a virtually unlimited amount of object data at very low prices, and Amazon CloudFront can easily be configured to deliver data stored in S3 to a global array of edge servers.

Storage is an integral part of any organization's cloud usage. When used correctly, servers are short-lived and replaceable. This means that having a durable, available storage service is critical to persisting and sharing state.

Here is a high-level summary of the storage services AWS offers:

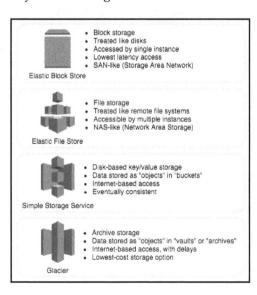

Storage services from AWS

In this chapter, we will cover the following recipes:

- Setting up a secure Amazon S3 bucket
- Hosting a static website in S3
- Caching a website with CloudFront
- Working with network storage provided by **Elastic File System** (**EFS**)
- Backing up data for compliance

Amazon Elastic Block Store and Amazon EFS offer options to suit a range of data storage needs. In this chapter, you will learn the basics of each of these services.

Setting up a secure Amazon S3 bucket

Amazon S3 is one of the main services offered by AWS. It is hard to imagine implementing even the most trivial architecture without using S3 buckets. In this recipe, you will create buckets in three ways – by using the web console, the **command-line interface** (**CLI**), and with **CloudFormation**. You will create buckets with different properties each time to give you a sample of the various configurations that are possible.

S3 provides a web-based service for hosting files. Files are referred to as **objects** and grouped in **buckets**. An object is effectively a key-value pair, similar to a document database. Keys are used like file paths, with / used as a separator and grouping character. Buckets can be accessed easily, like a website via an automatically generated domain name.

 Due to being associated with a domain name, bucket names must be globally unique.

The following are some recommended use cases for S3:

- Static website assets
- Sharing large files
- Short-term (that is, warm) backups

How to do it...

In this recipe, you will create different buckets using the web console, the CLI, and CloudFormation so that you are exposed to a variety of bucket configurations.

Using the web console to create a bucket with versioning enabled

Follow these steps to create a basic versioning-enabled bucket:

1. Log in to your AWS account and go to the S3 dashboard.
2. Click **Create bucket**:

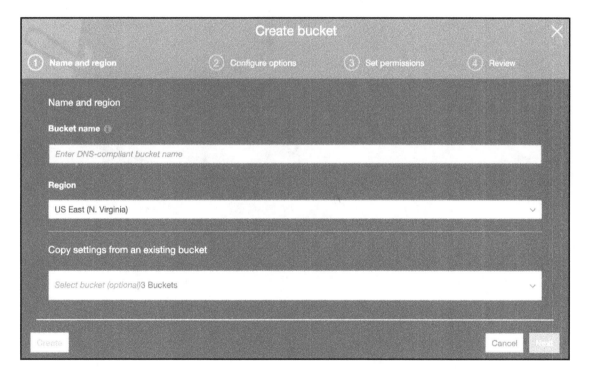

Creating a bucket

3. Give your bucket a globally unique name.
4. Click **Next**.
5. Check the box to **Keep all versions of an object in the same bucket**. This enables versioning so that you can revert objects to their former state if necessary:

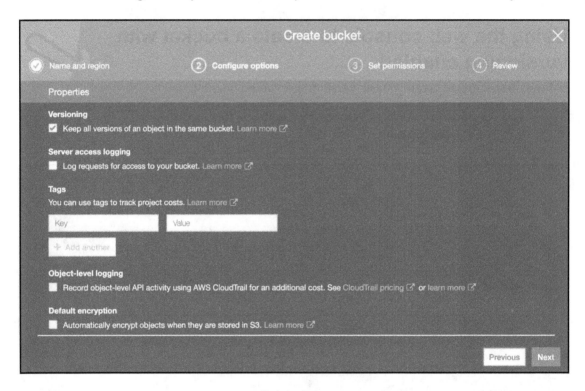

Versioning a bucket

6. Click **Next**.

7. On the next screen, leave the defaults as they are – we don't want our buckets to ever be made public:

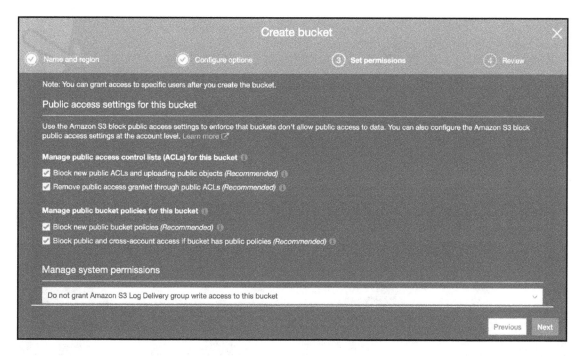

Bucket access

8. Click **Next**.

9. Review the bucket settings on the following screen and click **Create bucket**:

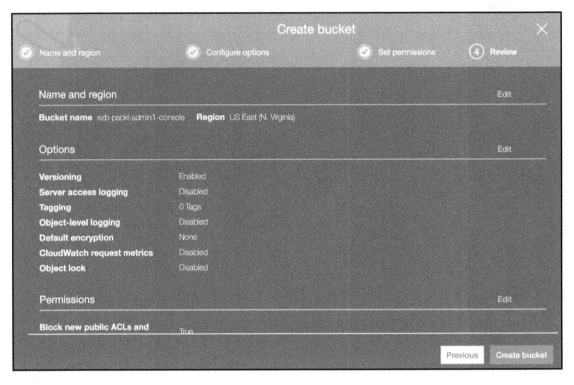

Reviewing the bucket settings

10. Once the bucket has been created, click on its name and take a look at the tools that are available to administer the new bucket:

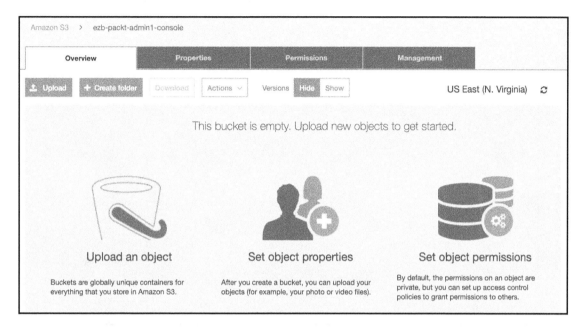

Bucket administration

11. Since we enabled versioning on this bucket, let's test it out to see how it works.

12. Create a text file on your desktop and add a single line to the file:

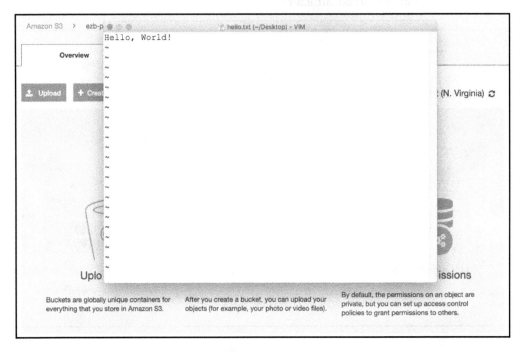

Creating a file to upload

13. Click the **Upload** button and upload that file to the new bucket:

Uploading a file

14. Click **Next**. Accept the defaults on the following screen and click **Next** again.

15. On the next screen, inspect the various storage classes that are available. It's worth spending some time learning the pros and cons of each class. Pick **Standard**:

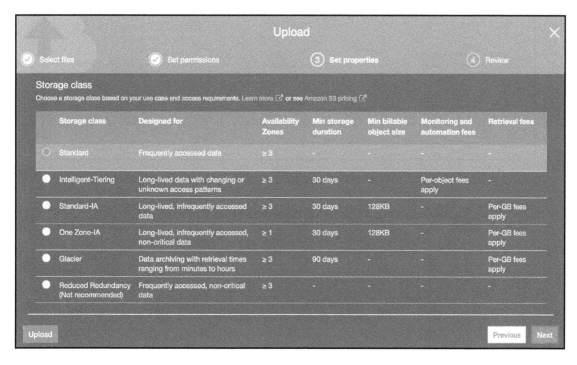

Storage class

16. Scroll down to the **Encryption** option. Select the **Amazon S3 master key**. The object will be encrypted seamlessly, without requiring you to manually encrypt or decrypt it. Encryption is handled behind the scenes for you.

17. On the final screen, click **Upload**:

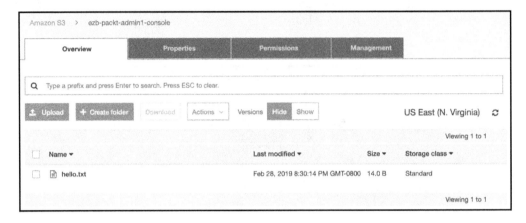

File upload

18. Click the object name to go to a screen dedicated to the object:

Object administration

19. Note that there is an object URL at the bottom, but if you click it, you will get an error since we didn't make this object public!

20. Click the **Download** button to retrieve a copy of the object. Open it to confirm that it's the same as what we uploaded.

21. Edit the file on your desktop to add a new line.

22. Go back to the bucket administration and click **Upload** again. Upload a new copy of the file using the same procedure we outlined in the previous steps.

23. Click the object name, and then click the **Latest version** link next to the name. Download each version to confirm that the content matches your expectations:

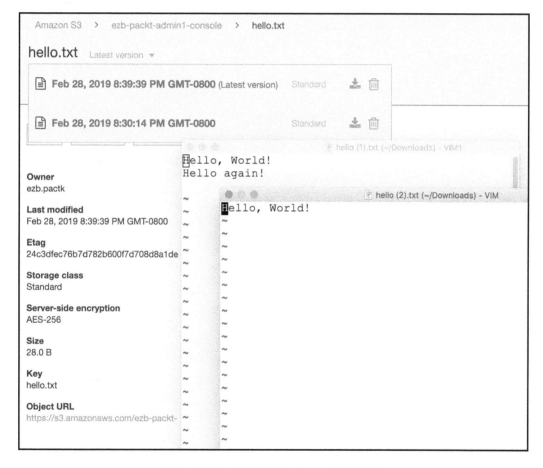

When versioning is enabled, all object versions are retained indefinitely

Using the CLI to create a bucket with cross-region replication enabled

In this recipe, we will do something slightly different than in the previous recipe. **Cross-region replication** can be a very important aspect of a solid disaster recovery plan, and it is often a requirement for various compliance certifications.

The first thing to understand about using S3 with the CLI is that there are two separate executables: s3 and s3api. These provide access to different tiers of functionality:

- We use s3 for simple high-level commands that are similar to Unix shell commands such as cp and ls.
- We use s3api to get complete access to the functionality offered by the entire S3 REST API.

In this recipe, you will use both tiers to create and manipulate buckets:

1. List all the buckets in your account with aws s3:

   ```
   $ aws s3 ls
   2019-02-02 17:43:46 cf-templates-1llvkn4p8d3dr-us-east-1
   2019-02-11 16:38:29 cf-templates-1llvkn4p8d3dr-us-west-1
   2019-03-01 04:14:05 ezb-packt-admin1-console
   2019-02-08 19:25:18 mycloudtrailbucketstack-mycloudtrailbucket-
   bf8yqwecopwv
   ```

2. Create a new bucket in us-east-1. This bucket will be the source of cross-region replication (replace the following bucket name with a globally unique name of your choosing):

   ```
   $ aws s3 mb --region us-east-1 s3://YOUR-SOURCE-BUCKET
   make_bucket: YOUR-SOURCE-BUCKET
   ```

3. Create a separate bucket in us-west-1 to act as the target of the replication:

   ```
   $ aws s3 mb --region us-west-1 s3://YOUR-TARGET-BUCKET
   make_bucket: YOUR-TARGET-BUCKET
   ```

4. Enable versioning on the source and target buckets:

```
$ aws s3api put-bucket-versioning \
    --bucket YOUR-SOURCE-BUCKET \
    --versioning-configuration Status=Enabled
$ aws s3api put-bucket-versioning \
    --bucket YOUR-TARGET-BUCKET \
    --versioning-configuration Status=Enabled
```

5. Create a role that will allow S3 to replicate objects on your behalf. Copy the following code into a file called `cr-role.json`:

```
{
    "Statement": [{
        "Effect": "Allow",
        "Principal": {
            "Service": "s3.amazonaws.com"
        },
        "Action": "sts:AssumeRole"
    }]
}
```

6. Create the role:

```
$ aws iam create-role --role-name my-cr-role --assume-role-policy-
document file://cr-role.json
```

7. Attach a policy to the role that allows S3 access to the source and target buckets. Create a file called `cr-policy.json`, replacing the placeholders with your bucket names:

```
{
    "Statement":[
        {
            "Effect": "Allow",
            "Action": [
                "s3:GetObjectVersionForReplication",
                "s3:GetObjectVersionAcl"
            ],
            "Resource": [
                "arn:aws:s3:::YOUR-SOURCE-BUCKET/*"
            ]
        },
        {
            "Effect": "Allow",
            "Action": [
                "s3:ListBucket",
                "s3:GetReplicationConfiguration"
```

```
                            ],
                            "Resource": [
                                "arn:aws:s3:::YOUR-SOURCE-BUCKET"
                            ]
                        },
                        {
                            "Effect": "Allow",
                            "Action": [
                                "s3:ReplicateObject",
                                "s3:ReplicateDelete",
                                "s3:ReplicateTags",
                                "s3:GetObjectVersionTagging"

                            ],
                            "Resource": "arn:aws:s3:::YOUR-TARGET-BUCKET/*"
                        }
                    ]
                }
```

8. Attach the policy to the role:

```
$ aws iam put-role-policy --role-name my-cr-role --policy-name my-
cr-role-policy --policy-document file://cr-policy.json
```

9. Configure cross-region replication on the first bucket using `aws s3api`. This is a complex command that is much easier to handle if you use a JSON file as input. Luckily, there is a way to output a template skeleton to get you started. In the following code, I used `put-bucket-replication`, along with the `--generate-cli-skeleton` parameter, and redirected the output to a file so that I could open it with a text editor:

```
$ aws s3api put-bucket-replication --generate-cli-skeleton >
pbr.json
$ vim pbr.json
```

10. Much of the skeleton is optional, so the file can be simplified. Use the following content for `pbr.json`. Make sure to replace the values for your role and your target bucket:

```
{
    "Role": "YOUR-ROLE-ARN",
    "Rules": [{
        "Status": "Enabled",
        "Prefix": "",
        "Destination": {
            "Bucket": "arn:aws:s3:::YOUR-TARGET-BUCKET"
        }
```

```
    }]
  }
```

11. Apply the replication configuration to the buckets:

```
$ aws s3api put-bucket-replication \
    --replication-configuration file://pbr.json \
    --bucket YOUR-SOURCE-BUCKET
```

12. Copy an object into the source bucket:

```
$ touch hello.txt
$ aws s3 cp hello.txt s3://YOUR-SOURCE-BUCKET
```

13. List the contents of the target bucket to confirm that the object
    was replicated successfully. Note that this might take a few seconds as the
    replication is eventually consistent:

```
$ aws s3 ls s3://YOUR-TARGET-BUCKET
2019-03-05 04:20:53 0 hello.txt
```

Using CloudFormation to create a bucket

In this recipe, you will use CloudFormation to create a bucket with resource tags that have
been configured to enable **cost-center reporting**, and with a rule to move the objects to
Glacier after 90 days:

1. Create a file called 03-04-Glacier.yml with the following content:

```yaml
Resources:
  MyCloudFormationBucket:
    Type: AWS::S3::Bucket
    Properties:
      LifecycleConfiguration:
        Rules:
        - Id: GlacierRule
          Prefix: glacier
          Status: Enabled
          Transitions:
            - TransitionInDays: '90'
              StorageClass: Glacier
      Tags:
        -
          Key: "COST_CENTER"
          Value: "Accounting"
        -
```

```
                   Key: "PROJECT_ID"
                   Value: "FY2019"
       Outputs:
         BucketName:
           Value: !Ref MyCloudFormationBucket
           Description: The bucket name
```

2. Create the `stack`:

```
$ aws cloudformation create-stack \
    --stack-name 03-04-Glacier.yml \
    --template-body file://03-04-Glacier.yml
```

How it works...

You might be wondering why you have to give S3 buckets globally unique names when S3 is a strictly regional construct. The reason for this is that each bucket is given a URL that can be accessed from anywhere, regardless of the region. There are a variety of strategies you can use to make sure your buckets are named consistently, and one of them is to use a variation of your domain name. For example, if your account is associated with `www.example.com`, you could prefix each of your buckets with `com-example-www-`. This would give you a reasonable chance of avoiding name conflicts.

S3 is a great example of the kind of resiliency you can get from Amazon's regional architecture that consists of multiple AZs, each of which a closely knit collection of data centers connected by high-speed data connections. Objects stored in S3 have 11 x 9s of durability, meaning they are 99.999999999% durable. The odds of permanently losing an object during our lifetimes are very slim.

There's more...

Several interesting and powerful services are built on top of S3. The following are some examples.

Athena

Athena allows you to query data within S3 as if it were a relational database (with limitations). Athena queries are written in standard SQL, which allows data analysts to reach beyond the data warehouse to query structured data stored in S3, which is extremely cost-efficient.

S3 Select

S3 Select is similar to Athena, but it allows you to select fragments out of a single object in S3.

See alo

- See the *Backing up for compliance* recipe in this chapter for a more detailed look at configuring Glacier.

Hosting a static website

It's really easy to host a **static website** on AWS. It turns out that it's also dirt cheap, fast, reliable, and massively scalable.

You do this by storing your content in an S3 bucket and configuring that bucket to behave like a website.

It's important to note that we're talking about static content only. This method doesn't work for websites requiring server-side processing or some other backend functionality. **WordPress**, for example, requires a **hypertext preprocessor** (**PHP**), which means you need a fully functional web server to run it. S3 won't interpret PHP pages for you; it will just serve files straight to the browser.

So, why would you want to host a static website in S3? Common scenarios we encounter include the following:

- Simply, your website is completely static and you don't change it very often.
- Your company is launching a new product or service. You're expecting very large numbers of customers to visit a mini-site within a short time period, which is likely to be more traffic than your existing web-hosting environment can handle.

- You need somewhere to host a failover or down-for-maintenance style page that is separate from your existing web-hosting environment:

> HTTPS is not supported by S3 when it is used to serve static content. If you require HTTPS, configure CloudFront along with Amazon Certificate Manager.

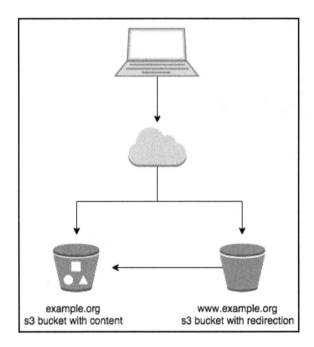

Serving static content from S3

How to do it...

This recipe provides you with CloudFormation, which is necessary to create the following:

- An S3 bucket for hosting your content
- A Route 53-hosted zone and necessary DNS records
- A redirection from `www` to `root/apex` for your domain

After running CloudFormation, you will, of course, need to upload your content to the buckets that CloudFormation created for you.

Creating S3 buckets and hosting content

In this example, we're actually going to create two S3 buckets for our site (http://www.example.org/). They correspond to www.example.org and example.org hostnames:

1. We're going to put all our content in our example.org bucket and tell S3 that requests to www.example.org should be redirected to the other bucket. Here's what the relevant parts of CloudFormation would look like for creating these buckets (note that we'll be expanding on this example as we proceed through this recipe). Create a new CloudFormation template file called 03-01-Website.yaml and enter the following code:

```
Resources:
  ApexBucket:
    Type: AWS::S3::Bucket
    Properties:
      BucketName: !Ref DomainName
  WWWBucket:
    Type: AWS::S3::Bucket
    Properties:
      BucketName: !Sub
        - www.${Domain}
        - Domain: !Ref DomainName
```

 This might be a good time to remind you that S3 bucket names are globally unique. You'll need to replace example.org with a domain that you own.

2. We won't be hardcoding our domain name into the bucket names. Instead, we're going to supply our domain as a parameter to the CloudFormation template in order to maximize its reusability, and then reference it via !Ref DomainName. To keep this recipe as simple as possible, we're going to set up a single-page website. In the real world, your website will, of course, consist of multiple files, but the process you need to follow is exactly the same.

3. Now, we need to configure the index document:
   - The **index** document is the file that S3 will serve by default when someone types your domain name into the address bar in their browser. This precludes the user from having to type the full path to a file, that is, example.org/index.html.
   - Typically, your index document will be called index.html. We'll provide a code snippet for this file toward the end of this chapter.

4. Next, we need to configure the error document:
   - The **error** document is the file S3 will serve if something goes wrong (missing files, forbidden access, bad requests, and so on). To keep things consistent, we're going to call ours `error.html`. Again, we'll provide a code snippet for this later in this chapter.

5. Now, we need to enable website hosting on our bucket:
   - As we mentioned previously, we're going to need to tell S3 that it should serve static website content from our `example.org` bucket. Often, users will perform this configuration through the S3 web console. We're going to do it in CloudFormation, however. The CLI also offers a nice one-liner for doing this. You're not going to need to run this command; we're just adding it here for reference:

```
aws s3 website s3://example.org/ \
    --index-document index.html --error-document
error.html
```

6. Next, we will set up a redirection from the `www` hostname:
   - When performing this task manually, you have little option but to fire up the web console and configure the `www.example.org` bucket to redirect to the `example.org` bucket. There's no handy one-line CLI command for this one. Fortunately, it's easy in CloudFormation, as you'll soon see in the upcoming CloudFormation snippet.

7. Let's configure some permissions:
   - The last bucket setup task is to configure permissions. By default, S3 buckets are private, and only the bucket owner can see its contents. This is not much use to us in this scenario because we need everyone to be able to see our bucket's contents. This is a public website, after all.

8. If we were configuring our bucket manually, we would apply a bucket policy, which looks something like this:

```
{
   "Version":"2012-10-17",
   "Statement": [{
     "Sid": "Allow Public Access to everything in our bucket",
     "Effect": "Allow",
     "Principal": "*",
     "Action": "s3:GetObject",
     "Resource": "arn:aws:s3:::example.org/*"
   }
```

```
    ]
  }
```

9. Fortunately, in CloudFormation, the task is much simpler. Building on the previous example, the `Resources` section of our CloudFormation template now looks like this:

```
Resources:
  ApexBucket:
    Type: AWS::S3::Bucket
    Properties:
      BucketName:
        Ref: DomainName
      AccessControl: PublicRead
      WebsiteConfiguration:
        IndexDocument: index.html
        ErrorDocument: error.html
  WWWBucket:
    Type: AWS::S3::Bucket
    Properties:
      BucketName:
        Fn::Join: [ ., [ www, Ref: DomainName ] ]
      AccessControl: BucketOwnerFullControl
      WebsiteConfiguration:
        RedirectAllRequestsTo:
          HostName:
            Ref: ApexBucket
```

We still have more changes to make to the file, as described in the following section.

Creating a hosted zone

To start adding DNS records, we need to add a hosted zone to Route 53. As you can see in the following code, this is reasonably simple to do. The `Name` we are going to supply will be provided as a parameter to our CloudFormation template. Add the following code to the top of the file:

```
Parameters:
  DNSHostedZone:
    Type: "AWS::Route53::HostedZone"
    Properties:
      Name:
        Ref: DomainName
```

Creating DNS records

Follow these steps to create your DNS records:

1. Now that we have a hosted zone, we can go ahead and create DNS records for it. For this, we use the AWS resource type known as `AWS::Route53::RecordSetGroup`.

2. We're going to create an `A` record for our domain's `root/apex` entry, and we'll make it an alias. This alias will be configured to point to the AWS endpoint for S3-hosted websites in the particular region we choose to run this CloudFormation in.

3. To achieve region portability in our template, we'll use a `mapping` to provide all the endpoints. The values in this map are published by AWS in their API endpoints documentation. You won't need to look these up, however, because our code sample provides the most up-to-date endpoints (at the time of writing). The endpoints tend not to change, but the list obviously grows when AWS adds more regions.

4. The mapping will look like this:

```
us-east-1:
  S3HostedZoneID: Z3AQBSTGFYJSTF
  S3AliasTarget: s3-website-us-east-1.amazonaws.com
us-east-2:
  S3HostedZoneID: Z2O1EMRO9K5GLX
  S3AliasTarget: s3-website.us-east-2.amazonaws.com
```

We'll also need a `CNAME` for `www`, which will point at our `WWWBucket` so that redirection can take place. The final resource for our DNS records will look like this:

```
DNSRecords:
  Type: "AWS::Route53::RecordSetGroup"
  Properties:
    HostedZoneId:
      Ref: DNSHostedZone
    RecordSets:
      - Name:
          Ref: DomainName
        Type: A
        AliasTarget:
          HostedZoneId:
            Fn::FindInMap: [ RegionMap, Ref: "AWS::Region",
              S3HostedZoneID ]
          DNSName:
            Fn::FindInMap: [ RegionMap, Ref: "AWS::Region",
```

```
                    S3AliasTarget ]
        - Name:
            Fn::Join: [ ., [ www, Ref: DomainName ] ]
          Type: CNAME
          TTL: 300
          ResourceRecords:
            - Fn::GetAtt: WWWBucket.DomainName
```

5. Now, we're ready for launch. It's time to create our CloudFormation stack. You can download the complete template file from the GitHub repository for this book. Create the stack using the following CLI command:

```
aws cloudformation create-stack \
  --stack-name static-website-1 \
  --template-body file://03-01-Website.yaml \
  --parameters \
  ParameterKey=DomainName,ParameterValue=<your-domain-name>
```

Once the stack completes, you will be able to add some content to your new website.

Uploading website content

Now, it's time to upload some content to our S3 buckets. Here are the snippets we promised you earlier. There's nothing fancy here. Once you've got these examples working, you can try replacing them with your real website content.

Save this content as index.html:

```
<html>
  <head>
    <title>Welcome to example.org</title>
  </head>
  <body>
    <h1>example.org</h1>
    <p>Hello World!</p>
  </body>
</html>
```

Save this content as error.html:

```
<html>
  <head>
    <title>Error</title>
  </head>
  <body>
    <h1>example.org</h1>
```

```
        <p>Something went wrong!</p>
    </body>
</html>
```

How it works...

That's it! As soon as S3 has an `index.html` file to serve up, you will be hosting a single-page website on S3. Go ahead and test it out. The CloudFormation example that's supplied will output a URL you can use to see your new website. After you've verified it's working, you can go ahead and upload your real static website and enjoy fast, cheap, and server-free hosting.

There's more...

Let's look at some additional things to consider.

Delegating your domain to AWS

While we've created a hosted zone and some DNS records in Route 53, no one can actually see them yet. To send your website visitors to your new S3 static website, you'll need to delegate your domain to Route 53. This is left to you as an exercise; however, there are some important things to remember:

- The DNS servers to delegate your domain to can be found in the NS record for your hosted zone.
- If your domain is already live and production-like, you'll need to make sure all your DNS records for your zone are recreated in Route 53, including things such as **MX records**, which are critical for the continuity of your email service.
- Before delegating to AWS, you may consider reducing the **time to live** (TTL) values on your DNS records. This will be useful if, for some reason, you need to redelegate or make changes to them. Once your DNS setup is stable, you can increase TTLs.

Cross-origin resource sharing (CORS)

It's worth discussing CORS here because the more static web content hosting you do in S3, the higher your chances are of needing to know about this, particularly where web fonts are concerned.

Some browsers implement a same-origin policy restriction. This prevents the browser from loading certain kinds of assets from hostnames that are different than the page being displayed to the user. Web fonts fall under this restriction and are an often-cited example, because, when they don't load correctly, your website will usually look a lot different than how you intended. The solution to this is to add a CORS configuration to your bucket to allow its content to be loaded by the particular origin or hostname that requested it.

We'll leave the CORS configuration out of our full example, but if you need to add one to your bucket, here's how you can do it. Update your `AllowedOrigins` property to look similar to the following CloudFormation, and you should be all set:

```
ApexBucket:
  Type: AWS::S3::Bucket
  Properties:
    BucketName: !Ref DomainName
    AccessControl: PublicRead
    WebsiteConfiguration:
      IndexDocument: index.html
      ErrorDocument: error.html
    CorsConfiguration:
      CorsRules:
      - AllowedOrigins:
          - example.net
          - www.example.net
          - example.com
          - www.example.com
        AllowedMethods:
          - GET
        MaxAge: 3000
        AllowedHeaders:
          - Content-*
          - Host
```

See also

- In this section, we covered how to simply and easily convert a public bucket into a website. But wait – aren't we always hearing about how it's bad practice to make an S3 bucket public? While a static website is one of the few legitimate use cases for a public bucket, there is a better way. See the next recipe, *Caching a website with CloudFront*, to learn how to securely host the contents of a private bucket using **Amazon CloudFront**.

Caching a website with CloudFront

In this recipe, we'll show you how to use AWS CloudFront to cache your website.

The primary reasons you'll want to consider doing this are as follows:

- Copies of your content will be geographically located closer to your end users, thereby improving their experience and delivering content to them faster.
- The burden for serving content will be removed from your fleet of servers. This could potentially result in a large cost saving if you're able to turn off some servers or reduce your bandwidth bill.
- You may need to be shielded from large and unexpected spikes in traffic.
- While not the focus of this chapter, CloudFront gives you the ability to implement a **Web Application Firewall (WAF)** as an added layer of protection from the bad guys.
- You can serve the contents of a private S3 bucket using TLS, which gives your site the secure HTTPS prefix.

 Unlike most AWS services, which are region-specific, CloudFront is a global service.

Getting ready

First of all, you're going to need a publicly accessible website. This could be a static website hosted in S3, or it could be a dynamically generated website hosted in EC2. In fact, your website doesn't even need to be hosted in AWS for you to use CloudFront. As long as your website is publicly accessible, you should be good to go.

You'll also need to have the ability to modify the DNS records for your website. Instead of pointing to your web server (or S3 bucket), we'll eventually point them to CloudFront.

About dynamic content

If your website consists of mostly dynamic content, you can still benefit from implementing CloudFront.

First, CloudFront will maintain a pool of persistent connections with your origin servers. This lessens the time it takes for files to be served to your users because the number of three-way handshakes they'll need to perform is reduced.

Second, CloudFront implements some additional optimizations around TCP connections for high performance. More data is able to be transferred over the wire initially because CloudFront uses a wider initial TCP window.

Finally, implementing a CDN such as CloudFront *does* give you the opportunity to review your caching strategy and how you use cache-control headers. If your home page is dynamically generated, you'll get some benefit straight away by serving it via CloudFront, but the benefits will be much greater if you let CloudFront cache it for a few minutes. Again, cost, end user, and backend performance are all things you should take into consideration.

Configuring CloudFront distributions

Distributions can be configured with a fairly wide array of options. Our recipe is going to be quite simple so that you can get up and running as quickly as possible. However, we will talk about some of the more common configuration options:

- **Origins**: A distribution needs to have at least one origin. An origin, as its name indicates, is where your website content originates from your public-facing website. The properties you'll most likely be concerned with are as follows:
  - **Origin Domain Name**: This is the hostname of your public-facing website. The CloudFormation template we supply accepts this hostname as a parameter.
  - **Origin Path**: It's possible to configure the distribution to fetch content from a directory or subfolder at the origin, for example, `/content/images`, if you were using CloudFront to cache images only. In our case, we are caching our entire website, so we don't specify an origin path at all.
  - **Origin ID**: This is particularly important when you are using non-default cache behavior settings, and therefore have configured multiple origins. You need to assign a unique ID to the origins so that the cache behaviors know which origin to target. There'll be more discussion on cache behaviors later.

- **HTTP Port, HTTPS Port**: If your origin is listening on nonstandard ports for HTTP or HTTPS, you would use these parameters to define those ports.
- **Origin Protocol Policy**: You are able to configure the distribution to talk to your origin via the following:
    - **HTTP Only**
    - **HTTPS Only**
    - **Match Viewer**

The **Match Viewer** option forwards requests to the origin based on which protocol the user requested in their browser. Again, we are keeping things quite simple in this recipe, so we'll be opting for **HTTP Only**.

- **Logging**: Keep in mind that because less traffic will be hitting your origin, fewer access logs will also be captured. It makes sense to have CloudFront keep these logs for us in an S3 bucket. This is included in CloudFormation provided with this recipe:
    - **Cache behaviors**: In this recipe, we'll configure a single (default) cache behavior, which will forward all the requests to our origin.
    - **CloudFront**: This allows you to get quite fine-grained with the behaviors you configure. You might, for example, want to apply a rule to all the `.js` and `.css` files on your origin. Perhaps you want to forward query strings to the origin for these file types. Similarly, you might want to ignore the TTL the origin is trying to set for image files, instead of telling CloudFront to cache for a minimum of 24 hours.
- **Aliases**: These are additional hostnames you want the distribution to serve traffic for. For example, if your **Origin Domain Name** is configured to `loadbalancer.example.org`, then you probably want aliases that look something like this:
    - `example.org`
    - `www.example.org`

The CloudFormation template provided with this recipe expects one or more aliases to be provided in the form of a comma-delimited list of strings.

- **Allowed HTTP methods**: By default, CloudFront will only forward GET and HEAD requests to your origin. This recipe doesn't change those defaults, so we don't declare this parameter in the template provided. If your origin is serving dynamically generated content, then you will likely want to declare this parameter and set its values to GET, HEAD, OPTIONS, PUT, POST, PATCH, and DELETE.

- **TTLs (minimum/maximum/default)**: Optionally, you can define how long you'd like objects to stay in CloudFront's caches before they expire and are fetched from the origin. Again, we've opted to stick to CloudFront's default values to keep this recipe simple, so we've omitted this parameter from our template. The defaults are as follows:
  - **Minimum TTL**: 0 seconds
  - **Default TTL**: 1 day
  - **Maximum TTL**: 1 year

- **Price Class**: By default, CloudFront will serve your content from all of its edge locations, giving you the maximum performance possible. We're going to deploy our distribution using the lowest possible price class, Price Class 100. This corresponds to edge locations in the United States, Canada, and Europe. Users from Australia would not benefit too much from this price class, but you're also paying less for it. Price Class 200 adds Asian regions, and Price Class All adds South America and Australia.

> A comprehensive list and detailed explanation on which values can be specified when creating a CloudFront distribution can be found at http://docs.aws.amazon.com/AmazonCloudFront/latest/DeveloperGuide/distribution-web-values-specify.html.

How to do it...

The first (and only) thing we need to do is configure a CloudFront distribution, as shown in the following diagram:

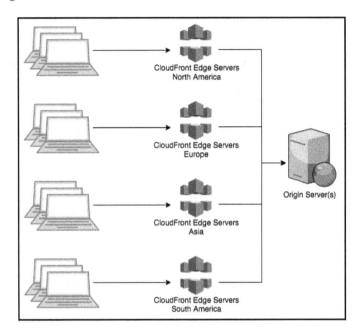

CloudFront Edge servers

Let's see how we can do that:

1. Create a new CloudFormation template and start with the following code, which can be found in this book's GitHub repository. Name the file `03-02-Caching.yaml`:

```
AWSTemplateFormatVersion: '2010-09-09'
    Parameters:
      OriginDomainName:
        Description: The hostname of your origin
          (i.e.
www.example.org.s3-website-ap-southeast-2.amazonaws.com)
        Type: String
      Aliases:
        Description: Comma delimited list of aliases
          (i.e. example.org,www.example.org)
        Type: CommaDelimitedList
```

2. Continue with the resources:

```
Resources:
  DistributionALogBucket:
    Type: AWS::S3::Bucket
  DistributionA:
    Type: AWS::CloudFront::Distribution
    Properties:
      DistributionConfig:
        Origins:
        - DomainName:
            Ref: OriginDomainName
          Id: OriginA
          CustomOriginConfig:
            OriginProtocolPolicy: http-only
        Enabled: true
```

3. Continue with the following code:

```
        Logging:
          IncludeCookies: false
          Bucket:
            Fn::GetAtt: DistributionALogBucket.DomainName
          Prefix: cf-distribution-a
        Aliases:
          Ref: Aliases
        DefaultCacheBehavior:
          TargetOriginId: OriginA
          ForwardedValues:
            QueryString: false
          ViewerProtocolPolicy: allow-all
        PriceClass: PriceClass_100
```

4. Finally, we need to define the outputs:

```
Outputs:
      DistributionDomainName:
        Description: The domain name of the CloudFront
Distribution
        Value:
          Fn::GetAtt: DistributionA.DomainName
      LogBucket:
        Description: Bucket where CloudFront logs will be stored
        Value:
          Ref: DistributionALogBucket
```

5. Using the template we created, go ahead and create your CloudFront distribution. Expect to wait around 20-25 minutes for this stack to finish being created. It takes a while for your distribution configuration to be pushed out to all the AWS CloudFront locations:

```
aws cloudformation create-stack \
        --stack-name cloudfont-cache-1 \
        --template-body file://03-02-Caching.yaml \
        --parameters \
        ParameterKey=OriginDomainName,ParameterValue=<your-
domain-name> \
        ParameterKey=Aliases,ParameterValue='<alias-1>\,<alias-2>'
```

How it works...

Content delivery is designed to quickly and efficiently distribute content to users. The best way to do this is to leverage a **Content Delivery Network (CDN)**. Amazon's CDN service is **Amazon CloudFront**.

At the time of writing, AWS has 20 regions, and it has an additional 115 edge locations that can be used as part of CloudFront. This gives you a massive global network of resources that you can use to improve your users' experience of your application.

CloudFront works closely with S3 to serve static assets. In addition to this, it can be configured to cache dynamic content. This gives you an easy way to improve the performance of applications that are not even aware of CloudFront.

CloudFront websites are referred to as **distributions**, which describes their CDN role.

 Distributions can also be used to provide a common frontend for multiple, disparate sources of content.

Working with network storage provided by EFS

In this recipe, we will use Amazon EFS to provide network-based storage to instances.

Some of the benefits of using EFS compared to other AWS services are as follows:

- There is a guaranteed write order between distributed clients.
- There is automatic resizing – no need to pre-allocate and no need to downsize.
- You only pay for the space you use (per GB) – there's no transfer or extra costs.

EFS provides a file storage service that can be accessed simultaneously by many instances, similar to **Network Attached Storage** (**NAS**). While not as fast as EBS, it still provides low-latency access. Since it may be accessed by multiple clients at a time, it can reach much higher levels of throughput than EBS. EFS filesystems also scale dynamically in size and so do not need to be pre-allocated or modified during use. Filesystems are stored redundantly across AZs.

The following are some recommended use cases for EFS:

- Home directories
- Serving shared web content
- Content management

> EFS performance scales according to the filesystem's size. As the filesystem's size is not pre-allocated, the only way to increase your performance is to add more data to it.

Getting ready

This recipe works with the default VPC and subnets that are present in all AWS accounts when they are created. Even if you have changed your network configuration, all you need is a working VPC with two or more subnets in different AZs for this recipe.

How to do it...

Follow these steps to create a secure filesystem and mount points that can be attached to your EC2 instances:

1. Open your favorite text editor and start a new CloudFormation template by defining `AWSTemplateFormatVersion` and `Description`:

```
AWSTemplateFormatVersion: "2010-09-09"
        Description: Create an EFS file system and endpoints.
```

2. Create a top-level `Parameters` section and define the required parameters, `VpcId` and `SubnetIds`, inside it:

```
VpcId:
  Description: VPC ID that contains the subnets that will
    access the file system
  Type: AWS::EC2::VPC::Id
SubnetIds:
  Description: Subnet IDs allowed to access the EFS file system
  Type: List<AWS::EC2::Subnet::Id>
```

3. Create a top-level `Resources` property, which will contain all the resources we've defined.

4. Under the `Resources` property, add the `EFS FileSystem` resource:

```
FileSystem:
  Type: AWS::EFS::FileSystem
  Properties:
    FileSystemTags:
      - Key: Name
        Value:
          Fn::Sub: "${AWS::StackName} EFS File System"
    PerformanceMode: generalPurpose
```

5. Add some mount target resources so that they can connect to the filesystem you just created:

```
MountTargetA:
  Type: AWS::EFS::MountTarget
  Properties:
    FileSystemId:
      Ref: FileSystem
    SecurityGroups:
      - Fn::GetAtt: MountTargetSecurityGroup.GroupId
    SubnetId:
      Fn::Select: [ 0, Ref: SubnetIds  ]
MountTargetB:
  Type: AWS::EFS::MountTarget
  Properties:
    FileSystemId:
      Ref: FileSystem
    SecurityGroups:
      - Fn::GetAtt: MountTargetSecurityGroup.GroupId
    SubnetId:
      Fn::Select: [ 1, Ref: SubnetIds  ]
```

6. Create a security group to control access to the mount targets:

```
MountTargetSecurityGroup:
  Type: AWS::EC2::SecurityGroup
  Properties:
    GroupDescription: EFS endpoint security group
    Tags:
      - Key: Name
        Value: MountTargetSecurityGroup
    VpcId:
      Ref: VpcId
```

7. Create a security group to access the mount target security group you created in the previous step:

```
MountTargetAccessSecurityGroup:
  Type: AWS::EC2::SecurityGroup
  Properties:
    GroupDescription: EFS endpoint access security group
  Tags:
    - Key: Name
      Value: MountTargetAccessSecurityGroup
  VpcId:
    Ref: VpcId
```

8. Define the ingress and egress rules for the mount target security group:

```
MountTargetIngress:
  Type: AWS::EC2::SecurityGroupIngress
  Properties:
    FromPort: 2049
    GroupId:
      Fn::GetAtt: MountTargetSecurityGroup.GroupId
    IpProtocol: tcp
    SourceSecurityGroupId:
      Fn::GetAtt: MountTargetAccessSecurityGroup.GroupId
    ToPort: 2049
MountTargetEgress:
  Type: AWS::EC2::SecurityGroupEgress
  Properties:
    DestinationSecurityGroupId:
      Fn::GetAtt: MountTargetAccessSecurityGroup.GroupId
    FromPort: 2049
    GroupId:
      Fn::GetAtt: MountTargetSecurityGroup.GroupId
    IpProtocol: tcp
    ToPort: 2049
```

9. Define the ingress and egress rules for the mount target access security group:

```
MountTargetAccessIngress:
  Type: AWS::EC2::SecurityGroupIngress
  Properties:
    FromPort: 22
    GroupId:
      Fn::GetAtt: MountTargetAccessSecurityGroup.GroupId
    IpProtocol: tcp
    CidrIp: 0.0.0.0/0
    ToPort: 22
MountTargetAccessEgress:
  Type: AWS::EC2::SecurityGroupEgress
  Properties:
    DestinationSecurityGroupId:
      Fn::GetAtt: MountTargetSecurityGroup.GroupId
    FromPort: 2049
    GroupId:
      Fn::GetAtt: MountTargetAccessSecurityGroup.GroupId
    IpProtocol: tcp
    ToPort: 2049
```

10. Save your template with the name `03-03-NetworkStorage.yml`.

11. Launch the CloudFormation stack with the following AWS CLI command, substituting your own `VpcId` and `SubnetIds`:

```
aws cloudformation create-stack \
  --stack-name wwns1 \
  --template-body file://03-03-NetworkStorage.yml \
  --parameters \
  ParameterKey=VpcId,ParameterValue=<your-vpc-id> \
  ParameterKey=SubnetIds,ParameterValue="<subnet-id-1>\, \
   <subnet-id-2>"
```

How it works...

Here is what the created resources will look like at the end of this recipe:

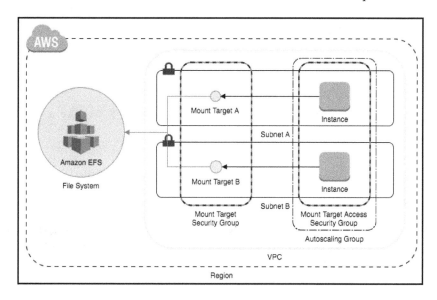

Working with network storage

We start by creating the standard CloudFormation template properties in *step 1*.

In *step 2*, we define the template's parameters that will be used when configuring the resources.

Steps 3 and *4* are where the EFS resources are specified. They consist of an EFS filesystem and mount targets in each of the AZs that will access it.

We then create the security groups in *steps 5* and *6* – one for the mount targets, and one for the instances that are allowed to connect to the mount targets.

As these two security groups contain two-way (or circular) references to each other, we must define the rules between them in separate resources, which we did in *steps 7* and *8*.

In *step 9*, you save the template with a specific filename so that it can be referenced in the command to launch the stack in *step 10*.

There's more...

To confirm that your EFS filesystem, mount targets, and security groups are working, you can also provide some client instances to connect to them. Add the following resources and parameters to the template you have already created:

1. Add the following parameters to your top-level `Parameters` section to configure your instances:

```
MountPoint:
  Description: The path on disk to mount the EFS file system
  Type: String
  Default: /mnt/efs
KeyName:
  Description: The SSH key pair allowed to connect to the client
    instance
  Type: AWS::EC2::KeyPair::KeyName
```

2. Add an `AutoScalingGroup` under the `Resources` section. Regardless of which AZ your servers are provisioned to, they will have access to the `EFS` filesystem via the local mount point:

```
AutoScalingGroup:
  Type: AWS::AutoScaling::AutoScalingGroup
  DependsOn: MountTargetA
  Properties:
    MinSize: 2
    MaxSize: 2
    LaunchConfigurationName:
      Ref: LaunchConfiguration
    Tags:
      - Key: Name
        Value:
          Fn::Sub: "${AWS::StackName} EFS Client"
        PropagateAtLaunch: true
    VPCZoneIdentifier:
      Ref: SubnetIds
```

3. While still in the `Resources` section, add a `LaunchConfiguration`:

```
LaunchConfiguration:
  Type: AWS::AutoScaling::LaunchConfiguration
  DependsOn: FileSystem
  Properties:
    ImageId: ami-1e299d7e
  SecurityGroups:
    - Ref: MountTargetAccessSecurityGroup
```

```
InstanceType: t2.micro
KeyName:
  Ref: KeyName
UserData:
  Fn::Base64:
  Fn::Sub: |
    #!/bin/bash -xe
    mkdir -p ${MountPoint}
    echo 'Waiting for mount target DNS to propagate'
    sleep 90
    echo '${FileSystem}.efs.${AWS::Region}.amazonaws.com:/
    ${MountPoint} nfs4
    nfsvers=4.1,rsize=1048576,wsize=1048576,hard,timeo=600,
    retrans=2 0 0' >>
    /etc/fstab
    mount -a\nchown ec2-user: ${MountPoint}\n"
```

4. Launch the `cloudformation` stack with the following AWS CLI command, substituting your own parameter values:

```
aws cloudformation create-stack \
  --stack-name wwns1 \
  --template-body file://03-03-NetworkStorage.yml \
  --parameters \
  ParameterKey=VpcId,ParameterValue=<vpc-id> \
  ParameterKey=SubnetIds,ParameterValue='<subnet-id-1>\, \
    <subnet-id-1>' \
  ParameterKey=MountPoint,ParameterValue=<local-path-to-mount-efs> \
  ParameterKey=KeyName,ParameterValue=<existing-key-pair-name>
```

Once the new stack is ready, you will be able to **Secure Shell** (**SSH**) to your instances and verify that they have mounted the EFS filesystem.

Amazon FSx for Windows File Server

AWS recently launched a Windows version of EFS so that users who prefer Windows EC2 instances can enjoy all of the same benefits. Follow this recipe to find out how to create an FSx file share using PowerShell.

Getting ready

You will need a Windows EC2 instance that is joined to a domain to complete this recipe. If you already have one, skip to the *How to do it* section. If not, follow these steps to create a **Directory Service** directory and an EC2 instance that is joined to your domain:

 Note that the resources you create in this recipe will not fall under the free tier! There will be charges associated with them, even if you tear down the resources after you finish this chapter.

1. Go to the **Directory Service** dashboard and click **Set up a directory**:

Directory Service

2. Select **AWS Managed Microsoft AD** from under **Directory types**:

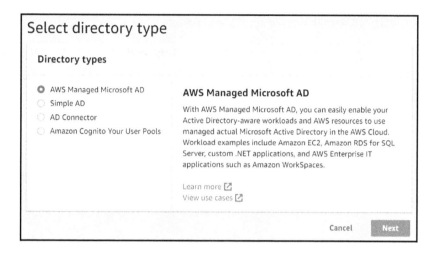

Selecting the directory type

3. Configure the directory information on the next screen. Again, note that this recipe does not fall into the free tier! There will be charges associated with these resources:

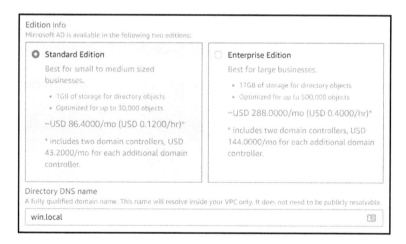

Directory information

4. Be sure to remember the password you set in the previous step. You will need to log in to your EC2 instance with the domain user account – not with the machine administrator account – via the EC2 console.

5. Choose your **VPC** and **Subnets**. To keep things simple, choose your default **VPC**:

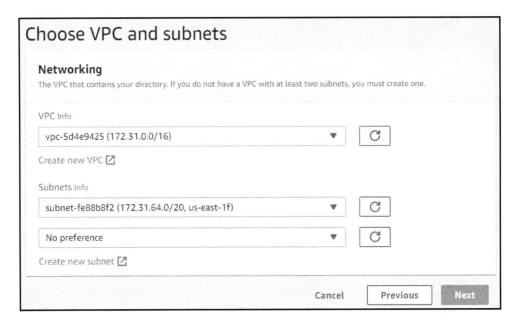

Choosing the VPC and subnets

6. On the next screen, confirm your settings and click **Create directory**.
7. Wait for the directory to be created.
8. Go to the EC2 dashboard and click **Launch Instance** to create a new Windows instance.

9. Select **Microsoft Windows Server 2019 Base**:

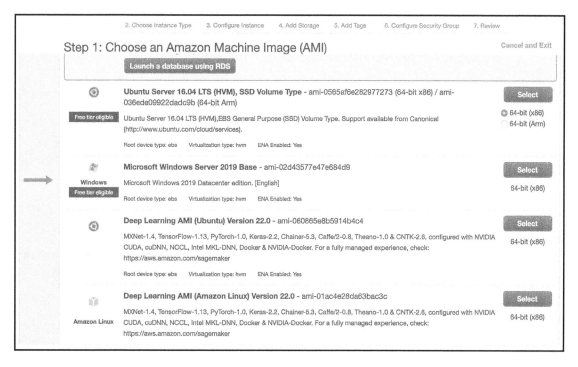

Choosing an Amazon Machine Image (AMI)

10. On the following screen, select an instance type. Choose **t2.micro** to stay in the free tier. However, be aware that the performance of Windows Server on this small instance will be very slow. A larger instance type will perform much better, but it will incur a cost until you terminate it.

11. Click **Next: Configure Instance Details**.

12. On the following screen, select a **Subnet** that matches the subnet that's used by your Active Directory instance. Also, choose the directory in the **Domain join directory** dropdown.

13. Click **Next: Add Storage** and accept the defaults.

14. Click **Next: Add Tags** and optionally tag the instance with a unique name so that you can recognize it on the dashboard.

15. Click **Next: Configure security group** and choose the default VPC security group.

16. Click **Review and Launch** and launch your instance.

How to do it...

Once you are logged in to your instance as the `Admin` domain user (this is the user you created when you were configuring the directory in *step 3*, not the machine administrator!), follow these steps to create and access an FSx file share:

1. Open up a PowerShell terminal.
2. Enter the following commands to enable script execution, import `AWS Tools for Windows PowerShell`, and then check the version to make sure everything works as expected:

```
PS C:\Users\Admin> Set-ExecutionPolicy RemoteSigned
PS C:\Users\Admin> Import-Module AWSPowerShell
PS C:\Users\Admin> Get-AWSPowerShellVersion

AWS Tools for Windows PowerShell
Version 3.3.462.0
Copyright 2012-2018 Amazon.com, Inc. or its affiliates. All Rights
Reserved.

Amazon Web Services SDK for .NET
Core Runtime Version 3.3.31.11
Copyright 2009-2015 Amazon.com, Inc. or its affiliates. All Rights
Reserved.

Release notes: https://aws.amazon.com/releasenotes/PowerShell

This software includes third party software subject to the
following copyrights:
- Logging from log4net, Apache License
[http://logging.apache.org/log4net/license.html]
```

3. Set your access key and secret key:

```
PS C:\Users\Admin> Set-AWSCredential -AccessKey [YOUR-ACCESS-KEY] -
SecretKey [YOUR-SECRET-KEY]
```

4. Create the filesystem. After running this command, you will get an output that describes the filesystem. You can use `ClientRequestToken` to make queries relating to this specific filesystem as it is being created. Make sure you use the same subnet as your EC2 instance:

```
PS C:\Users\Admin> New-FSXFileSystem -ClientRequestToken MyToken -
FileSystemType WINDOWS -StorageCapacity 300 -SubnetId
YOUR_SUBNET_ID -WindowsConfiguration
@{ThroughputCapacity=8;ActiveDirectoryId='YOUR_DIRECTORY_ID'}
```

5. Check its progress. The following command returns information for all filesystems. It can take several minutes for the filesystem to become available, which is indicated by `Lifecycle: AVAILABLE` in the output:

```
PS C:\Users\Admin> Get-FSXFileSystem
```

6. Once it's available, map the network drive via the file explorer, or use the following command:

```
PS C:\Users\Admin> net use E: \\[YOUR-FILESYSTEM-ID].[YOUR-DOMAIN]\share /persistent:yes
```

7. Now, you should be able to read and write to the network share mapped to the `E:` drive. To test it, open `notepad.exe` and create a new file on the `E:` drive.

8. To avoid further charges, terminate the instance, delete the filesystem, and remove Active Directory when you have finished this recipe.

How it works...

FSx for Windows combines the functionality of a Microsoft Windows domain with the resilient file storage of EFS so that Windows users can interact with a network share in exactly the same way they would if the share were created using native Windows filesystem commands within a domain. FSx is compatible with SMB versions 2.0 to 3.1.1, which allows backward compatibility to Windows Server 2008 and Windows 7, and even allows for connections from Linux machines.

Backing up data for compliance

We work with a lot of companies (especially in the finance industry) that have strict rules regarding the minimum time data needs to be kept for. This can become quite onerous and expensive if you need to keep customer records for a minimum of seven years, for example.

Using S3, Glacier, and life cycle rules, we can create a flexible long-term backup solution while also automating the archiving and purging of backups and reducing costs.

We are also going to utilize versioning in order to mitigate the damage caused by a file being accidentally deleted or overwritten in our backup bucket.

How to do it...

Execute the following steps to create an S3 bucket with life cycle policies to migrate data to Glacier:

1. First, we need to define a few parameters:

   - `ExpirationInDays`: This is the maximum amount of time we want to have our files kept in backup for. We've set a default for this value of 2,555 days (seven years).

   - `TransitionToInfrequentAccessInDays`: After a backup has been copied to S3, we want to move it to the infrequently accessed class to reduce our costs. This doesn't affect the durability of the backup, but it does have a small impact on its availability. We'll set this to 30 days.

   - `TransitionToGlacierInDays`: After the backup has been kept in the infrequently accessed class for a while, we want to move it to Glacier. Again, this helps us reduce our costs at the expense of retrieval times. If we need to fetch a backup from Glacier, the wait time will be approximately 3 to 5 hours. We'll set the default for this to 60 days.

   - `PreviousVersionsExpirationInDays`: Given that we will have versioning enabled on our bucket, we want to make sure old versions of files aren't kept forever – we're only using this feature to mitigate accidents. We'll set this value to 60 days, which gives us more than enough time to identify and recover from accidental deletion or overwrite.

   - `PreviousVersionsToInfrequentAccessInDays`: Just like our other backup files, we want to move our old versions to the infrequently accessed class after a period of time in order to minimize costs. We'll set this to 30 days:

```
AWSTemplateFormatVersion: '2010-09-09'
Parameters:
 ExpirationInDays:
   Description: The maximum amount of time to keep
files
       for
   Type: Number
   Default: 2555
 TransitionToInfrequentAccessInDays:
   Description: How many days until files are moved to
     the Infrequent Access class
   Type: Number
   Default: 30
```

```
TransitionToGlacierInDays:
  Description: How many days until files are moved
    to Glacier
  Type: Number
  Default: 60
PreviousVersionsExpirationInDays:
  Description: The maximum amount of time to keep
previous
    versions of files for
  Type: Number
  Default: 60
PreviousVersionsToInfrequentAccessInDays:
  Description: How many days until previous versions
    of files are moved to the Infrequent Access class
  Type: Number
  Default: 30
```

2. Next, we'll need to create the S3 bucket in which to store our backups. Note that we're omitting the `name` property for this bucket in order to avoid bucket name conflicts and maximize region portability. We're also enabling versioning and adding our life cycle rules from our previous `Parameters`:

```
Resources:
  BackupBucket:
    Type: AWS::S3::Bucket
    Properties:
      VersioningConfiguration:
        Status: Enabled
      LifecycleConfiguration:
        Rules:
          - Status: Enabled
            ExpirationInDays:
              Ref: ExpirationInDays
            Transitions:
              - StorageClass: STANDARD_IA
                TransitionInDays:
                  Ref: TransitionToInfrequentAccessInDays
              - StorageClass: GLACIER
                TransitionInDays:
                  Ref: TransitionToGlacierInDays
            NoncurrentVersionExpirationInDays:
              Ref: PreviousVersionsExpirationInDays
            NoncurrentVersionTransitions:
              - StorageClass: STANDARD_IA
                TransitionInDays:
                  Ref: PreviousVersionsToInfrequentAccessInDays
```

3. Finally, let's add some output so that we know which bucket to store our backups in:

```
Outputs:
  BackupBucket:
    Description: Bucket where backups are stored
    Value:
      Ref: BackupBucket
```

How it works...

Go ahead and launch this CloudFormation stack. If you're happy with the default values for the parameters, you don't need to provide them with the CLI command:

```
aws cloudformation create-stack \
  --stack-name backup-s3-glacier-1 \
  --template-body file://03-backing-up-data-for-compliance.yaml
```

Once the stack has been created, you'll be all set to start copying backups to the S3 bucket and start worrying less about your backups' life cycle and management. If you decide that the expiry or transition times need to change after you've created the bucket, you can do this by simply updating the parameters for the stack.

There's more...

Glacier is a companion service to S3, but it is the **cold** storage option. Cold storage is a service where you are unable to directly access your data; you must lodge a request for data to be restored (to S3), and you will be notified when it is ready. A physical example of cold storage might be backup tapes that are stored in a secure location. Similar to S3, files are referred to as **objects**. Files are grouped together and stored in **archives**. Archives can be created and deleted but never modified. Archives are grouped together into **vaults**, which allow you to control access.

The shortest restoration time is 1 to 5 minutes (with limitations). Standard restoration times take 3 to 5 hours, with some other options available.

The following are some recommended use cases for Glacier:

- Long-term (that is, cold) backups
- Compliance backups

4
AWS Compute

This chapter covers some of the fundamental building blocks of the **computing** category of AWS cloud services. It's hard to accomplish much in the cloud without computing resources, which gives you a place to run your code. The most common computing resource is a virtual server, and you will get a thorough introduction to Amazon **Elastic Compute Cloud (EC2)** in this chapter. However, server-less environments are becoming more and more prevalent, so you will also have the opportunity to create and configure an AWS Lambda function.

Amazon Elastic Cloud Compute (EC2) is by far the most utilized service in the AWS catalog, and it comes with a very rich and deep set of functionality. More than just virtual machines, EC2 provides a framework of sub-services to help you secure and manage your instances elastically, such as Elastic Load Balancing, Autoscaling, Security Groups, and Elastic Block Store.

AWS Systems Manager offers a consolidated view of large numbers of resources, such as EC2 instances, and gives administrators ways to automate things such as deploying security patches in a consistent manner.

AWS Lambda is quickly becoming the glue that holds together many architectures, and it can completely replace your EC2 instances if you embrace the serverless mindset.

In this chapter, we will cover the following recipes:

- Creating a key pair
- Launching an instance
- Attaching storage
- Autoscaling an application server

- Creating security groups
- Creating a load balancer
- Using AWS Systems Manager to log in to instances from the console
- Creating serverless functions with AWS Lambda

Creating a key pair

A key pair is used to access your instances via SSH. Key pairs are an integral part of asymmetrical cryptography and are an encryption technique that makes use of two non-identical keys to encrypt and decrypt data. A user's public key can be shared freely, and data that is encrypted with the public key can only be decrypted with the private key. When you create a key pair with EC2, the key can be associated with any number of instances, and you download a .pem file, which is similar to a .ppk file in Putty or an id_rsa file on Linux machines.

Getting ready

To complete this recipe, you must have your AWS CLI tool configured correctly. Follow the guidance in Chapter 1, *AWS Fundamentals*, to configure your CLI.

How to do it...

Follow these steps to create and download a key pair:

1. Create the key pair and save it to disk, as follows:

Note that this is intended to be a secret key and must be protected accordingly! Don't store the key in a public place.

```
aws ec2 create-key-pair \
    --key-name MyEC2KeyPair \
    --query 'KeyMaterial' \
    --output text > ec2keypair.pem
```

2. Change the permissions on the created file:

```
chmod 400 ec2keypair.pem
```

How it works...

This call requests a new private key from EC2. The response is then parsed using a `JMESPath` query, and the private key (in the `KeyMaterial` property) is saved to a new key file with the `.pem` extension. The public key is stored in the region so that it can be copied to new EC2 instances. You cannot copy keys from region to region, and you cannot retrieve the full key pair after initial creation.

Finally, we change the permissions on the key file so that it cannot be read by other users – this is required before SSH will allow you to use it.

Launching an instance

There will be scenarios – usually when testing and developing your infrastructure code – where you need quick access to an instance. Creating it via the AWS CLI is the quickest and most consistent way to create one-off instances.

There are other recipes in this book that will require a running instance. This recipe will get you started.

Getting ready

For this recipe, you must have an existing key pair.

Here, we will be launching an instance of AWS Linux using an **Amazon Machine Image (AMI)** ID in the `us-east-1` region. If you are working in a different region, you will need to update your `image-id` parameter, since AMIs are stored in each region with unique identifiers.

You must have configured your AWS CLI tool with working credentials.

How to do it...

Run the following AWS CLI command using your own key pair name. It creates an EC2 instance using a specific AMI and instance type, which, in this case, is the economical t2.micro:

```
aws ec2 run-instances \
  --image-id ami-9be6f38c \
  --instance-type t2.micro \
  --key-name <your-key-pair-name>
```

How it works...

This example uses the **command-line interface** (**CLI**) instead of the web console. Choosing the CLI over the console is largely a matter of preference, but they both result in the same underlying API calls being made in your account to create resources.

While the key-name argument is optional, you will not be able to connect to your instance unless you have preconfigured some other way of logging in. When the instance is created, the public half of the key is written to ~/.ssh/known_hosts so that, when you use your SSH client with the private key, the instance recognizes you as an authorized user.

 The t2.micro instance type that's used in this recipe is included in the AWS free tier. You can run one micro instance per month for free during the first 12 months of your usage. See https://aws.amazon.com/free for more information.

Since no **Virtual Private Cloud** (**VPC**) or security groups are specified, the instance will be launched in your account's default VPC and security group. You can modify an instance's security groups after it is launched without stopping it.

There's more...

If you have created your own AMI, then you can change the image-id argument to quickly launch your specific AMI.

Take note of the InstanceId value in the response from the API, as you will need it for future commands.

See also

- The *Creating a key pair* recipe
- The *Creating machine images* recipe

Attaching storage

Ideally, you will have defined all your storage requirements (disk size, IOPs, and so on) up-front as code using a service such as CloudFormation. However, sometimes, that isn't possible due to application restrictions or changing requirements.

You can easily add additional storage to your instances while they are running by attaching a new volume.

Getting ready

For this recipe, you will need the following:

- A running instance's ID. It will start with `i-`, followed by alphanumeric characters.
- The AZ the instance is running in. This looks like the region name with a letter after it; for example, `us-east-1a`.

In this recipe, we are using an Amazon Linux 2 instance. If you are using a different operating system, the steps to mount the volume will be different. We will be running an instance in the AZ `us-east-1a` region.

You must have configured your AWS CLI tool with working credentials for this to work.

How to do it...

Follow these steps to create an **Elastic Block Store** (**EBS**) volume and attach it to an instance. EBS is the AWS service that provides disk storage to EC2 instances. While some instance types come with local disk storage, in the vast majority of cases, you will be working with EBS. You can think of EBS as being similar to a **Storage Attached Network** (**SAN**) or **Network Attached Storage** (**NAS**), but there are significant advantages to EBS over those technologies, which will be covered later:

1. Create a volume:

   ```
   aws ec2 create-volume --availability-zone us-east-1a --size 8
   ```

    Take note of the returned `VolumeId` in the response. It will start with `vol-`, followed by alphanumeric characters.

2. Attach the volume to the instance using the volume ID we noted in the previous step and the instance ID you started with:

   ```
   aws ec2 attach-volume \
     --volume-id <your-volume-id> \
     --instance-id <your-instance-id> \
     --device /dev/sdf
   ```

3. Run the `lsblk` command on the instance. You will see that the device name has been changed from `/dev/sdf` to `/dev/xvdf`:

   ```
   sh-4.2$ lsblk
   NAME MAJ:MIN RM SIZE RO TYPE MOUNTPOINT
   xvda 202:0 0 8G 0 disk
   `-xvda1 202:1 0 8G 0 part /
   xvdf 202:80 0 8G 0 disk
   ```

4. On Amazon Linux 2, you can see that `/dev/sd*` is linked to `/dev/xvd*`:

   ```
   sh-4.2$ ls -l /dev/sd*
   lrwxrwxrwx 1 root root 4 Jun 17 20:12 /dev/sda -> xvda
   lrwxrwxrwx 1 root root 5 Jun 17 20:12 /dev/sda1 -> xvda1
   lrwxrwxrwx 1 root root 4 Jun 17 20:15 /dev/sdf -> xvdf
   ```

5. Create a filesystem on the device with the `mkfs` command. Make sure that you use the correct identifier for the new, unformatted device, as you might corrupt an existing data drive if you get it wrong:

```
sudo mkfs -t xfs /dev/xvdf
```

6. Create a new directory and run the `mount` command on the instance to mount the volume device:

```
sudo mkdir /mydata
sudo mount /dev/xvdf /mydata
```

After running those commands, the new EC2 volume will be mounted to `/mydata` and will be available for use.

How it works...

In this recipe, we started by creating a volume. Volumes are created from snapshots. If you don't specify a snapshot ID, it uses a blank snapshot, and you get a blank volume.

While volumes are hosted redundantly, they are only hosted in a single AZ, so they must be provisioned in the same AZ the instance is running in. The data on a volume is stored in several places in the AZ to ensure a high level of durability, but they are only made available in a single AZ to ensure consistent low latency performance.

The `create-volume` command returns a response that includes the newly created volume's `VolumeId`. We then use this ID in the next step.

It can sometimes take a few seconds for a volume to become available. If you are scripting these commands, use the `aws ec2 wait` command to wait for the volume to become available.

In *step 2*, we attached a volume to the instance. When attaching to an instance, you must specify the name of the device that it will be presented to the operating system with. Unfortunately, this doesn't guarantee what the device will appear as. In the case of AWS Linux, `/dev/sdf` becomes `/dev/xvdf`.

Device naming is kernel-specific, so if you are using something other than AWS Linux, the device name may be different.
See `http://docs.aws.amazon.com/AWSEC2/latest/UserGuide/device_na ming.html` for full details.

See also

- The *Launching an instance* recipe
- The *Working with network storage* recipe in `Chapter 3`, AWS *Storage and Content Delivery*

Autoscaling an application server

Autoscaling is a fundamental component of computing in the cloud. To understand autoscaling, you need to understand the concepts of vertical and horizontal scaling. With vertical scaling, a single machine is upgraded to a more powerful instance by adding more CPU power, more RAM, or more disk capacity. This can be effective to an extent, but eventually, the complexity and costs associated with vertical scaling make it impractical. With horizontal scaling, an application workload is spread out over several smaller machines, and adding new machines provides a nearly linear increase in the load that can be managed by the application. Adding extra machines is called **scaling up**, and removing machines that are no longer needed is called **scaling down.**

EC2 autoscaling provides not only the ability to scale up and down in response to application load but also redundancy. It does this by ensuring that capacity is always available. Even in the unlikely event of an AZ outage, the autoscaling group will ensure that instances are available to run your application if you have configured it to provision instances in all AZs.

Autoscaling also allows you to pay for only the EC2 capacity you need because underutilized servers can be automatically deprovisioned.

Getting ready

You must supply two or more subnet IDs for this recipe to work.

The following example uses an AWS Linux AMI in the `us-east-1` region. Update the parameters as required if you are working in a different region.

How to do it...

Follow these steps to create a CloudFormation template that launches a stack with an autoscaling group:

1. Start by defining the template version and description:

```
AWSTemplateFormatVersion: "2010-09-09"
Description: Create an Auto Scaling Group
```

2. Add a `Parameters` section with the required parameters that will be used later in the template:

```
Parameters:
  SubnetIds:
    Description: Subnet IDs where instances can be launched
    Type: List<AWS::EC2::Subnet::Id>
```

3. Still under the `Parameters` section, add the optional instance configuration parameters:

```
AmiId:
  Description: The application server's AMI ID
  Type: AWS::EC2::Image::Id
  Default: ami-9be6f38c # AWS Linux in us-east-1
InstanceType:
  Description: The type of instance to launch
  Type: String
  Default: t2.micro
```

4. Still under the `Parameters` section, add the minimum and maximum sizes:

```
MinSize:
  Description: Minimum number of instances in the group
  Type: Number
  Default: 1
MaxSize:
  Description: Maximum number of instances in the group
  Type: Number
  Default: 4
```

5. Then, add the settings for the CPU thresholds:

```
ThresholdCPUHigh:
  Description: Launch new instances when CPU utilization
    is over this threshold
  Type: Number
```

```
         Default: 60
       ThresholdCPULow:
         Description: Remove instances when CPU utilization
           is under this threshold
         Type: Number
         Default: 40
       ThresholdMinutes:
         Description: Launch new instances when over the CPU
           threshold for this many minutes
         Type: Number
         Default: 5
```

6. Add a `Resources` section and define the autoscaling group resource:

```
   Resources:
     AutoScalingGroup:
       Type: AWS::AutoScaling::AutoScalingGroup
       Properties:
         MinSize: !Ref MinSize
         MaxSize: !Ref MaxSize
         LaunchConfigurationName: !Ref LaunchConfiguration
         Tags:
           - Key: Name
             Value: !Sub "${AWS::StackName} server"
             PropagateAtLaunch: true
         VPCZoneIdentifier: !Ref SubnetIds
```

7. Still under the `Resources` section, define the launch configuration that's used by the autoscaling group:

```
     LaunchConfiguration:
       Type: AWS::AutoScaling::LaunchConfiguration
       Properties:
         ImageId: !Ref AmiId
         InstanceType: !Ref InstanceType
         UserData:
           Fn::Base64: !Sub |
             #!/bin/bash -xe
             # This will be run on startup, launch your application
   here
```

8. Next, define two scaling policy resources – one to scale up and the other to scale down:

```
     ScaleUpPolicy:
       Type: AWS::AutoScaling::ScalingPolicy
       Properties:
         AdjustmentType: ChangeInCapacity
```

```
        AutoScalingGroupName: !Ref AutoScalingGroup
        Cooldown: 60
        ScalingAdjustment: 1
  ScaleDownPolicy:
    Type: AWS::AutoScaling::ScalingPolicy
    Properties:
      AdjustmentType: ChangeInCapacity
      AutoScalingGroupName: !Ref AutoScalingGroup
      Cooldown: 60
      ScalingAdjustment: -1
```

9. Define an alarm that will alert you when the CPU goes over the
   `ThresholdCPUHigh` **parameter:**

```
  CPUHighAlarm:
    Type: AWS::CloudWatch::Alarm
    Properties:
      ActionsEnabled: true
      AlarmActions:
        - !Ref ScaleUpPolicy
      AlarmDescription: Scale up on CPU load
      ComparisonOperator: GreaterThanThreshold
      Dimensions:
        - Name: AutoScalingGroupName
          Value: !Ref AutoScalingGroup
      EvaluationPeriods: !Ref ThresholdMinutes
      MetricName: CPUUtilization
      Namespace: AWS/EC2
      Period: 60
      Statistic: Average
      Threshold: !Ref ThresholdCPUHigh
```

10. Finally, define an alarm that will alert you when the CPU goes under the
    `ThresholdCPULow` **parameter:**

```
  CPULowAlarm:
    Type: AWS::CloudWatch::Alarm
    Properties:
      ActionsEnabled: true
      AlarmActions:
        - !Ref ScaleDownPolicy
      AlarmDescription: Scale down on CPU load
      ComparisonOperator: LessThanThreshold
      Dimensions:
        - Name: AutoScalingGroupName
          Value: !Ref AutoScalingGroup
      EvaluationPeriods: !Ref ThresholdMinutes
      MetricName: CPUUtilization
```

```
Namespace: AWS/EC2
Period: 60
Statistic: Average
Threshold: !Ref ThresholdCPULow
```

11. Save the template with the filename `04-01-AutoScaling.yml`.

12. Launch the template with the following AWS CLI command, supplying your subnet IDs in place of `<subnet-id-1>` and `<subnet-id-2>`:

```
aws cloudformation create-stack \
--stack-name asg \
--template-body file://04-01-AutoScaling.yml \
--parameters \
ParameterKey=SubnetIds,ParameterValue='<subnet-id-1>\,<subnet-id-2>'
```

13. At this point, the CFN service is provisioning all the resources in the template and will take a few minutes to complete. Once the stack has reached a `CREATE_COMPLETE` status, you can confirm that the autoscaling group is working correctly by checking for a new EC2 instance with the name `asg-server`.

14. Delete the stack to prevent future charges for the resources that were created in this recipe.

How it works...

This example defines an autoscaling group and dependent resources. These include the following:

- A launch configuration to use when launching new instances. Launch configurations are templates that describe the settings for newly launched instances.
- Two scaling policies: one to scale the number of instances up, and an inverse policy to scale back down.
- A CloudWatch alarm to alert when the CPU crosses a certain threshold for a certain number of minutes. CloudWatch is the AWS logging and monitoring solution and is covered in more detail in `Chapter 5`, *Monitoring the Infrastructure*.

The autoscaling group and launch configuration resource objects in this example use mostly default values. You will need to specify your own `SecurityGroups` and a `KeyName` parameter in the `LaunchConfiguration` resource configuration if you want to be able to connect to the instances (for example, via SSH).

AWS will automatically take care of spreading your instances evenly over the subnets you have configured, so make sure that they are in different AZs! When scaling down, the oldest instances will be removed before the newer ones.

Scaling policies

The scaling policies detail how many instances to create or delete when they are triggered. It also defines a `Cooldown` value, which helps prevent **flapping** servers – when servers are created and deleted before they have finished starting and are useful. Often, an EC2 instance will have startup scripts that install third-party packages and custom application software that takes several minutes to complete. The scaling policies allow you to fine-tune the timing to avoid putting a machine into rotation before it is ready.

> While the scaling policies in this example use equal values, you might want to change that so that your application can **scale up** quickly and **scale down** slowly for the best user experience.

Alarms

The `CPUHighAlarm` parameter will alert you when the average CPU utilization goes over the value set in the `ThresholdCPUHigh` parameter. CPU utilization and other instance metrics are tracked by CloudWatch. This alert will be sent to the `ScaleUpPolicy` resource that's provisioning more instances, which will bring the average CPU utilization down across the whole autoscaling group. As the name suggests, the `CPULowAlarm` parameter does the opposite when the average CPU utilization goes under the `ThresholdCPULow` parameter.

This means that new instances will be launched until the CPU utilization across the autoscaling group stabilizes somewhere between 40-60% (based on the default parameter values) or the `MaxSize` of instances is reached.

> It is very important to leave a gap between the high and low alarms thresholds. If they are too close together, the alarms will not stabilize and you will see instances being created and destroyed almost continually.

Creating security groups

AWS describes security groups as **virtual firewalls**. While this analogy helps newcomers to the EC2 platform understand their purpose and function, it's probably more accurate to describe them as a firewall-like method of authorizing traffic. They don't offer all the functionality you'd find in a traditional firewall, but this simplification makes them much easier to use and troubleshoot since they do just a single job and do it reliably.

We're going to go through a basic scenario involving a web server and a load balancer. Load balancers are vital components of a scalable web application as they allow requests to be spread out over a fleet of instances, instead of sending traffic to a single point of failure. We want the load balancer to respond to HTTP requests from everywhere, and we want to isolate the web server from everything except the load balancer. This is a good security practice as it shields instances from direct external connections.

Getting ready

Before we get started, there's a small list of things you'll need to have ready:

- AmiId: This is the ID of an AMI in your region. For this recipe, we'd recommend using an AWS Linux AMI because our instance will attempt to run some yum commands on startup.
- VPCID: This is the ID of the VPC you wish to launch the EC2 server into.
- SubnetIDs: These are the subnets that our EC2 instance can launch in.

How to do it...

Follow these steps to create a CloudFormation template that launches a stack with a new security group, a load balancer, and an EC2 instance:

1. Open up your text editor and create a new CloudFormation template. We're going to start by adding a few Parameters, as follows:

```
AWSTemplateFormatVersion: '2010-09-09'
  Parameters:
    AmiId:
      Type: AWS::EC2::AMI::Id
      Description: AMI ID to launch instances from
    VPCID:
      Type: AWS::EC2::VPC::Id
      Description: VPC where load balancer and instance will launch
```

```
SubnetIDs:
   Type: List<AWS::EC2::Subnet::Id>
   Description: Subnets (pick at least 2)
```

2. Let's take a look at a security group we'll be applying to a public load balancer:

```
Resources:
  ExampleELBSecurityGroup:
     Type: AWS::EC2::SecurityGroup
     Properties:
        GroupDescription: Security Group for example ELB
        SecurityGroupIngress:
           - IpProtocol: tcp
             CidrIp: 0.0.0.0/0
             FromPort: 80
             ToPort: 80
```

Anything that resides in this security group will allow inbound TCP connections on port 80 from anywhere (0.0.0.0/0). Note that a security group can contain more than one rule; we'd almost certainly want to also allow HTTPS (443), but we've left it out to simplify this recipe.

3. Now, let's look at a security group for a web server sitting behind our load balancer:

```
ExampleEC2InstanceSecurityGroup:
   Type: AWS::EC2::SecurityGroup
   Properties:
      GroupDescription: Security Group for example Instance
      SecurityGroupIngress:
         - IpProtocol: tcp
           SourceSecurityGroupName:
              Ref: ExampleELBSecurityGroup
           FromPort: 80
           ToPort: 80
```

Here, you can see that we aren't specifying a source IP range. Instead, we're specifying a source security group, which we will accept connections from. In this case, we're saying that we want to allow anything from our ELB security group to connect to anything in our EC2 instance security group on port 80.
Since this is the only rule we're specifying, our web server will not accept connections from anywhere except our load balancer, to port 80 or otherwise. Our web server isn't wide open to the internet, and it is even isolated from other instances in our VPC.

Remember that multiple instances can reside in a security group. In a scenario where you have multiple web servers attached to this load balancer, it would be unnecessary, inefficient, and somewhat of an anti-pattern to create a new security group for each web server. Given that all the web servers attached to this load balancer would be serving the same role or function, it makes sense to apply the same security group to them.

This is where the power of security groups really comes in. If an EC2 instance is serving multiple roles – let's say you have an outbound HTTP proxy server in your VPC that you also want to act as an SMTP relay – then you can simply apply multiple security groups to it.

4. Next, we need to add our load balancer. This is probably the most basic load balancer configuration you'll come across. The following code will give you a load balancer and a listener:

```
ExampleLoadBalancer:
  Type:
AWS::ElasticLoadBalancingV2::LoadBalancer
    Properties:
      Subnets:
        - Fn::Select: [ 0, Ref: SubnetIDs ]
        - Fn::Select: [ 1, Ref: SubnetIDs ]
      SecurityGroups:
        - Fn::GetAtt: ExampleELBSecurityGroup.GroupId
  ExampleListener:
    Type: AWS::ElasticLoadBalancingV2::Listener
    Properties:
      LoadBalancerArn:
        Ref: ExampleLoadBalancer
      DefaultActions:
        - Type: forward
          TargetGroupArn:
            Ref: ExampleTargetGroup
      Port: 80
      Protocol: HTTP
```

5. Then, we need to add the target group:

```
ExampleTargetGroup:
  Type: AWS::ElasticLoadBalancingV2::TargetGroup
  Properties:
    Port: 80
    Protocol: HTTP
    VpcId:
        Ref: VPCID
```

```
                Targets:
                  - Id:
                      Ref: ExampleEC2Instance
```

6. The last resource we'll add to our template is an EC2 server. This server will install and start `nginx` when it boots:

```
        ExampleEC2Instance:
          Type: AWS::EC2::Instance
          Properties:
            InstanceType: t2.nano
            UserData:
              Fn::Base64:
                Fn::Sub: |
                  #!/bin/bash -ex
                  yum install -y nginx
                  service nginx start
                  exit 0
          ImageId:
            Ref: AmiId
          SecurityGroupIds:
            - Fn::GetAtt: ExampleEC2InstanceSecurityGroup.GroupId
          SubnetId:
            Fn::Select: [ 0, Ref: SubnetIDs ]
```

7. Lastly, we're going to add some `Outputs` to the template to make it a little more convenient to use our ELB and EC2 instances after the stack is created:

```
        Outputs:
          ExampleEC2InstanceHostname:
            Value:
              Fn::GetAtt: [ ExampleEC2Instance, PublicDnsName ]
          ExampleELBURL:
            Value:
              Fn::Join:
                - ''
                - [ 'http://', { 'Fn::GetAtt': [ ExampleLoadBalancer,
        DNSName ] }, '/' ]
```

8. Go ahead and launch this template using the CloudFormation web console or the AWS CLI.

There's more...

You'll eventually run into circular dependency issues when configuring security groups using CloudFormation. Let's say you want all the servers in `ExampleEC2InstanceSecurityGroup` to be able to access each other on port 22 (SSH). To achieve this, you would need to add this rule as the separate resource type, `AWS::EC2::SecurityGroupIngress`. This is because a security group can't refer to itself in CloudFormation when it hasn't been created yet. This is what the extra resource type looks like:

```
ExampleEC2InstanceIngress:
  Type: AWS::EC2::SecurityGroupIngress
  Properties:
    IpProtocol: tcp
    SourceSecurityGroupName:
      Ref: ExampleEC2InstanceSecurityGroup
    GroupName:
      Ref: ExampleEC2InstanceSecurityGroup
    FromPort: 22
    ToPort: 22
```

Unfortunately, circular dependencies sometimes crop up with CloudFormation, but there is usually an effective workaround.

Differences from traditional firewalls

The following are some of the ways in which a security group differs from traditional firewalls:

- Security groups can't be used to explicitly block traffic. Only rules of a permissive kind can be added; deny style rules are not supported. Essentially, all inbound traffic is denied unless you explicitly allow it.
- Your rules may not refer to source ports; only destination ports are supported.
- When security groups are created, they will contain a rule that allows all outbound connections. If you remove this rule, new outbound connections will be dropped. It's a common pattern to leave this rule in place and filter all your traffic using inbound rules only.

- If you do replace the default outbound rule, it's important to note that only new outbound connections will be filtered. Any outbound traffic being sent in response to an inbound connection will still be allowed. This is because security groups are **stateful**.
- Unlike security groups, network ACLs are not stateful and support DENY rules. You can use them as a complementary layer of security inside your VPC, especially if you need to control traffic flow between subnets.

Creating a load balancer

AWS offers several kinds of load balancers:

- Classic load balancer
- Application load balancer
- Network load balancer

We're going to focus on the application load balancer in this section. It's effectively an upgraded, second-generation version of the ELB service, and it offers a lot more functionality than the classic load balancer. HTTP/2 and WebSockets are supported natively, for example. The hourly rate also happens to be cheaper.

 Application load balancers do not support layer-4 load balancing. For this kind of functionality, you'll need to use a classic load balancer.

How to do it...

Follow these steps to create a load balancer using CloudFormation:

1. Open up your text editor and create a new CloudFormation template. We're going to require a VPC ID and some subnet IDs as Parameters. Add them to your template, as follows:

```
AWSTemplateFormatVersion: '2010-09-09'
Parameters:
  VPCID:
    Type: AWS::EC2::VPC::Id
    Description: VPC where load balancer and instance will launch
  SubnetIDs:
    Type: List<AWS::EC2::Subnet::Id>
```

```
        Description: Subnets where load balancer and instance will launch
(pick at least 2)
```

2. Next, we need to add some Mappings of ELB account IDs. We'd like to be able to store logs for our ELB and store them in an S3 bucket. This requires updating the bucket policy on our S3 bucket to allow access to the associated AWS Account ID. We'll use this Mappings section to store these. Your mappings should look like this:

 You can find the complete list of ELB account IDs here: http://docs.aws.amazon.com/elasticloadbalancing/latest/classic/enable-access-logs.html#attach-bucket-policy.

```
Mappings:
  ELBAccountMap:
    us-east-1:
  ELBAccountID: 127311923021
    ap-southeast-2:
  ELBAccountID: 783225319266
```

3. Now, we can start adding Resources to our template. First, we're going to create an S3 bucket and bucket policy so that we can store our load balancer logs. To make this template portable, we'll omit a bucket name, but, for convenience, we'll include the bucket name in our outputs so that CloudFormation will echo the name back to us:

```
Resources:
  ExampleLogBucket:
    Type: AWS::S3::Bucket
  ExampleBucketPolicy:
    Type: AWS::S3::BucketPolicy
    Properties:
      Bucket:
        Ref: ExampleLogBucket
      PolicyDocument:
        Statement:
          -
            Action:
              - "s3:PutObject"
            Effect: "Allow"
            Resource:
              Fn::Join:
                - ""
                -
                  - "arn:aws:s3:::"
```

```
                            - Ref: ExampleLogBucket
                            - "/*"
                        Principal:
                          AWS:
                            Fn::FindInMap: [ ELBAccountMap, Ref:
  "AWS::Region",

                            ELBAccountID ]
```

4. Next, we need to create a security group for our load balancer to reside in. This security group will allow inbound connections to port 80 (HTTP). To simplify this recipe, we'll leave out port 443 (HTTPS), but we'll briefly cover how to add this functionality later in this section. Since we're adding a public load balancer, we want to allow connections to it from everywhere (0.0.0.0/0). This is what our security group looks like:

```
ExampleELBSecurityGroup:
  Type: AWS::EC2::SecurityGroup
  Properties:
    GroupDescription: Security Group for example ELB
    SecurityGroupIngress:
      -
        IpProtocol: tcp
        CidrIp: 0.0.0.0/0
        FromPort: 80
        ToPort: 80
```

5. Now, we need to define a target group. Upon completion of this recipe, you can go ahead and register your instances in this group so that HTTP requests will be forwarded to it. Alternatively, you can attach the target group to an autoscaling group and AWS will take care of the instance registration and deregistration for you.

6. The target group is where we specify the health checks our load balancer should perform against the target instances. This health check is necessary to determine whether a registered instance should receive traffic. The example that's provided with this recipe includes these health check parameters, with the values all set to their defaults. Go ahead and tweak these to suit your needs, or, optionally, remove them if the defaults work for you:

```
ExampleTargetGroup:
  Type: AWS::ElasticLoadBalancingV2::TargetGroup
  Properties:
    Port: 80
    Protocol: HTTP
    HealthCheckIntervalSeconds: 30
    HealthCheckProtocol: HTTP
```

```
HealthCheckPort: 80
HealthCheckPath: /
HealthCheckTimeoutSeconds: 5
HealthyThresholdCount: 5
UnhealthyThresholdCount: 2
Matcher:
   HttpCode: '200'
VpcId:
   Ref: VPCID
```

7. We need to define at least one listener, which we will add to our load balancer. A listener will **listen** for incoming requests to the load balancer on the port and protocol we configure for it. Requests matching the port and protocol will be forwarded to our target group.

   The configuration of our listener is going to be reasonably simple. We're listening for HTTP requests on port 80. We're also setting up a default action for this listener, which will forward our requests to the target group we defined previously. There is a soft limit of 50 listeners per load balancer:

```
ExampleListener:
  Type: AWS::ElasticLoadBalancingV2::Listener
  Properties:
    LoadBalancerArn:
      Ref: ExampleLoadBalancer
    DefaultActions:
      - Type: forward
        TargetGroupArn:
          Ref: ExampleTargetGroup
    Port: 80
    Protocol: HTTP
```

8. Finally, now that we have all the Resources we need, we can go ahead and set up our load balancer. We'll need to define at least two subnets for it to live in – these are included as Parameters in our example template:

```
ExampleLoadBalancer:
  Type: AWS::ElasticLoadBalancingV2::LoadBalancer
  Properties:
    LoadBalancerAttributes:
      - Key: access_logs.s3.enabled
        Value: true
      - Key: access_logs.s3.bucket
        Value:
          Ref: ExampleLogBucket
      - Key: idle_timeout.timeout_seconds
        Value: 60
```

```
Scheme: internet-facing
Subnets:
  - Fn::Select: [ 0, Ref: SubnetIDs ]
  - Fn::Select: [ 1, Ref: SubnetIDs ]
SecurityGroups:
  - Fn::GetAtt: ExampleELBSecurityGroup.GroupId
```

9. Lastly, we're going to add some `Outputs` to our template for convenience. We're particularly interested in the name of the S3 bucket we created and the URL of the load balancer:

```
Outputs:
  ExampleELBURL:
    Value:
      Fn::Join:
        - ''
        - [ 'http://', { 'Fn::GetAtt': [ ExampleLoadBalancer,
              DNSName ] }, '/' ]
  ExampleLogBucket:
    Value:
      Ref: ExampleLogBucket
```

Once you have created this stack and finished this recipe, don't forget to delete the stack to avoid any future charges.

How it works...

As you can see, we're applying a logging configuration that points to the S3 bucket we've created. We're configuring this load balancer to be internet-facing, with an idle timeout of 60 seconds (the default).

All load balancers are internet-facing by default, so it's not strictly necessary to define a `Scheme` in our example; however, it can be handy to include this anyway. This is especially the case if your CloudFormation template contains a mix of public and private load balancers.

If you specify a logging configuration but the load balancer can't access the S3 bucket, your CloudFormation stack will fail to complete.

Private ELBs are not internet-facing and are only available to the resources that live inside your VPC.

There's more...

Load balancers on AWS are highly configurable and there are many options available to you. Here are some of the more frequent ELB options you'll encounter.

HTTPS/SSL

If you wish to accept HTTPS requests, you'll need to configure an additional listener. It will look something like the following:

```
ExampleHTTPSListener:
  Type: AWS::ElasticLoadBalancingV2::Listener
  Properties:
    Certificates:
      - CertificateArn:
          arn:aws:acm:ap-southeast-2:123456789012:
          certificate/12345678-1234-1234-1234-123456789012
    LoadBalancerArn:
      Ref: ExampleLoadBalancer
    DefaultActions:
      - Type: forward
        TargetGroupArn:
          Ref: ExampleTargetGroup
    Port: 443
    Protocol: HTTPS
```

The listener will need to reference a valid **Amazon Resource Name (ARN)** for the certificate you wish to use. It's really easy to have AWS Certificate Manager create a certificate for you, but it does require validation of the domain name you're generating the certificate for. You can, of course, bring your own certificate if you wish. You'll need to import it into AWS Certificate Manager before you can use it with your ELB (or CloudFront distribution).

Unless you have specific requirements around ciphers, a good starting approach is to not define an SSL Policy and let AWS choose what is currently their best recommendation.

Path-based routing

Once you are comfortable with the ELB configuration, you can start to experiment with path-based routing. In a nutshell, it allows you to inspect a request and proxy it to different targets based on the path that's requested.

One common scenario you might encounter is needing to route requests for /blog to a different set of servers running WordPress, instead of to your main server pool, which is running your Ruby on Rails application.

Using AWS Systems Manager to log in to instances from the console

AWS Systems Manager is a service that many administrators overlook, but if you take the time to learn its capabilities, you will find that it offers invaluable ways to group large numbers of resources together to issue batch operations quickly and efficiently. At the time of writing, it provides a quick overview of EC2 instances, S3 buckets, and RDS databases. One of its most common uses is patch management on a fleet of EC2 instances. If you have ever spent time manually patching a large number of instances, you know that it can be a tedious and error-prone process. Systems Manager solves this problem for you. But patching isn't all that it offers. In this recipe, you will learn how to take advantage of one of the newer features that has been added to Systems Manager so that you can log in to your EC2 instances directly from the console, with no key pairs or external terminal window required.

Getting ready...

You will need an EC2 instance to complete this recipe. If you already have an instance, you can skip these steps and move on to the *How to do it...* section:

1. Log in to your AWS account, go to the EC2 dashboard, and click **Launch Instance**.
2. Select the default instance type, which at the time of writing is **Amazon Linux 2 AMI (HVM) > SSD Volume Type.**
3. On the next screen, go with the default selection of **T2.micro** and click **Review and launch**.
4. Click **Launch** on the following screen to launch your instance.

5. On the key pair dialog, select **Proceed without a key pair**. Normally, this would make it impossible to access the instance using SSH, but the **Systems Manager Session Manager** will allow us to connect:

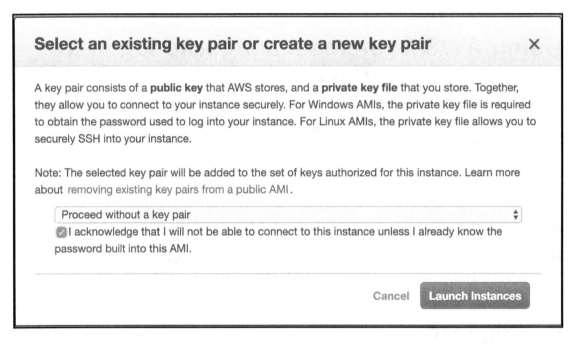

Select an existing key pair or create a new key pair ✕

A key pair consists of a **public key** that AWS stores, and a **private key file** that you store. Together, they allow you to connect to your instance securely. For Windows AMIs, the private key file is required to obtain the password used to log into your instance. For Linux AMIs, the private key file allows you to securely SSH into your instance.

Note: The selected key pair will be added to the set of keys authorized for this instance. Learn more about removing existing key pairs from a public AMI.

Proceed without a key pair ⇕

☑ I acknowledge that I will not be able to connect to this instance unless I already know the password built into this AMI.

Cancel   **Launch Instances**

Proceeding without a key pair

6. Click **Launch Instances** and wait until the instance is fully initialized.

An agent running on the EC2 instance is required to facilitate Systems Manager actions. In most cases, the SSM Agent will already be installed on your instances. If you have an instance that uses an operating system such as RedHat, you might need to install it manually. Follow the instructions on the following page to learn how to do this: `https://docs.aws.amazon.com/systems-manager/latest/userguide/ssm-agent.html`.

How to do it...

Follow these steps to log in to your instance using Systems Manager Session Manager:

1. Systems Manager needs permissions to access your instance, so you will need to create an instance profile and associate it with the instance. Instance profiles are containers for roles that apply to all applications running on the instance and are used to avoid the need for storing access keys and secrets on the machine. First, go to the **Identity and Access Management** (**IAM**) dashboard, select **Roles**, and then click **Create Role**.

2. Choose **EC2** as the service that will use this role and click **Next: Permissions**.

3. Search for and select **AmazonEC2RoleforSSM**:

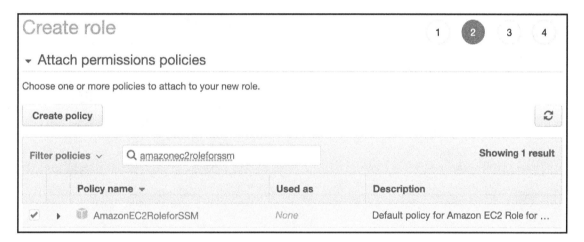

AmazonEC2RoleforSSM

4. Click **Next: Tags** and then **Next: Review**.

5. Name the role **MyEC2RoleForSSM** and click **Create role**.

6. Go back to the EC2 dashboard and select your running instance. Click **Actions > Instance Settings > Attach/Replace IAM Role**:

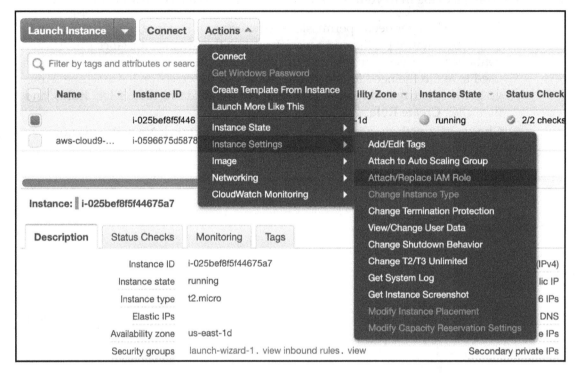

Attaching an IAM role to an EC2 instance

7. On the following screen, select the role you just created and click **Apply**.
8. Go to the **AWS Systems Manager** dashboard:

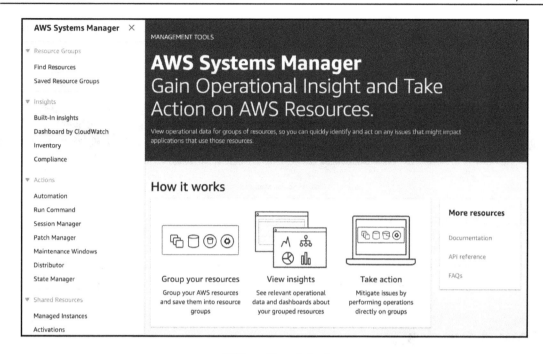

AWS Systems Manager dashboard

9. Select **Session Manager** from the menu on the left-hand side of the screen, and then click **Start Session**. You should see your EC2 instance in the list of available instances. If you don't see it, wait a few minutes and refresh the screen since it might take a while for **Systems Manager** to notice that you added the instance profile to your instance:

Starting a session

10. Select the instance and click **Start session**. A Terminal session will open in a new tab:

```
Session ID: ezb.packt.admin1-0d3450ab7ddb8a3bf    Instance ID: i-025bef8f5f44675a7    Terminate
sh-4.2$ cd ~
sh-4.2$ ls -a
.   ..   .bash_logout   .bash_profile   .bashrc
sh-4.2$ █
```

A Systems Manager Session Manager Terminal window

11. Terminate the EC2 instance to avoid future charges if you don't have any further use for it.

Session Manager is a great tool that simplifies gaining access to your EC2 instances, thus improving security by removing the need to manage an externally stored key pair.

How it works...

Systems Manager Session Manager allows you to log in to your instances without the need for SSH keys or Terminal clients. This allows you to rescue instances if you happen to lose your key pairs, and it can add an increased level of security since, if you never create a key pair in the first place, there is no chance that it could ever be compromised.

The SSM Agent, which is installed by default on Amazon Linux instances, combined with the instance profile that is attached to the instance, allows Systems Manager to take actions on that instance on your behalf.

There's more...

Session Manager is just the tip of the iceberg as far as Systems Manager is concerned! Take some time to explore the service to find out about its many organizational benefits that can increase your productivity and take the repetitive motions out of your administration routine.

Here are a few features that are offered by Systems Manager:

- **Resource Groups** allow you to create groups of instances that can easily be searched, and these groups can be acted on all at once. An example is applying a patch to all the instances in the group.
- Use **Built-in Insights** to check Config rule compliance, CloudTrail logs, and Trusted Advisor recommendations.
- Use the **Run** command to issue shell commands to a large batch of instances.

Creating serverless functions with AWS Lambda

AWS Lambda is quickly becoming an indispensable resource for building systems in the cloud. It fits in nicely for several utility use cases, such as running code each time an object is dropped into an S3 bucket, but it can also be used to construct entire applications. Lambda lends itself well to the microservices mentality, which is an important piece of the DevOps puzzle. A microservice is a small, fully independent component of an application. Microservices generally have a dedicated code repository and a dedicated data store so that they can be deployed in isolation from any other related services. By decomposing your architecture down to the individual function level, you can maximize your compute resources by configuring, deploying, and scaling each function separately.

How to do it...

Follow these steps to create a simple AWS Lambda function that processes messages from an Amazon **Simple Queue Service** (**SQS**) queue. The ability to automatically process all the messages in a queue with a Lambda function is an incredibly valuable feature that was announced by AWS in 2018. Anyone who has written code to poll a queue for messages knows that it can be surprisingly hard to do correctly, especially at scale with distributed systems. Adding this tool to your belt will allow you to tackle a wide variety of architectural challenges:

1. Go to the SQS dashboard and create a new queue. Name the queue `MySampleQ`, choose **Standard Queue**, and click **Quick-Create Queue**.
2. Go to the AWS Lambda dashboard and click **Create function**.
3. Choose **Author from scratch** and name the function `MyQReader`.

4. Choose **Node.js 8.10** as the runtime and click **Create function**.

5. Scroll down to the function code and paste in the following:

```
exports.handler = async (event) => {
    // Log the entire event
    console.info('event', JSON.stringify(event))
    let numRecordsProcessed = 0
    event.Records.forEach(record => {
        // Process the message from SQS here
        console.log(record.body);
        numRecordsProcessed++
    });
    const response = {
        statusCode: 200,
        body: JSON.stringify(`${numRecordsProcessed} messages
handled!`),
    };
    return response;
};
```

6. Your Lambda function needs additional privileges to interact with SQS. Scroll down to the execution role and click the role name to view it in the IAM console.

7. Expand the policy and click **Edit policy**.

8. Click the **JSON** tab and add the following policy statement to the array of statements that are already present in the policy. Note that the best practice is to replace the asterisk (*) in the Resource property with the actual ARN of your SQS queue:

```
{
    "Effect": "Allow",
    "Action": [
        "sqs:ReceiveMessage",
        "sqs:DeleteMessage",
        "sqs:GetQueueAttributes"
    ],
    "Resource": "*"
}
```

9. Go back to your browser tab with the **Lambda** function.
10. Scroll down to **Designer** and select **SQS** from the event sources.
11. Select `MySampleQ` from the dropdown under **Configure triggers**:

Configuring triggers

12. Click **Add** and then **Save** the function.
13. Open a new tab (leaving the **Lambda** tab open) and go to the SQS dashboard.

14. Select `MySampleQ` and, from the **Queue Actions** dropdown, select **Send a Message**:

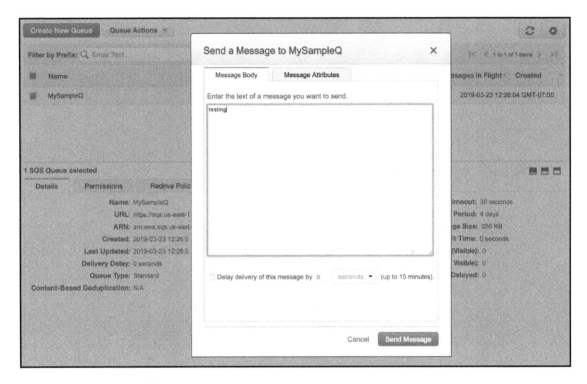

Sending a message

15. Type some text into the box and click **Send Message**.
16. Go back to the Lambda function and click the **Monitoring** tab. Click **View logs in CloudWatch**.

17. On the **CloudWatch** page, click the latest log stream and check out the log messages that have been sent from your Lambda function to confirm that the message was successfully processed:

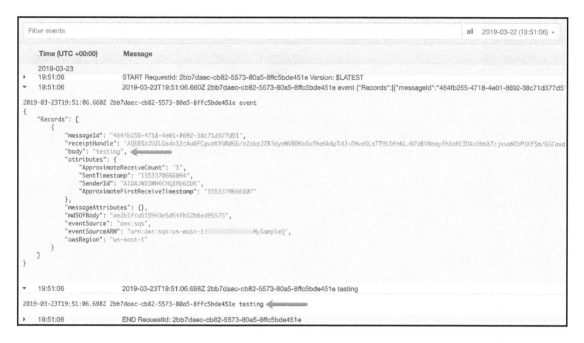

CloudWatch logs being sent from the Lambda function

18. Delete the Lambda function and the SQS queue to avoid future charges.

Delegating work to a queue can drastically improve the perceived performance of your web applications, and there is no easier way to accomplish queue processing than to wire up a Lambda function to SQS. Using a queue also helps you decompose your application into decoupled, separately deployable components, which reduces risks when you're making future changes.

How it works...

Lambda functions run in containers that are fully managed by AWS. All of the implementation details are hidden from you, and, in most cases, you don't need to know how or where your function runs. Of course, a little bit of knowledge of what's going on behind the scenes can help in some situations. For example, it's important to understand the penalty you pay when your function is run for the first time. This is called a **cold start**, and it can add a significant amount of latency if there are no ready resources that have already been provisioned to run your function.

For a busy application, this is often not a problem, since frequent function invocations guarantee that for most requests, your function will be warm. There are certain steps you can take to optimize your functions with cold starts in mind, such as increasing the configured memory size and making sure that you create resources such as database connection pools outside of your function code so that you don't pay the cold startup price every time your function runs.

There's more...

While it's possible to create and edit Lambda functions solely within the Lambda dashboard, it is highly recommended that you use a system such as the AWS **Serverless Application Model** (**SAM**) to structure your applications. Use SAM in combination with a version control system such as AWS `CodeCommit` so that you can maintain a revision history and share your code with colleagues.

SAM templates are a superset of AWS CloudFormation and use abbreviated commands that make creating Lambda functions much easier. The following screenshot shows an example SAM template that was created using AWS Cloud 9, an excellent web-based **Integrated Development Environment** (**IDE**) that you can run from your own account:

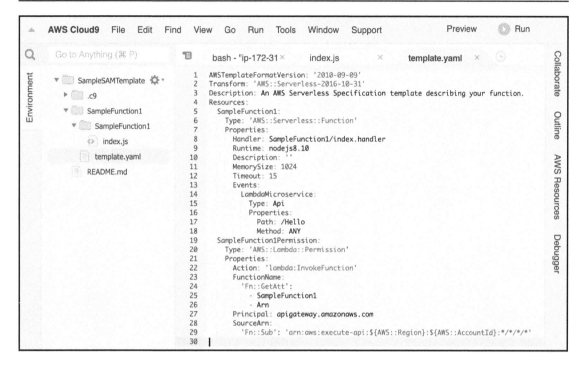

Cloud9 and the Serverless Application Model

SAM templates make it easier to create Lambda functions with **Infrastructure as Code (IaC)**, and they should be your default way of allowing your development teams to create serverless microservices.

See also

- Check out AWS CodeStar, a service that allows you to create a complete microservice or website, along with a code repository, development environment, and CI/CD pipeline, all in a single command that takes just a few minutes to run: https://aws.amazon.com/codestar/

Monitoring the Infrastructure

5

As with all administration, monitoring is a critical part of using AWS. Due to the ephemeral nature of cloud resources, and the ability to quickly provision large numbers of new resources, keeping track of and measuring your usage is even more important than when using on-premises systems.

One of the greatest benefits of the cloud is its ability to spin up new resources with the click of a button, or by the use of automation scripts and auto-scaling to create new resources in response to the greater load on the system. However, this advantage can come at a cost if you are not carefully monitoring the infrastructure. As an administrator, you will need to keep a close eye on the cost associated with resource usage, and you will be tasked with providing a view of **key performance indicators** (**KPIs**) for your business. This chapter will provide you with the tools and techniques that you need to always know what is happening in your AWS account.

In this chapter, we will cover the following recipes:

- AWS Trusted Advisor
- Resource tags
- AWS CloudWatch
- Billing alerts
- The ELK stack
- AWS CloudTrail
- Network logging and troubleshooting

These recipes will give you the foundation that you need in order to handle the routine monitoring of your AWS infrastructure. The value of collecting metrics is the ability to spot trends and relationships (often unknown or unexpected) between disparate systems. With this kind of visibility, you are able to identify and troubleshoot issues before they become an incident.

AWS Trusted Advisor

Trusted Advisor covers five main areas, and it is designed to give you some guidance around what are considered the best practices for your cloud deployment. The areas that are covered are as follows:

- Cost optimization
- Performance
- Security
- Fault tolerance
- Service limits

It's available to everyone and free to use for basic coverage. If you are paying for Business- or Enterprise-level support with AWS, you get access to additional checks that are important for production workloads. At the time of writing, there are 53 checks for cost optimization, performance, security, and fault tolerance, and 48 separate checks for service limits.

How to do it...

The good news is that you don't need to do anything at all to turn on Trusted Advisor. It's automatically enabled when your AWS account is created, and will continue to update for the lifetime of your account. Go ahead and navigate to the Trusted Advisor section of the AWS web console.

How it works...

The checks that are provided for free with this service are as follows:

- **Unrestricted ports**: This is a check on the highest-risk ports in your security groups. They'll be flagged if they're open to everyone ($0.0.0.0/0$).
- **IAM usage**: This is a fairly rudimentary check. If there isn't at least one IAM user in your account, this check won't pass. It's considered good practice to not use your root login credentials for your AWS account, and instead create IAM users with least privileged access.

- **MFA on root account**: You need to have MFA enabled for your root login in order for this check to pass. It's also a good idea to enable MFA for your IAM users as well, as we discussed in `Chapter 1`, *AWS Fundamentals*.
- **Amazon S3 bucket permissions**: This will alert you to any buckets that are configured for public access.
- **Service limits**: This one is quite handy—if you're approaching 80% of your service limits, this check won't pass. For example, it's nice to know if you're about to hit the cap of CloudFormation stacks or EC2 instances before you attempt to create them.
- **EBS and RDS public snapshots**: This checks to see if any of your snapshots are open to the general public.

Even though there is only a handful of checks here, these are some of the more useful ones, so we'd encourage you to pay attention to them. The console uses a color scheme to denote the status of each check:

- **Red**: It's recommended that you take action to remedy this check.
- **Yellow**: This check requires investigation and possible remediation.
- **Green**: This check is passing and needs no attention.

> Visit the **Preferences** page in the Trusted Advisor web console if you'd like to have a weekly report emailed to you.

There's more...

As well as opening up the entire suite of Trusted Advisor checks, a Business- or Enterprise-level support arrangement gives you access to the following:

- **Notifications**: You are able to have notifications delivered to you at a higher frequency using a number of delivery methods. Since Trusted Advisor is an available source in CloudWatch Events, you'll be able to create notifications that can be handled by SNS (email, push, SMS), or even notifications that will trigger Lambda functions.

- **API access**: You'll have access to a number of Trusted Advisor API methods, such as `DescribeTrustedAdvisorCheckResult` and `DescribeTrustedAdvisorCheckSummaries`. You can use these to integrate the results from checks into your own dashboards or monitoring systems. You'll also be able to use the APIs to refresh Trusted Advisor checks (after you've taken corrective action on them, for example).
- **Exclusion**: You can selectively mute checks that are failing. You'll sometimes want to do this for things such as RDS instances in your development environments that aren't in multi-AZ mode, or don't have backups enabled.

Finally, some of the more useful checks that we see for Business- and Enterprise-level support customers are as follows:

- **Reserved Instances**: This is a nice cost optimization if you have a reasonably static workload since a reserved instance allows you to pay upfront for EC2 instances when you know they will run steadily for long periods of time.
- **Unassociated Elastic IPs**: If IP addresses are not associated with a network interface (on an EC2 instance, for example), you will be charged for them. Also, if there are unassociated IPs floating around, that is usually a sign that they are being allocated manually, instead of with CloudFormation. Remember that the goal here is for more automation, not less.
- **Idle load balancers**: Again, these cost money, and are often easily orphaned in low-automation environments.
- **S3 bucket permissions**: It's not always obvious if the permissions on an S3 bucket have been misconfigured. This check helps you to avoid unintentionally leaking data.

As we have stated in other chapters, if you are running any production workload in an AWS account, you should have, as a minimum, a Business support contract, which will unlock the full functionality of Trusted Advisor.

Resource tags

Resource tags are an indispensable way of categorizing the resource that you create in your AWS account. Resource tags do not represent an AWS service by themselves, but are rather an attribute that is associated with a variety of services.

Resource tags are simply name-value pairs that are associated with a resource. You can attach as many as 50 tags, as of this writing, to any given resource.

Resource tags can be helpful with the following:

- Assigning a nametag to your EC2 instances so that it is easy to differentiate them in the console.
- Billing reports for cost center tracking. For example, you could tag resources with *Department = Finance* so that all the resources that are used by your finance department can be grouped in a billing report.
- Applying for tag-specific permissions in IAM so that users are limited to accessing resources with a given tag.
- Assigning specific tags that can then be acted on via automation (tying into your automation theme).

You can't use the `aws:` prefix in your tags. That is reserved for use by AWS to apply tags to certain resources in order to support advanced functionality.

How to do it...

In this recipe, you will use the **Tag Editor** to locate resources that do not have any tags. Ideally, all the resources in a production account will be tagged for various purposes. The **Tag Editor** can be a handy way to identify resources that you may have forgotten about:

1. Log in to your AWS account and click the **Resource Groups** link at the top navigation bar. Then, select **Tag Editor**.

2. Pick a resource type to search for. In the following example, I chose S3 buckets:

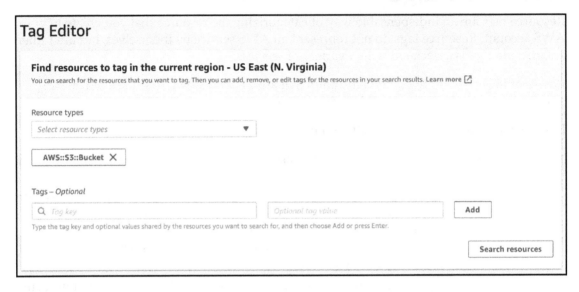

Tag Editor

If you don't see any resources listed, create a resource such as an S3 bucket or EC2 instance and come back to this screen to try the search again:

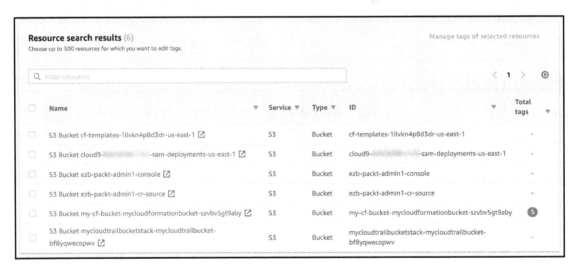

Resource search results

3. Select one of your resources that does not have a tag.
4. For S3, you could go to the bucket itself and edit the tags in the **Advanced** section under **Properties**. Alternatively, you can stay on this screen and edit the tags directly without leaving the search results.
5. Select the checkbox next to the resource and click the **Manage tags** button of the selected resources:

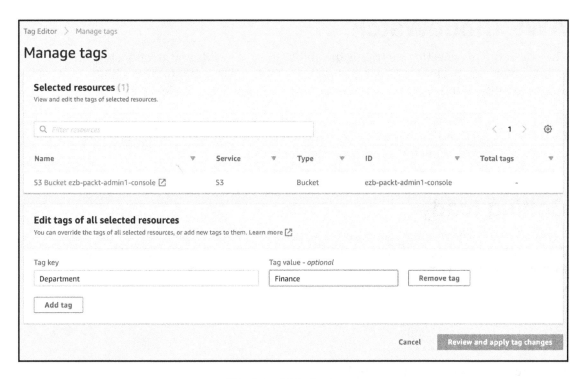

Editing the tags of all the selected resources

6. Add a tag and click **Review and apply tag changes**.
7. Click **Apply changes to all selected**.

How it works...

The Tag Editor is simply providing quick and easy access to all the resources that can be tagged, allowing you to audit your tag usage all in one place without having to dive into the details of each individual resource.

AWS CloudWatch

The real value of collecting metrics is the ability to spot trends and relationships (often unknown or unexpected) between disparate systems. With this kind of visibility, you are able to identify and troubleshoot issues before they become an incident.

In addition to providing a way to aggregate and view metrics from your systems, the CloudWatch service also makes it easy to create monitoring dashboards, allowing you to quickly and clearly view the most important metrics.

Getting ready

You will need to have some metrics already present in CloudWatch in order to create a dashboard. If you have been using AWS services (for example EC2, RDS, DDB, and so on), then you should have plenty—almost all of the AWS services populate metrics in CloudWatch by default.

How to do it...

In this recipe, you will set up a simple CloudWatch dashboard, and you will learn about the different kinds of widgets that can be added to a dashboard:

1. Log in to your AWS account and navigate to **CloudWatch**:

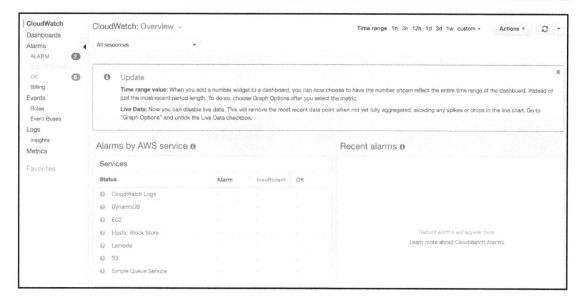

CloudWatch

2. Go to the **Dashboards** section of the console via the link on the left-hand menu and click the **Create dashboard** button:

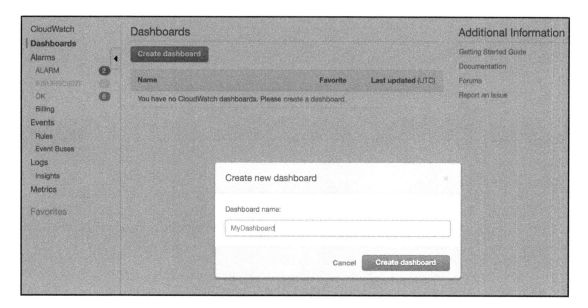

Creating a dashboard

3. Choose the type of widget that you want to use to display your metric. In this example, we will choose the most versatile, Line. Navigate to the **All metrics** tab to find the metric(s) you want to include, selecting it by clicking the tick box on the left of the metric details. You will see a preview of the metric(s) if there is any data to display:

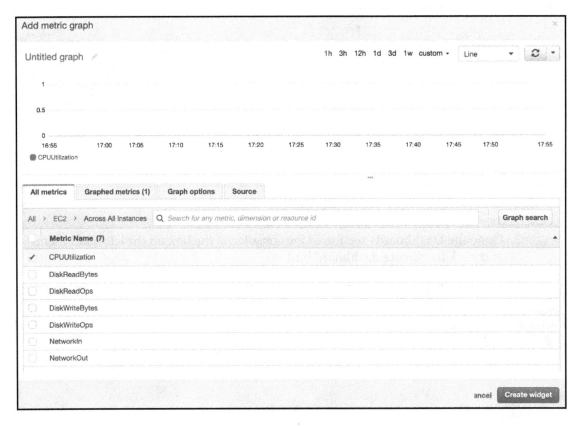

Add metric graph screen

4. Once selected, you can modify how the metric is displayed via the settings on the **Graphed metrics** tab. In this case, we have given the widget a name and changed the **Period** setting for our metric to **1 Minute** to reflect the additional granularity that is available:

Edit graph screen

5. Once you click **Create widget**, you will see your widget on the dashboard. Once you click **Save dashboard**, it will appear under the **Dashboards** heading on the left-hand menu:

Save dashboard screen

6. At the dashboard level, you can turn on **Auto refresh** and the **Refresh interval**. You can resize and rearrange your widgets by dragging them. Just remember to click **Save dashboard** to persist any changes. As you can see here, I have added widgets for DiskReadBytes and CPUCreditBalance to my dashboard:

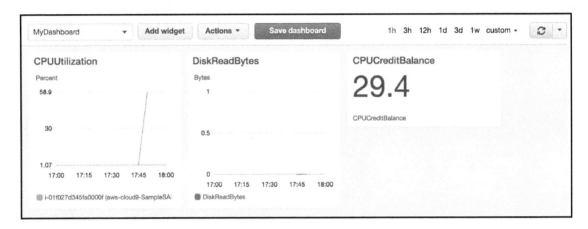

Adding widgets

How it works...

CloudWatch dashboard's value is the ease and simplicity with which it allows you to publicize your most important metrics.

As with any dashboard, make sure that the metrics you choose to display are relevant and actionable. There's no point in displaying a metric if there's no action required when it changes.

Widget types

Line graphs are not the only type of widget that can be displayed in a dashboard. The following types can also be displayed:

- Stacked area
- Number
- Text
- Query results

Depending on the type of metrics you are collecting or are interested in, you should experiment with different types of widgets to display them. Not all metrics are suited to line graphs.

 You can use the Amazon CloudWatch API to automate the creation of dashboard widgets in response to new resources that are being created or terminated in your environment.

Billing alerts

One of the main attractions of using AWS is its pay-as-you-go model. You only pay for what you use, no more and no less. Unfortunately, this can sometimes result in what's known as bill shock at the end of the month. This happens when you do something that you might not know is a charged service, or you do not know how much is charged for it, and you don't find out until it's too late. Especially when getting started, users may not fully appreciate the cost of the activities they're undertaking.

Creating a budget and setting up alerts that get sent when you exceed that budget is good practice for all AWS accounts. For a development account, where you are only testing things out for short periods of time, you may never expect to exceed the free tier, so you can set a $1 budget and get alerted if charges exceed that amount, and then quickly find and remove any resources that you forgot about.

While you can create budgets via the AWS CLI tool, it is useful to know how the **Billing** dashboard works for administration purposes, so we will use the AWS console for this recipe.

Getting ready

By default, IAM users do not have access to the **Billing** section of the AWS console. Follow these steps in order to delegate access to an IAM user so that you can follow best practices and not use the root account unless it is absolutely necessary:

1. Log in to your AWS account as the root user.
2. Click the name of your account at the upper right of the console and then click **My Account**.

3. Scroll down to **IAM User and Role Access to Billing Information**, as shown in the following diagram. Click **Edit**:

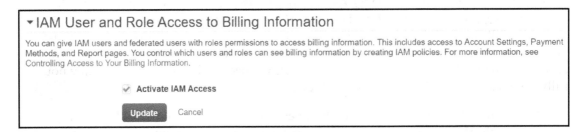

The Edit link to activate IAM access is subtle. It is indicated with the yellow arrow here.

4. Check the box to **Activate IAM Access**, and then click **Update**:

▾ IAM User and Role Access to Billing Information

You can give IAM users and federated users with roles permissions to access billing information. This includes access to Account Settings, Payment Methods, and Report pages. You control which users and roles can see billing information by creating IAM policies. For more information, see Controlling Access to Your Billing Information.

☑ **Activate IAM Access**

Update   Cancel

Activating access to billing information for IAM users

5. Go to the IAM dashboard and select the IAM user account (or group) that you wish to delegate for billing access.
6. Add the following policy:

```
{
    "Statement": [
        {
            "Effect": "Allow",
            "Action": [
                "aws-portal:ViewBilling",
                "aws-portal:ModifyBilling",
                "budgets:ViewBudget",
                "budgets:ModifyBudget"
            ],
            "Resource": [
                "*"
            ]
        }
    ]
}
```

Once these steps have been completed, you can log out of the root account and back in as the IAM user.

How to do it...

1. Log in as an IAM user who has the rights to create budgets (not as the root user!) and navigate to the **My Billing Dashboard** via the user menu, which can be accessed by clicking on your name in the top right.
2. The **Billing** dashboard displays your up-to-date usage for the month. Click on **Budgets** on the left-hand menu.
3. When you first arrive at the **Budgets** console, there will be no budgets to display. Click on the **Create budget** button to get started.
4. Start by filling out the budget details, such as **Cost** for the measurement type, **Monthly** for the period, and the budget amount. Select the **Start date** (which defaults to the first of the current month) and (optionally) the **End date**. Leave the **End date** field blank to create a rolling budget that is reset each month.
5. Next, enter the notification details. This includes the threshold for notification, which we will set to 80% (of our budget) in forecasted use. For email notifications, simply enter the email addresses you want to receive the notifications. Click **Create** when you're finished.
6. You will be returned to the **Budgets** section of the **Billing** dashboard, and you will be able to see your newly created budget.
7. For each of the budgets you create, you can select it to view its full details.

How it works...

The **Billing** dashboard is closely tied to the account itself, which is why it is not part of the regular services in the console. Accessing it via the user menu hints at the special access that it requires. Generally, you would configure a budget when you first open a new AWS account so that you don't get any surprises in your bill at the end of the month.

If you get access denied messages in the **Billing** dashboard, it is most likely because you are using an IAM user and IAM access has not been enabled. You must use your root account credentials (such as those that you used to create the account) or enable IAM access. IAM access can only be enabled by the root user.

When you first arrive at the **Billing** section, you will see a high-level summary of your usage and expenses. As I performed this example in a new account, there's not much to see at this point. The Month-to-Date Spend by Service graph on the right can be particularly useful if you want to find out what the most popular services you use are. This is a great place to start when you're trying to reduce or optimize your AWS spending. We then navigate to the **Budgets** section and create a new budget.

Most of the details should be self-explanatory, and obvious for the purposes of budgeting. Your main choice is to decide whether you want to alert users on usage or costs. Cost budgets work against the dollar (or appropriate billing currency) amount you will be charged. Usage budgets work against a selected unit of usage, for example, instance hours or data transfer for EC2. A usage budget can only track one type of usage unit, so you will need to create multiple budgets to track the various units that you might be charged for. This is one reason why we prefer a cost budget, as it takes into account multiple forms of usage.

Specifying email addresses to alert is the simplest way to send any alerts from the budget. For more advanced use cases, you can specify an SNS topic to receive notifications. An example might be if you wanted to receive budget alerts on your phone via an SMS message, or send the alert to a different system automatically (via HTTP/JSON). Once finished, you can view all your budgets on the dashboard. You can repeat the process to create multiple budgets. This means that you can create budgets for forecast usage and actual usage, as well as for different time periods.

The ELK stack

ELK stands for **Elasticsearch-Logstash-Kibana**, a combination of open source products that results in a very popular way to visualize logs in an AWS account:

- **Elasticsearch**: Based on Apache Lucene, this is a scalable indexing service that is custom built to handle full-text searching. It includes a number of flexible algorithms to help you optimize your search queries.

- **Logstash**: A project that enables high rates of data ingestion and includes plugins that can handle most of the common log file formats in use by mainstream applications.
- **Kibana**: A user interface tool that provides a means of visualizing data.

The Amazon Elasticsearch Service is a fully managed implementation of Elasticsearch, with built-in Kibana and supported integrations with Logstash.

How to do it...

In this recipe, you will learn how to create an Elasticsearch domain, configure the CloudWatch Logs agent on an EC2 instance, and stream those logs to Elasticsearch so that you can search them with Kibana:

1. Log in to your account and go to the Elasticsearch dashboard. Click **Create a new domain**:

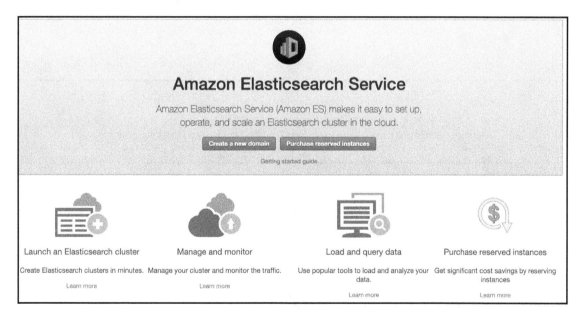

Amazon Elasticsearch Service

2. Choose **Development and testing** to limit the size of the cluster. Be aware that this recipe will not fall under the free tier! There will be charges associated with setting up a test domain:

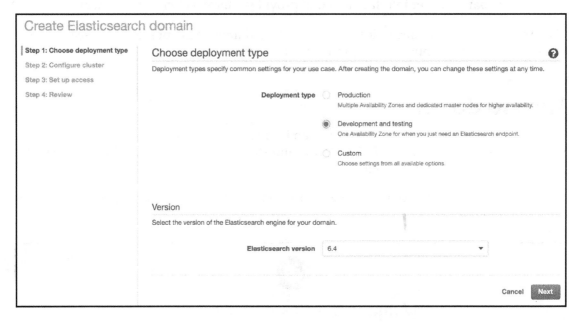

Development and testing domain

3. Give the domain a unique name. Stick with the default instance type:

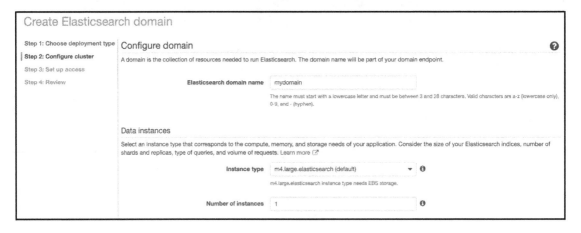

Elasticsearch domain name

4. On the next screen, configure the network. The simplest choice for a quick test is **Public access**, but of course for a production application, you will want to lock down access to the domain. If you choose **VPC access (Recommended)**, be warned that gaining access to your Kibana endpoint will involve a VPN or a proxy server of some kind:

Elasticsearch VPC configuration

5. The last step is to set up your domain access policy. To limit access to a single user, select **Allow or deny access to one or more AWS accounts or IAM users**, or simply allow open access (do not make this selection for production systems!). After you complete the setup wizard by clicking **Confirm** on the final screen, the domain will take a while to become active. When it does, you will have access to the Kibana URL:

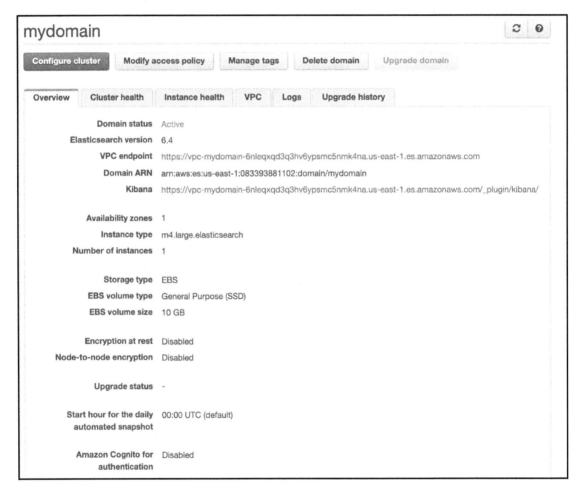

Active Elasticsearch domain with Kibana URL

6. Now, you need some logs to ingest into Elasticsearch. The quickest way to do this is to log in to one of your EC2 instances. (Create an Amazon Linux instance using the *Launch an instance* recipe in `Chapter 4`, *AWS Compute*, if you don't already have a running instance.)

7. Add an instance profile to the instance that has the `CloudWatchAgentAdminPolicy` so that the instance will have permission to write to CloudWatch Logs.

8. Log into the instance using **SSM Session Manager**, like we did in `Chapter 4`, *AWS Compute*, and run the following commands to install and start the CloudWatch Logs agent on the instance:

```
$ sudo yum update -y
$ sudo yum install -y awslogs
$ sudo service awslogs start
```

9. The default setting should be sufficient to send system logs to CloudWatch, but you can edit the configuration file if you wish:

```
$ vim /etc/awslogs/awslogs.conf
```

10. You should see a new log group show up in the CloudWatch Logs console. If you don't, check the error logs in `/var/logs/awslogs.log`:

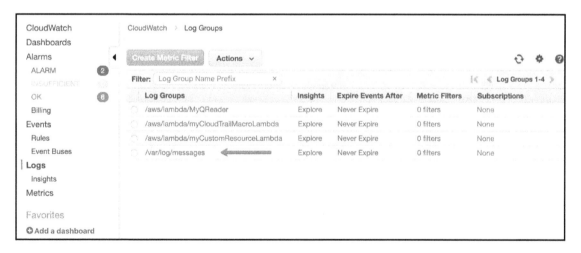

CloudWatch Log Groups

11. Select the new `/var/log/messages` log group and then select **Stream to Amazon Elasticsearch Service** from the **Actions** dropdown menu:

Stream to Amazon Elasticsearch Service option

12. Select your domain and create a new role that will be used by a Lambda function that CloudWatch creates to broker the ingestion. Add the `AWSLambdaVPCAccessExecutionRole` policy to the default role that is created for you:

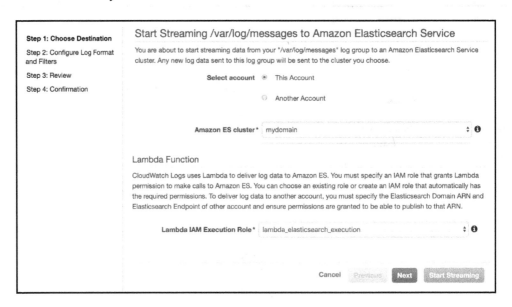

Start streaming logs to Elasticsearch

TIP

Note that streaming data from CloudWatch to Elasticsearch can result in high-usage charges! Be sure to set a budget and monitor your charges carefully.

13. Click **Next**, then choose **Common Log Formant** on the next screen. Click **Next** on the following two screens, then click **Start Streaming**.

14. Now, you are ready to visualize your logs in Kibana. Click the Kibana URL on the Elasticsearch domain console:

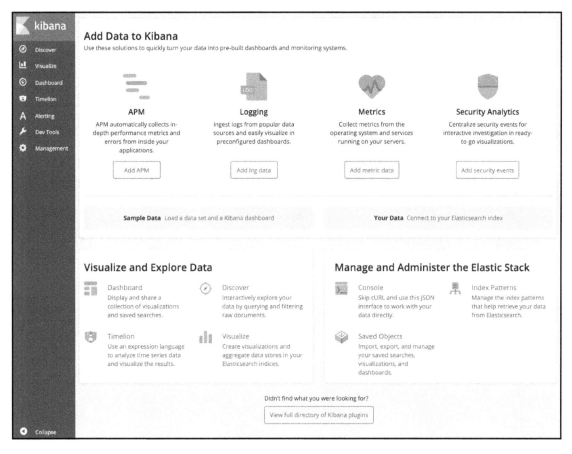

Kibana

15. Click **Discover** and then create an **Index Patterns** for CloudWatch Logs—`cwl-*`:

Create an index pattern

16. On the next screen, choose `@timestamp` as a filter, and then after the index pattern is created, go back to the **Discover** tab to start querying your data:

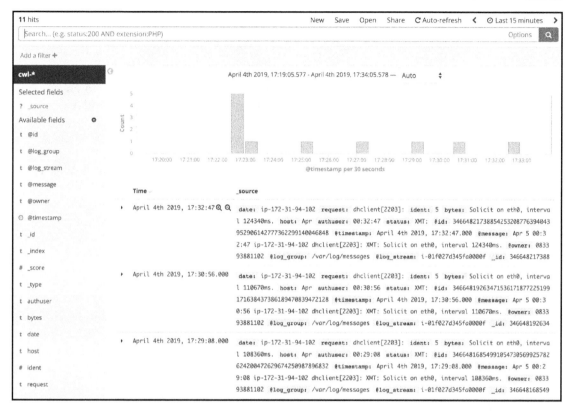

Search logs with Kibana

17. Once you have explored what's possible with Kibana, delete the Elasticsearch domain in order to prevent future charges associated with the resources that you created in this recipe.

How it works...

When you configure an Elasticsearch domain, an instance is provisioned for you behind the scenes to run the open source software that comprises Elasticsearch and Kibana. The CloudWatch Logs agent that runs on the instances that you want to monitor watches log files according to the configuration that you specify and sends the logs to CloudWatch in batches. CloudWatch, in turn, passes those log entries on to the Elasticsearch domain. Once they have been ingested by Elasticsearch, you can query and search them with Kibana.

One important thing to keep in mind with this logging solution is that application logs on your instances often log sensitive data, so be sure to safeguard all the aspects of this solution in the same way that you would safeguard customer databases. Many infamous data breaches are the result of web application developers logging things such as usernames and passwords to log files, and then those log files are passed to an unprotected system. Don't be one of those administrators who simply assume that log files are innocuous and don't deserve rigorous data protection controls!

In the preceding recipe, you had the option of configuring an open domain that allows access to the public. While this made completing the recipe easy, when it comes to production applications, lock your domain down to a VPC and apply the lessons you have learned about security to limit access to a small subset of your users.

There's more...

AWS released a feature called CloudWatch Logs Insights that provides much of the functionality offered by Kibana. There may be use cases where the ELK stack is still the right choice for your application, but in many cases, CloudWatch Logs Insights will get the job done, with much less cost and complexity. The Insights feature provides a custom query language that gives you a flexible way to build powerful visualizations of your CloudWatch Logs:

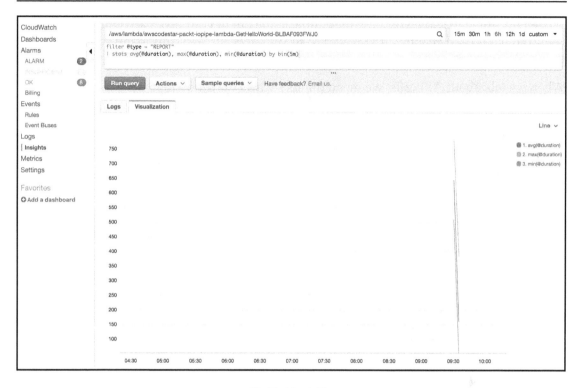

CloudWatch Logs Insights

As you can see from the preceding screenshot, a simple query produces a visualization of Lambda function latency characteristics.

AWS CloudTrail

A vital feature of any IT environment is the ability to record a detailed audit log of the changes made, who made the changes, and when they were made. Audits are a requirement of many compliance standards, and are the best practice to ensure that security breaches can be detected and investigated. AWS CloudTrail provides this functionality by allowing you to set up trails that record specific activity within your account.

We're now going to show you how to set up CloudTrail in your AWS account. Once CloudTrail has been enabled, it will start to record all of the API calls made in your account to the AWS service, and then deliver them to you as log files in an S3 bucket.

When we talk about API calls, we mean things such as the following:

- Actions performed in the AWS console.
- Calls made to AWS APIs using the CLI or SDKs.
- Calls made on your behalf by AWS services. Think CloudFormation or the auto-scaling service.

Each entry in the log will contain useful information, such as the following:

- The service that was called
- The action that was requested
- The parameters that were sent with the request
- The response that was returned by AWS
- The identity of the caller (including IP address)
- The date and time of the request

How to do it...

Follow these steps to set up a new trail with CloudFormation. A trail is a single configuration for logging audit records using CloudTrail. Multiple trails can be configured:

1. Create a new CloudFormation template file named `05-01-CloudTrail.yml`; you're going to define the following resources:

    - An S3 bucket for our CloudTrail log files to be stored in
    - A policy for our S3 bucket that allows the CloudTrail service to write to our bucket
    - A CloudTrail trail

It's actually good practice to avoid giving names to your CloudFormation resources. Let CloudFormation name then for you—by doing this, you are guaranteed to avoid naming conflicts. Use output parameters and cross-stack references instead of copying and pasting hardcoded names.

2. First, define an S3 bucket. We don't need to give it a name; we'll add the bucket name to the list of `Outputs` later:

```
Resources:
  ExampleTrailBucket:
    Type: AWS::S3::Bucket
```

3. Next, you need to define a policy for your bucket. This section is a little wordy, so you may prefer to get this from the code samples instead. This policy essentially allows CloudTrail to do two things to our bucket: `s3:GetBucketAcl` and `s3:PutObject`:

```
ExampleBucketPolicy:
  Type: AWS::S3::BucketPolicy
  Properties:
    Bucket: !Ref ExampleTrailBucket
    PolicyDocument:
      Statement:
        - Sid: AWSCloudTrailAclCheck20150319
          Effect: Allow
          Principal:
            Service: cloudtrail.amazonaws.com
          Action: s3:GetBucketAcl
          Resource: !Join
            - ""
            -
              - "arn:aws:s3:::"
              - !Ref ExampleTrailBucket
        - Sid: AWSCloudTrailWrite20150319
          Effect: Allow
          Principal:
            Service: cloudtrail.amazonaws.com
          Action: s3:PutObject
          Resource: !Join
            - ""
            -
              - "arn:aws:s3:::"
              - !Ref ExampleTrailBucket
              - "/AWSLogs/"
              - !Ref AWS::AccountId
              - "/*"
          Condition:
            StringEquals:
              s3:x-amz-acl: bucket-owner-full-control
```

4. Now, you can set up your trail. One thing to note here is that we use `DependsOn` to make CloudFormation create this trail after it has created the S3 bucket and policy. If you don't do this, you'll likely encounter an error when you create the stack because CloudTrail won't be able to access the bucket. Also, setting `IsMultiRegionTrail` to `true` is considered good practice. Add `Trail` to your template:

```
ExampleTrail:
  Type: AWS::CloudTrail::Trail
  Properties:
    EnableLogFileValidation: true
    IncludeGlobalServiceEvents: true
    IsLogging: true
    IsMultiRegionTrail: true
    S3BucketName: !Ref ExampleTrailBucket
  DependsOn:
    - ExampleTrailBucket
    - ExampleBucketPolicy
```

5. Finally, you're going to output the name of the S3 bucket where your CloudTrail logs will be stored:

```
Outputs:
  ExampleBucketName:
    Value: !Ref ExampleTrailBucket
    Description: Bucket where CloudTrail logs will be stored
```

6. Run your CloudFormation stack using the following command:

```
aws cloudformation create-stack \
--template-body file://05-01-CloudTrail.yml \
--stack-name example-cloudtrail
```

How it works...

This template will set up CloudTrail with the following configuration:

- CloudTrail will be turned on for all regions in your account. This is a sensible place to start because it gives you visibility over where your AWS resources are being created. Even if you are the sole user of your AWS account, it can be handy to know if you are making API calls to other regions by mistake (it's easy to do). When you create a multi-region trail, new regions will automatically be included when they come online with no additional effort on your part.

- Global service events will also be logged. Again, this is a sensible default because it includes services that aren't region-specific. CloudFront and IAM are two examples of AWS services that aren't region-specific.
- Log file validation is turned on. With this feature enabled, CloudTrail will deliver a digest file on an hourly basis that you can use to determine if your CloudTrail logs have been tampered with. CloudTrail uses SHA-256 for hashing and signing (RSA). The AWS CLI can be used to perform ad hoc validation of CloudTrail logs. For a quick view of your CloudTrial logs with some basic search and filter functionality, you can head to the AWS web console.

There's more...

Here are more details about CloudTrail:

- Server-side encryption is used to encrypt log files in S3. This encryption is transparent to you, but you can opt to encrypt these files with your own **Customer Master Key (CMK)** if you wish. CMKs are a feature of the **Key Management Service (KMS)**, which is used to encrypt data keys for envelope encryption.
- API calls are logged by CloudTrail in under 15 minutes.
- Logs are shipped to your S3 bucket every five minutes.
- It's possible to aggregate CloudTrail events across many accounts into a single bucket. This is a pattern often used to log AWS activity into a SecOps, or similar, account for auditing.
- By default, CloudTrail keeps your API activity for seven days.
- You can create more than one trail. You might consider creating a trail for your developers that is separate from the trail that is consumed by security. Be aware that trails beyond the first, and trails that record data plane activity, will incur additional costs that could be significant if your account has a large amount of activity.
- If a CloudFormation stack creates an S3 bucket and that S3 bucket has objects in it, the delete operation will fail if and when you choose to delete the stack. You can manually delete the S3 bucket in the S3 web console if you wish to work around this.

Network logging and troubleshooting

One of the benefits of using a virtualized infrastructure is that you can get a level of introspection that is difficult or costly with physical hardware. Being able to quickly switch on logging at a network-device level is an extremely useful feature, especially when getting used to the interactions between VPCs, subnets, NACLs, routing, and security groups. A common use case would be figuring out why a specific user is not able to connect to an EC2 instance inside one of your VPCs.

In this recipe, we will turn on logging for our network resources by using VPC Flow Logs. You could do this all the time to give yourself another layer for monitoring and auditing, or you could selectively enable it during troubleshooting, saving yourself any additional data storage charges. VPC Flow Logs allow you to capture and analyze information (but not individual packets) about traffic that is flowing to and from network interfaces within your account.

Getting ready

For this recipe, you must have a VPC to log activity on.

How to do it...

Follow these steps to set up a flow-log:

1. Start by defining the template version and description:

    ```
    AWSTemplateFormatVersion: "2010-09-09"
    Description: Flow logs for networking resources
    ```

2. Define `Parameters` for the template. In this case, it is just the `VpcId` where we will enable flow-logs:

    ```
    Parameters:
      VpcId:
        Type: String
        Description: The VPC where we will enable flow logs
    ```

3. Create the `Resources` section of the template and define the log group to use to send our flow logs to:

```
Resources:
  LogGroup:
    Type: AWS::Logs::LogGroup
    Properties:
      LogGroupName: LogGroup
```

4. Next, we define the IAM role that will give the flow-logs service permission to write the logs:

```
IamRole:
  Type: AWS::IAM::Role
  Properties:
    AssumeRolePolicyDocument:
      Version: "2012-10-17"
      Statement:
        -
          Effect: Allow
          Principal:
            Service: vpc-flow-logs.amazonaws.com
          Action: sts:AssumeRole
    Policies:
      -
        PolicyName: CloudWatchLogsAccess
        PolicyDocument:
          Version: "2012-10-17"
          Statement:
            -
              Action:
                - logs:CreateLogGroup
                - logs:CreateLogStream
                - logs:PutLogEvents
                - logs:DescribeLogGroups
                - logs:DescribeLogStreams
              Effect: Allow
              Res
```

5. Finally, we define the flow-log itself:

```
FlowLog:
  Type: AWS::EC2::FlowLog
  DependsOn: LogGroup
  Properties:
    DeliverLogsPermissionArn: !GetAtt IamRole.Arn
    LogGroupName: LogGroup
    ResourceId: !Ref VpcId
```

```
ResourceType: VPC
TrafficType: ALL
```

6. Save the template and give it a filename such as `05-02-NetworkLogging.yaml`.

7. Create the flow-logs and associated resources by creating the template with the following command:

```
aws cloudformation create-stack \
    --stack-name VpcFlowLogs \
    --template-body file://05-02-NetworkLogging.yml \
    --capabilities CAPABILITY_IAM \
    --parameters ParameterKey=VpcId,ParameterValue=<your-vpc-id>
```

Once launched (and assuming you have network activity), you will be able to see your flow-log in the CloudWatch Logs console. If you don't see any flow-logs, you may need to create a resource such as an EC2 instance and SSH into it.

How it works...

The only parameter that is required for this template is the VPC ID to target. We specifically target a VPC to turn on flow-logging for because it gives us the most *bang for buck*. While you can enable flow-logs for subnets and **Elastic Network Interfaces** (**ENIs**) individually, if you enable them on a VPC, you get flow-logs for all the networking resources contained in that VPC, which includes subnets and ENIs.

In the `Resources` section, we start by explicitly defining the log group to *hold* the flow-logs. If you don't create the log group yourself (and specify it in your flow-log resource configuration), a log group will be created for you. This means that you will still be able to use flow-logs, but the log group won't be managed by CloudFormation and will have to be maintained (for example, deleted) manually. We have also set a **deletion policy** of *delete* for our log group. This means that it will be deleted if the CloudFormation stack is deleted.

Next, we define the IAM role to use. Via the `AssumeRolePropertyDocument` value, we give the AWS flow-logs service permission to assume this role. Without this access, the flow-logs service cannot access the account. In the `Policies` property, we give the role permission to create and update log groups and streams.

Finally, now that we have created the dependent resources, we define the flow-log resource itself. You don't need to define the resources in order of dependencies, but it is usually easier to read if you do. In the resource, we also define a `DependsOn` relationship to the log group that we defined earlier so that the log group is ready to receive the flow-logs when it is created.

The final step is to launch the template that you have created, passing the VPC ID as a parameter. As this template creates an IAM role to allow the VPC service to send logs to CloudWatch Logs, the command to create the stack must be given the `CAPABILITY_IAM` flag in order to signify that you are aware of the potential impact of launching this template.

There's more...

Turning on logging is just the start of the troubleshooting process. There are a few other things that you should be aware of when using flow-logs:

- Log format
- Updates
- Omissions

Log format

Once logging is enabled, you can view the logs in the CloudWatch Logs console. Here is a summary of the type of information that you will see in the flow-log (in order):

- The VPC flow-logs version
- The AWS account ID
- The ID of the network interface
- The source IPv4 or IPv6 address
- The destination IPv4 or IPv6 address
- The source port of the traffic
- The destination port of the traffic
- The **Internet Assigned Numbers Authority (IANA)** protocol number of the traffic
- The number of packets transferred
- The number of bytes transferred
- The start time of the capture window (in Unix seconds)
- The end time of the capture window (in Unix seconds)
- The action associated with the traffic; for example, `ACCEPT` or `REJECT`
- The logging status of the flow-log; for example, `OK`, `NODATA`, or `SKIPDATA`

To identify the protocol, check the protocol number field against the IANA protocol numbers list
at `http://www.iana.org/assignments/protocol-numbers/protocol-numb`
`ers.xhtml`.

Updates

You cannot update the configuration of an existing flow-log; you must delete it and recreate it if you want to change any of the associated settings. This is another reason why it is good to explicitly create and manage the associated log group.

Omissions

Some traffic is not captured by the flow-logs service, as follows:

- Traffic to the Amazon DNS server (`x.x.x.2` in your allocated range)
- Traffic for Amazon Windows license activation (only applicable to Windows instances).
- Traffic to and from the instance metadata service (that is, IP address, `169.254.169.254`), which gives the services that are running on the machine a way to get information on the instance's configuration
- DHCP traffic
- Traffic to the reserved VPC IP address for the default VPC router (`x.x.x.1` in your allocated range)

See also

- The *Virtual Private Cloud (VPC)* recipe in `Chapter 7`, *AWS Networking Essentials*

6
Managing AWS Databases

Having a persistent storage service is a key component of effectively using the AWS cloud for your systems. By ensuring that you have a highly available, fault-tolerant location to store your application state in, you can stop depending on individual servers for your data. AWS provides several different database choices, so you have plenty of flexibility to pick the database that best matches your use case.

In this chapter, we will cover the following topics:

- Creating an RDS database with automatic failover
- Creating an RDS database read replica
- Promoting an RDS read replica to master
- Creating a one-time RDS database backup
- Restoring an RDS database from a snapshot
- Migrating an RDS database
- Managing Amazon Aurora databases
- Create a DynamoDB table with a Global Secondary Index
- Calculating Amazon DynamoDB capacity
- Managing Amazon Neptune graph databases

By understanding the characteristics of the various database technologies offered on AWS, you will be equipped to design and administer architectures that meet any data storage need.

Creating an RDS database with automatic failover

In this recipe, we're going to create a MySQL **Relational Database Service (RDS)** database instance configured in multi-**AZ (Availability Zone)** mode to facilitate automatic failover. This is a best practice and should be done for all production databases. The standby database in a separate AZ is not the same thing as a read replica—its sole purpose is to enable **High Availability (HA)**.

Getting ready

The default VPC will work fine for this example. Once you are comfortable with creating databases, you may want to consider a VPC containing private subnets that you can use to segment your database away from the internet and other resources (in the style of a three-tier application). Either way, you'll need to note down the following:

- The ID of the VPC
- The CIDR range of the VPC
- The IDs of at least two subnets in your VPC—these subnets need to be in different AZs, for example, `us-east-1a` and `us-east-1b`

How to do it...

Create a new CloudFormation template. We're going to add a total of 12 parameters to it:

1. The first three parameters will contain the values we mentioned in the *Getting ready* section:

```
Parameters:
  VPCId:
    Type: AWS::EC2::VPC::Id
    Description: VPC where DB will launch
  SubnetIds:
    Type: List<AWS::EC2::Subnet::Id>
    Description: Subnets where the DB will launch (pick at least 2)
  SecurityGroupAllowCidr:
    Type: String
    Description: Allow this CIDR block to access the DB
    Default: "172.30.0.0/16"
```

2. We're also going to add the database credentials as parameters. This is better than storing credentials in our infrastructure source code, but you should also investigate AWS Secret Manager and Parameter Store for even more secure options. Note that the password contains the NoEcho parameter set to true. This stops CloudFormation from outputting the password wherever the CloudFormation stack details are displayed:

```
DBUsername:
  Type: String
  Description: Username to access the database
  MinLength: 1
  AllowedPattern: "[a-zA-Z][a-zA-Z0-9]*"
  ConstraintDescription: must start with a letter, must
    be alphanumeric
DBPassword:
  Type: String
  Description: Password to access the database
  MinLength: 1
  AllowedPattern: "[a-zA-Z0-9]*"
  NoEcho: true
  ConstraintDescription: must be alphanumeric
```

3. The next block of parameters pertains to cost and performance. They should be mostly self-explanatory. Refer to the AWS documentation on database instance types should you wish to change the instance class for this example. We're supplying a default value of 10 GB for the storage size and choosing a magnetic (standard) volume for the storage type. gp2 offers better performance, but it costs a little more:

```
DBInstanceClass:
  Type: String
  Description: The instance type to use for this database
  Default: db.t2.micro
DBStorageAmount:
  Type: Number
  Description: Amount of storage to allocate (in GB)
  Default: 10
DBStorageType:
  Type: String
  Description: Type of storage volume to use
    (standard [magnetic] or gp2)
  Default: standard
  AllowedValues:
    - standard
    - gp2
```

4. We need to set some additional parameters for our database. These are the MySQL engine version and port. Refer to the AWS documentation for a list of all of the available versions. We are setting a default value for this parameter as the latest version of MySQL at the time of writing:

```
DBEngineVersion:
  Type: String
  Description: DB engine version
  Default: "5.7.26"
DBPort:
  Type: Number
  Description: Port number to allocate
  Default: 3306
  MinValue: 1150
  MaxValue: 65535
```

5. Finally, we are going to define some parameters relating to backup and availability. We want our database to run in *multi-AZ* mode; we set this to true by default. We also set a backup retention period of 1 day by default; you might want to choose a period larger than this. If you set this value to 0, backups will be disabled (not recommended!):

```
DBMultiAZ:
  Type: String
  Description: Should this DB be deployed in Multi-AZ
configuration?
  Default: true
  AllowedValues:
    - true
    - false
DBBackupRetentionPeriod:
  Type: Number
  Description: How many days to keep backups (0 disables backups)
  Default: 1
  MinValue: 0
  MaxValue: 35
```

6. We're done with the parameters for this template; we can now go ahead and start defining our `Resources` parameters. First of all, we want a security group for our DB to reside in. This security group allows inbound access to the database port from the CIDR range we've defined:

```
Resources:
  ExampleDBSecurityGroup:
    Type: AWS::EC2::SecurityGroup
    Properties:
```

```
        GroupDescription: Example security group for inbound access
    to DB
        SecurityGroupIngress:
          - IpProtocol: tcp
            CidrIp: !Ref SecurityGroupAllowCidr
            FromPort: !Ref DBPort
            ToPort: !Ref DBPort
        VpcId: !Ref VPCId
```

7. Next, we need to define a `DBSubnetGroup` resource. This resource is used to declare which subnet(s) our DB will reside in. We define two subnets for this resource so that the primary and standby servers will reside in separate AVs:

```
ExampleDBSubnetGroup:
  Type: AWS::RDS::DBSubnetGroup
  Properties:
    DBSubnetGroupDescription: Example subnet group for example DB
    SubnetIds:
      - Fn::Select: [ 0, Ref: SubnetIds ]
      - Fn::Select: [ 1, Ref: SubnetIds ]
```

8. Finally, we define our RDS instance resource. We specify it as being a MySQL database and the rest of the properties are made up of the parameters and resources that we've defined previously. Lots of `!Ref` is required here:

```
ExampleDBInstance:
  Type: AWS::RDS::DBInstance
  Properties:
    AllocatedStorage: !Ref DBStorageAmount
    BackupRetentionPeriod: !Ref DBBackupRetentionPeriod
    DBInstanceClass: !Ref DBInstanceClass
    DBSubnetGroupName: !Ref ExampleDBSubnetGroup
    Engine: mysql
    EngineVersion: !Ref DBEngineVersion
    MasterUsername: !Ref DBUsername
    MasterUserPassword: !Ref DBPassword
    MultiAZ: !Ref DBMultiAZ
    StorageType: !Ref DBStorageType
    VPCSecurityGroups:
      - !GetAtt ExampleDBSecurityGroup.GroupId
```

9. For good measure, we can add an output to this template that will return the hostname for this RDS database:

```
Outputs:
  ExampleDbHostname:
    Value: !GetAtt ExampleDBInstance.Endpoint.Address
```

10. You can provision the database via the CloudFormation web console or use a CLI command like so:

```
aws cloudformation create-stack \
--stack-name rds1 \
--template-body \
file://06-create-database-with-automatic-failover.yaml \
--parameters \
ParameterKey=DBUsername,ParameterValue=<username> \
ParameterKey=DBPassword,ParameterValue=<password> \
ParameterKey=SubnetIds,"ParameterValue='<subnet-id-a>, \
<subnet-id-b>'" \
ParameterKey=VPCId,ParameterValue=<vpc-id>
```

Be sure to delete the stack if you have no further use for it, to avoid any future charges.

How it works...

In a multi-AZ configuration, AWS will provision a standby MySQL instance in a separate AZ. Changes to your database will be replicated to the standby DB instance synchronously. If there is a problem with your primary DB instance, AWS will automatically fail over to the standby, promote it to be the primary DB, and provision a new standby.

You don't have access to query standby databases directly. So, you can't use it to handle all of your read queries, for example. If you wish to use additional database instances to increase read capacity, you'll need to provision a *read replica*. We'll cover those in a separate recipe.

Backups will always be taken from the standby instance, which means there is no interruption to your DB availability. This is not the case if you opted against deploying your DB in multi-AZ mode.

When you deploy this example, it will take roughly 20 minutes or more for the stack to report completion. This is because the RDS service needs to go through the following process to provide a fully working multi-AZ database:

- Provision the primary database.
- Back up the primary database.
- Provision the standby database using the backup from the primary.
- Configure both databases for synchronous replication.

Warning
Be careful about making changes to your RDS configuration after you've started writing data to it, especially when using CloudFormation updates. Some RDS configuration changes require the database to be re-provisioned, which can result in data loss. We'd recommend using CloudFormation changesets, which will allow you to see which changes are about to cause destructive behavior. The CloudFormation RDS documentation also provides some information on this.

There's more...

You can define a maintenance window for your RDS instance. This is the period when AWS will perform maintenance tasks such as security patches or minor version upgrades. If you don't specify a maintenance window (which we don't in this example), one is chosen for you.

Creating an RDS database read replica

This recipe will show you how to create an RDS read replica. You can use read replicas to increase the performance of your application by off-loading database reads to a separate database instance. You can provision up to five read replicas per source DB.

Getting ready

You will need an RDS DB deployed with backup retention enabled. We are going to build upon the DB deployed in the previous recipe.

You're going to need the following values:

- The identifier for your source RDS instance, for example, `eexocwv5k5kv5z`
- A unique identifier for the read replica we're going to create, for example, `read-replica-1`

How to do it...

In the AWS CLI, type this command:

```
aws rds create-db-instance-read-replica \
  --source-db-instance-identifier <source-db-identifier> \
  --db-instance-identifier <unique-identifier-for-replica>
```

RDS will now go ahead and create a new read replica for you.

How it works...

Some parameters are inherited from the source instance and can't be defined at the time of creation:

- Storage engine
- Storage size
- Security group

The CLI command accepts some parameters that we could have defined but didn't to keep things simple. They will instead be inherited from the source database. The main two are as follows:

- `--db-instance-class`: The same class as the source instance is used.
- `--db-subnet-group-name`: The source instance's subnet group will be used and a subnet is chosen at random (hence, an AZ is chosen at random).

There's more...

Here is some additional information about read replicas:

- Read replicas are deployed in a single AZ; there is no standby read replica.
- It's not possible to enable backups on read replicas during the time of creation. This must be configured afterward.
- The default storage type is standard (magnetic). You can increase performance by choosing gp2 or using provisioned IOPS.
- It's possible to add MySQL indexes directly to a read replica to further increase read performance. These indexes are not required to be present on the primary DB.

- Using read replicas for availability purposes is more of a complementary DR strategy and shouldn't be used in place of multi-AZ RDS. A multi-AZ configuration gives you the benefit of failure detection and automatic failover.
- It is possible to deploy a read replica in an entirely different region.
- Unlike the replication between a primary and standby DB (which is synchronous), replication to a read replica is asynchronous. This means that a read replica can fall behind the primary. Keep this in mind when sending time-sensitive read queries to your read replicas.

Promoting an RDS read replica to master

We're going to show you how to promote an RDS read replica to be a primary instance. There are a few reasons you might like to do this:

- To handle a table migration that would typically cause a large amount of downtime, especially when messing with columns or indexes
- Because you need to implement sharding
- Recovery from failure, should you choose not to deploy your existing primary in multi-AZ mode (not recommended)

Getting ready

You're going to need the unique ID that has been assigned to an RDS read replica. If you followed the *Creating a database with automatic failover* and *Creating a database read replica* recipes, then you'll be all set.

It's also a good idea to have backups enabled on this read replica before promoting it. This shortens the promotion process because you won't need to wait for a backup to be taken. You'll want to set the backup retention period to a value between 1 and 8.

Enabling backups on your read replica will cause it to reboot!

To enable backups, you can use the following CLI command:

```
aws rds modify-db-instance \
    --db-instance-identifier <identifier-for-read-replica> \
    --backup-retention-period <days-to-keep-backups-for> \
    --apply-immediately
```

You can drop the `--apply-immediately` parameter if you prefer to wait for the reboot to happen during the configured maintenance window. But you'll still want to wait until after the reboot happens before you continue with the promotion process.

To ensure that you have the most up-to-date data before promotion, you'll want to stop all write traffic to the current source primary DB before going ahead. It's also a good idea to make sure that the replication lag on your read replica is 0 (you can check this in CloudWatch).

How to do it...

Complete the following steps to learn how to promote a read replica to master:

1. Run the following command to promote your read replica to a primary DB instance. This command will cause your read replica to reboot:

```
aws rds promote-read-replica \
    --db-instance-identifier <identifier-for-read-replica>
```

2. If you wish to then go ahead and configure your new primary RDS instance to run in a multi-AZ configuration, then you'll need to run this additional command. Expect to wait a while for this operation to complete:

```
aws rds modify-db-instance \
    --db-instance-identifier <identifier-for-new-primary> \
    --multi-az \
    --apply-immediately
```

How it works...

Promoting a read replica can serve several different purposes, such as allowing you to apply time-consuming schema changes without disrupting your primary instance, or to split your database into shards by partitioning data onto multiple primary instances.

The read replica reboots when you promote it and the promotion can take a while since there are significant changes that have to be made to the database configuration to disconnect it as a replica and bring it up as a primary. Configuration items such as backup retention and parameter groups are copied from the original primary to the newly promoted primary.

Transactions to the read replica must be stopped before promotion, and the database must be in a read-only state.

Creating a one-time RDS database backup

We're now going to show you how to make a one-off snapshot of your database. You might opt to do this if you have a specific requirement around keeping a point-in-time backup of your DB. You might also want to take a snapshot to create a new working copy of your dataset.

Getting ready

To proceed, you're going to need the following:

- The identifier for the RDS instance you wish to back up
- A unique identifier that you'd like to assign to this snapshot

The snapshot identifier has some constraints:

- It needs to start with a letter.
- It must not be longer than 255 characters.

 If your primary database isn't running in a multi-AZ configuration, then be aware that creating a snapshot will cause an outage. In a multi-AZ configuration, the snapshot is taken on the standby instance so no outage occurs.

How to do it...

Type the following AWS CLI command to initiate the creation of a snapshot:

```
aws rds create-db-snapshot \
  --db-instance-identifier <primary-rds-id> \
  --db-snapshot-identifier <unique-id-for-snapshot>
```

You'll need to wait for a few minutes for the snapshot to complete before you can use it.

How it works...

A snapshot is an image of the entire storage volume for your database, not just a single instance as you get with a native database backup. If you have a multi-AZ setup, as described in a previous recipe, there is no I/O cost associated with the creation of the snapshot. Snapshots are stored in S3, so you get the built-in durability of S3 buckets for your snapshot. You give the snapshot a unique identifier so that you can reference it if you need to restore the snapshot later.

Restoring an RDS database from a snapshot

We'll now talk through how to restore a database from a snapshot. This process creates a new database that will retain a majority of the configuration of the database that the snapshot was taken from.

Getting ready

You'll need the following pieces of information:

- The ID of the snapshot you wish to restore from
- A name or identifier that you wish to give to the database we're about to create

AWS does not allow RDS services in your account to share the same identifier. If the source database is still online, you'll need to make sure to choose a different identifier (or rename the source database).

How to do it...

Follow these steps to restore an RDS snapshot:

1. Type the following command:

```
aws rds restore-db-instance-from-db-snapshot \
  --db-snapshot-identifier <name-of-snapshot-to-restore > \
  --db-instance-identifier <name-for-new-db> \
  --db-subnet-group-name <your-db-subnet-group> \
  --multi-az
```

2. You may have noticed that this command creates a new database in the default security group. This happens because `restore-db-instance-from-db-snapshot` doesn't accept a security group ID as a parameter. You'll have to run a second command to assign a non-default security group to the new database:

```
aws rds modify-db-instance \
  --db-instance-identifier <name-of-newly-restored-db> \
  --vpc-security-group-ids <id-of-security-group>
```

The `modify-db-instance` command will return an error unless the state of the target database is `available`.

Also, security group names aren't valid with this command; you'll need to use a security group ID instead, for example, `sg-7603d50a`.

How it works...

RDS backups use the snapshot process to make a copy of the entire database instance, not just individual databases or schemas. When restoring the snapshot, you must create a new instance instead of restoring to the original instance. Be sure to associate the restored instance with the original parameter group so that the correct settings are applied to the instance.

There's more...

The `restore-db-instance-from-db-snapshot` command includes the parameter for enabling multi-AZ on the new DB. If you'd like the new DB to be running in single-AZ mode only, then can you simply remove this flag.

Managing Amazon Aurora databases

Amazon Aurora is a managed relational database that is compatible with either MySQL or PostgreSQL. You might be wondering why we have Amazon Aurora when Amazon RDS already supports MySQL and PostgreSQL. The keyword with Aurora is *compatible*—whereas RDS manages the full open source implementation of those databases, Aurora was built from the ground up using AWS storage technologies to offer databases that look and feel like MySQL and PostgreSQL to external tools and clients but offer improved performance and availability.

If you already have an application built on one of these open source databases running on-premises or in the cloud, you can safely migrate it to Aurora with no changes and enjoy a significant performance boost, along with automatic replication across three AZs.

How to do it...

In this recipe, you will configure a new Aurora database instance, securely store the administrative password in Secrets Manager, add a read replica, and perform a backup and restore of the database. Note that the resources you create in this recipe will incur charges on your AWS bill:

1. Log in to your AWS account and go to the RDS dashboard (Aurora is considered a component of RDS).
2. Click the **Create database** button. Choose **Amazon Aurora** from the **Engine options** on the following page. Select **Amazon Aurora with MySQL compatibility** as the **Edition**:

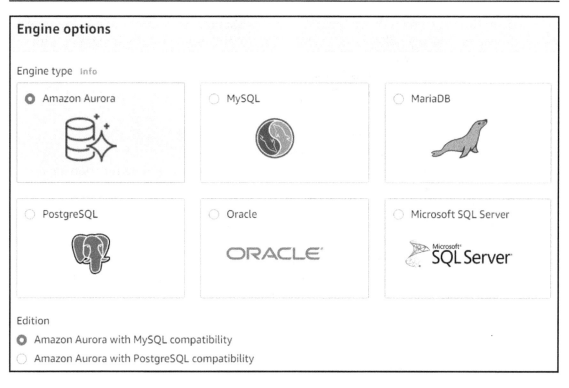

Engine options

3. Leave the rest of the settings at the defaults:
   - Regional database location
   - One writer and multiple readers
   - Production template
   - db.r5.large database instance size
   - Multi-AZ deployment
   - Default VPC

4. Click **Create database**.
5. You will see a button to view credential details on the next screen as the database is being created. Click that button and copy the password, along with the connection details. Wait until the database is available.

6. In this step, you will use the AWS Secrets Manager to store the admin password. Secrets Manager allows you to store secrets and automatically integrates with other AWS services to handle password rotation for you. Open a new browser tab and go to the **Secrets Manager** dashboard. Click **Store new secret**.

7. Select **Credentials for the RDS database** and paste in the username and password.

8. Select the database you just created from the options.

9. Click **Next** and give the secret a name.

10. Enable automatic credential rotation, give the rotation lambda function a name, and click **Next**.

11. On the final **Secrets Manager** review screen, take note of the code samples that are relevant for your application and click **Store**.

12. Go back to the Aurora dashboard and view your databases. Note that the top-level node represents the entire cluster. Underneath, you can see the primary writer instance and the read replica. Note that your region and AZs might be different:

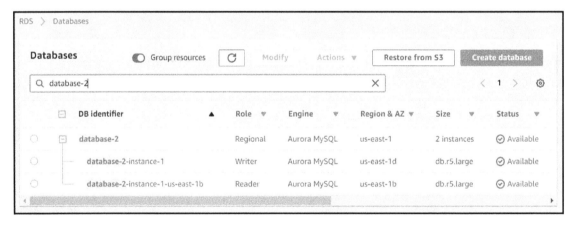

Aurora databases

13. Click on the cluster and note the various tabs that are available for configuration. Take some time to explore each tab:

Aurora cluster configuration

14. From the **Actions** menu at the top of the screen, select **Add reader**.
15. On the next screen, accept all defaults, enter a unique DB instance identifier, and click **Add reader**.
16. From the left-hand menu, select **Snapshots**, then click **Take snapshot**.

17. Choose the DB instance, give the snapshot a name, and click **Take snapshot**:

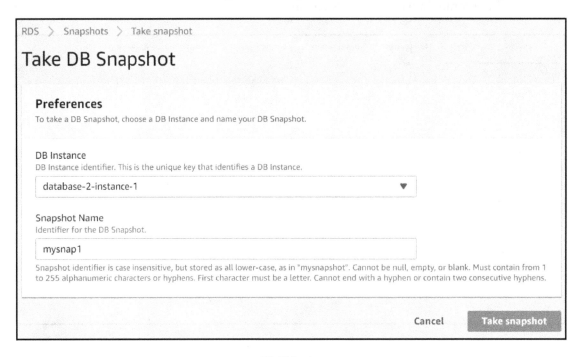

Take DB Snapshot

18. You could create a new cluster based on the snapshot, or you can do a point-in-time recovery.
19. From the **Actions** menu, select **Restore snapshot**.
20. Note that the following screen is basically the same as the screen to create a new database since you are not overwriting the original.
21. Accept the defaults, give the restored copy a unique **DB instance name**, and click **Launch DB instance**.
22. When you have completed all steps in this recipe, be sure to delete all instances to avoid further charges!

How it works...

The storage layer for Amazon Aurora is custom-built to provide a high degree of durability and availability. A total of six copies of your data are spread across three AZs, and snapshot backups are sent to S3 to give you the ability to do a point-in-time restore if your data becomes corrupted. Read replicas in Aurora share the underlying storage with the primary instance, so the replica lag typically associated with reading replicas is much shorter, and there is little to no performance impact on the primary.

Failover for Aurora works a bit differently than with a normal RDS database. Since the storage and compute layers are separate, and storage is spread out over three different AZs, failures that can occur with relational databases due to storage issues are much less likely. If an underlying compute instance needs to be restarted due to a crash, nothing needs to be done to correct or repair the data, and the buffer cache is separate from database processes, so your application will be back up and running at full speed quickly. Another benefit is if you have a cross-region replica set up, you can also fail the database over to the other region.

There's more...

Aurora serverless is an option that allows you to automatically scale the size of your database up and down depending on usage. If your app is not in use constantly, the instance will be shut down to save money, and then it will be quickly spun back up in response to activity. While not a good choice for applications that see 24/7 usage, it is definitely an option to consider for departmental line-of-business databases that only see use during business hours.

Another interesting feature of Aurora is the ability to create custom endpoints that point to a subset of read replicas. This gives you the ability to create replicas with configurations tuned toward specific workloads and direct those queries at just those replicas.

Managing Amazon Neptune graph databases

Amazon Neptune is a graph database that was created specifically to process data that includes a large number of interconnected records. This may not be a familiar use case to everyone, so first, we need to start with a basic description of a graph database.

Let's say you are building a social networking application, where users can friend each other and comment on each other's posts. You will end up with data structures that quickly exceed what relational databases were designed to handle. You may have users with millions of followers, and you may want to quickly traverse the relationship graph to find followers that have interests that match the content of your popular users' latest updates. A purpose-built graph database will give you the best performance in this kind of scenario.

The objects in your graph (entities such as users) are referred to as vertices. A vertex is sort of like a row in a relational database table or an item in a DynamoDB table, but it is enhanced by its relationships to other vertices, which are known as edges. You can think of edges as the lines you draw between vertices in a diagram:

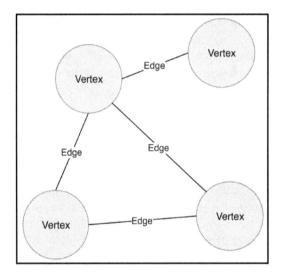

Vertices and edges

Imagine the preceding diagram with billions of interconnected vertices. Amazon Neptune can handle queries across such a graph in milliseconds, and it allows for the creation of multiple read replicas to support high-volume applications.

How to do it...

In this recipe, you will create a Neptune cluster, back it up, and restore it:

1. Log in to your AWS account and go to the **Neptune** dashboard.
2. Click **Launch Amazon Neptune**.
3. In the database creation screen, select the default **DB engine version** and choose `db.r4.large` as the **DB instance class**:

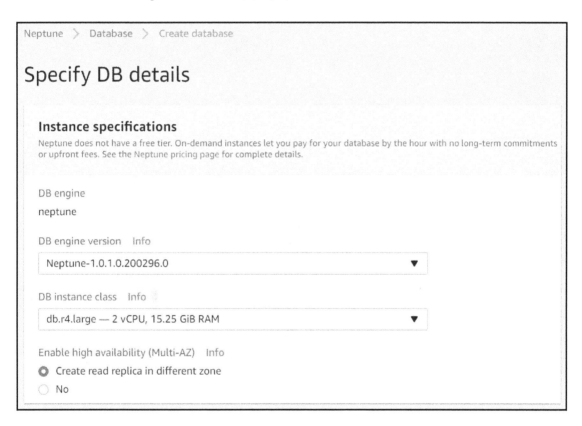

Specify DB details

4. In the **Settings** section, give the cluster a unique identifier and click **Next**:

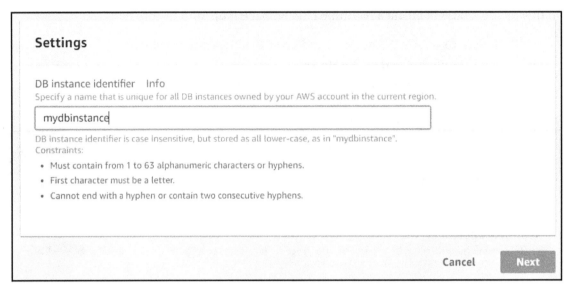

DB instance identifier

5. On the following screen for advanced settings, go with the defaults and click **Create database**. On the next screen, you can wait for cluster creation to complete:

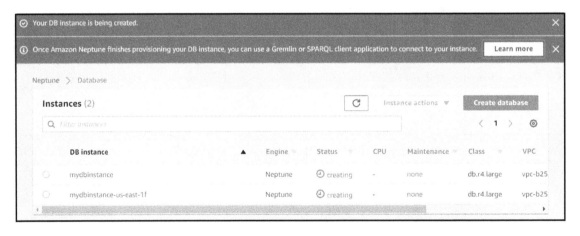

Creating a DB instance

6. Loading data into the cluster and querying that data is outside the scope of this recipe. Check out the extensive documentation on the AWS website for instructions on how to load and query data.

7. Go to the left-hand menu and choose **Snapshots**. Click **Take snapshot**:

Take snapshot

8. On the next screen, choose the database instance and give the snapshot a name. Click **Take snapshot**.

9. Once the snapshot becomes available, select **Restore snapshot** from the **Actions** menu. Note that you also have the option to share this snapshot with another account, which can be the basis of a sound disaster recovery plan for your application.

10. On the following screen, you will configure a new cluster, just as if you were creating one from scratch. The restored snapshot is not overwriting an existing database.

How it works...

When you create a Neptune cluster to host your graph data, several resources are created and managed for you:

- **The primary database instance**: This database is available for both reads and writes.
- **Read replicas**: You can create up to 15 read replicas. As the name implies, these instances can only be used for reads, allowing you to scale out read-intensive workloads. If the primary database instance fails, Neptune fails over to one of the read replicas, which gives it a reported availability of 99.99%.
- **Cluster volumes**: The data is stored across multiple AZs for high availability. All database instances, both the primary and the read replicas, connect to the same cluster volume. If a disk fails in the underlying storage system, it is automatically repaired by Neptune without causing downtime.

Neptune allows you to encrypt the data with **Key Management Service** (**KMS**) keys, which are applied not only to the primary cluster volumes but also to snapshots and any other copies of the database.

You connect to your Neptune cluster using one of several endpoints, which are URLs dedicated to a specific purpose:

- The cluster endpoint is the read/write connection to the primary database instance.
- The reader endpoint provides round-robin connections to all readable database instances. It cannot be used for writes. Note that the way the round-robin works is by changing the DNS record to resolve to a different IP address, so clients that cache the DNS record will keep connecting to the same replica.
- Instance endpoints point to specific cluster replica instances. Normally, you won't need these endpoints, but in some scenarios, it may make sense to connect directly to a replica.

Neptune allows you to use two popular query languages (although they cannot be intermixed):

- Apache Tinkerpop Gremlin is a popular graph traversal language.
- SPARQL allows you to query the **Resource Definition Framework** (**RDF**) graphs.

Advocates for graph databases claim that they are a more natural way to represent real-world objects and could eventually rival the popularity of relational databases. It's worth spending some time to acquaint yourself with Neptune so that you can recognize valid use cases and administer graph databases successfully.

Create a DynamoDB table with a global secondary index

Amazon DynamoDB is a managed key-value store that was one of the first NoSQL databases to be made available in the cloud. A NoSQL database is an alternative to the traditional relational databases that have been used for a variety of purposes in the industry for decades. DynamoDB does not offer many of the standard features of an RDBMS, such as table joins and ACID semantics. ACID stands for Atomic, Consistent, Isolated, and Durable. Consistency is one of the key trade-offs normally made with a NoSQL database since these systems are designed to run in a distributed fashion across a multitude of commodity machines. That being said, it is possible to make consistent reads with DynamoDB, and now you can even initiate transactions across operations, so the lines are being blurred somewhat.

There are still big differences with how you have to approach DynamoDB. It is a key-value store, and you do not use SQL to create, read, update, or delete records. You cannot write ad hoc queries across multiple tables, and in fact, tables are completely disconnected from one another. Each table has its own configuration, and in fact, if you find yourself creating multiple tables for a single service, you may not be following design best practices. Each DynamoDB table should have a single, simple job to perform, which aligns well with microservice design patterns and the overall DevOps philosophy.

How to do it...

In this recipe, you will create a DynamoDB table to hold user account records, and you will add a **global secondary index** (**GSI**) to allow fast lookups by email address. GSIs give you an additional way to sort the data in your table, which allows for some degree of design flexibility after the table has been created:

1. Log in to your account and go to the **DynamoDB** dashboard. Click **Create table**.
2. Give the table a unique name and then enter `UserID` as the **Partition key**. A primary key in DynamoDB is either a partition key by itself or the combination of a partition key and a sort key. In this case, we will leave the sort key blank:

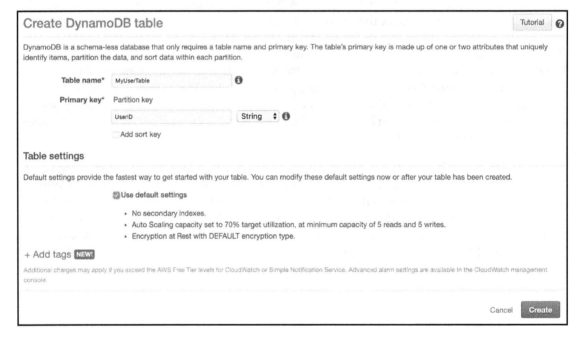

Create DynamoDB table

3. Uncheck **Use default settings**.
4. For **Read-write capacity mode**, choose **On-demand**. This will keep costs low while not using the table and enables rapid auto-scaling to meet increased demand. This should be your default choice for any unpredictable workload that does not have a relatively steady access pattern.
5. Leave the other settings as defaults and click **Create**.
6. It can take a few minutes for your table to become available. Once it does, go to the **Items** tab and click **Create item**.
7. Note that, unlike a relational database, there is no structure for the item beyond the `UserID`. Enter a unique value for `UserID`:

Create item

8. Click the + and enter a few more values, such as `EmailAddress` and `LastName`. With DynamoDB, each record can have unique property names, which allows for some very flexible design patterns. Save the record.
9. Create a new item and this time, give it different properties, such as `Username` and `FullName`.

10. In the item summary, note how each of the unique column names you have used is visible, but don't let this fool you—each record only knows about the properties that were assigned to it. This is not a relational database schema. One of the benefits of DynamoDB is the ability to define new properties at runtime without the need to run **Data Definition Language** (**DDL**) commands as you would with an RDBMS:

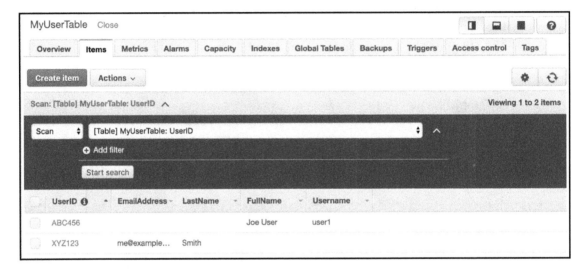

Item summary

11. Click on the **Indexes** tab, then click **Create index**.

12. Enter `EmailAddress` as the **Partition key** and click **Create index**. Leaving the
    Projected attributes as the default of **All** means that all properties will be
    available when looking up items by the index key:

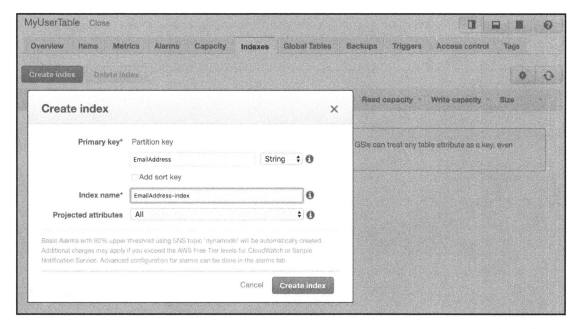

Creating an index

13. Wait a few minutes for the index to be created. The status will change to **Active** when the index is ready.

14. Go back to the **Items** tab and refresh the page so that the new index is recognized.

15. Change **Scan** to **Query** and select your new index. Enter an email address to match one of your earlier entries into the table and click **Start search**:

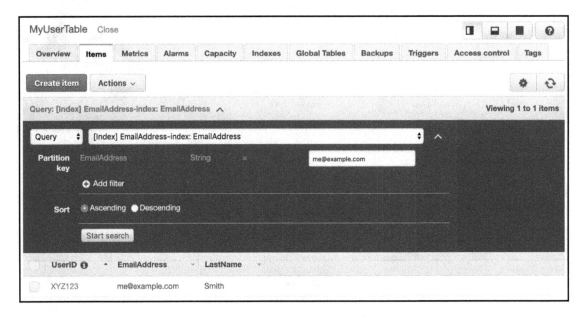

Querying an index

16. Note that the record only displays the columns that are actually entered on that item. By querying the index, you will get a response back in milliseconds, even if the table had millions or billions of records.

17. Take some time to explore the other tabs and see the many configuration options available to you.

18. Be sure to delete the table when you are finished with this recipe, to prevent future charges.

How it works...

The partition key for a DynamoDB table is used to spread the data out over partitions, which are 10 GB slices of data located across a large number of physical machines. It's best to use something like a UUID (GUID) or something with a similarly high level of cardinality for the partition key to preventing too much data from being concentrated on one partition. A combination of partition and sort key can be used in cases where you want buckets of data sorted under your keys, which can be useful in many scenarios but are very application-specific.

Once a table is created, data records can be retrieved by the key very quickly, but if you want to search by any of the other properties, lookups are very slow because you are forced to scan the entire table. For a table with millions or billions of records, this is obviously not practical. That's where GSIs come in. A GSI functions much like a separate table, holding the same data, but indexed by a different key. The benefit is that you don't have to manage that secondary table yourself. DynamoDB handles it for you, making sure the index is always kept up to date according to changes made on the table (in an eventually consistent manner).

While primary keys on the primary table must be unique, the same rule is not enforced for index keys. A query operation specifying a key for a GSI can return multiple records. Any items with index keys that are missing from the primary table do not take up any space in the GSI, which allows for efficient storage of items with different sets of properties.

Another concept that is important to understand is the difference between auto-scaling and on-demand settings for table capacity. It's also possible to manually set the read and write capacity of a table, but since we always want to look for ways to automate, this option should not be your first choice. Choosing auto-scaling can result in lower costs if you carefully choose your settings, and if your application scales slowly and smoothly, without abrupt changes in usage or long periods of no activity at all. On-demand is a relatively new choice that is much more appropriate for bursty workloads, and it handles quick changes better than auto-scaling, but in some scenarios, it can end up being more expensive.

Calculating Amazon DynamoDB capacity

Amazon DynamoDB is the managed NoSQL database service from AWS, described in the previous recipe.

As DDB pricing is based on the amount of read and write capacity units provisioned, it is important to be able to calculate the requirements for your use case. This recipe uses a written formula to estimate the required **Read Capacity Units** (**RCUs**) and **Write Capacity Units** (**WCUs**) that should be allocated to your DDB table.

It is also crucial to remember that, while new partitions will be automatically added to a DDB table, they cannot be automatically taken away. This means that excessive partitioning can cause long-term impacts on your performance, so you should be aware of them.

Getting ready

All of these calculations assume that you have chosen a good partition key for your data. A good partition key ensures the following:

- Data is evenly spread across all the available partitions.
- Read and write activity is spread evenly in time.

Unfortunately, choosing a good partition key is very data-specific, and beyond the scope of this recipe.

All reads are assumed to be strongly consistent.

How to do it...

Follow these steps to calculate your DynamoDB capacity:

1. Start with the size of the items, in **Kilobytes** (**KB**):

    ItemSize = Size of the items (rows) in KB

2. Work out the required number of RCUs required by dividing the number by 4 and rounding up:

    RCU Per Item = ItemSize / 4 (rounded up)

3. Define the expected number of reading operations per second. This is one of the numbers you will use to provision your table with:

   Required RCU = Expected Number of Reads * RCU Per Item

4. Divide the number by 3,000 to calculate the number of DDB partitions required to reach the capacity:

   Read Partitions = Required RCU / 3,000

5. Next, work out the write capacity required by dividing the item size by 1 and rounding up:

   WCU Per Item = ItemSize / 1 (rounded up)

6. Define the expected number of write operations per second. This is one of the numbers you will use to provision your table with:

   Required WCU = Expected Number of Writes * WCU Per Item

7. Divide the number by 1,000 to calculate the number of DDB partitions required to reach the capacity:

   Write Partitions = Required WCU / 1,000

8. Add these two values to get the capacity partitions required (rounding up to a whole number):

   Capacity Partitions = Read Partitions + Write Partitions (rounded up)

9. Work out the minimum number of partitions required by the amount of data you plan to store:

   Size Partitions = Total Size in GB / 10 (rounded up)

10. Once you have the partition requirements for your use case, take the maximum of your previous calculations:

Required Partitions = Maximum value between Capacity Partitions and Size Partitions

11. Since your allocated capacity is spread evenly across partitions, divide the RCU and WCU values to get the per-partition performance of your table:

Partition Read Throughput = Required RCU / Required Partitions

Partition Write Throughput = Required WCU / Required Partitions

For example, let's say you have an item size of 3 KB. The RCU per item is 1 (3/4 rounded up). We expect 100 reads per second, so the expected RCUs are 100. The WCU per item is 3, and if we expect 20 writes per second, then the expected WCUs are 60. Since each of those is less than 1,000, we need two total partitions to handle the reads and writes. If we plan to store 1 billion items, then the number of partitions we expect is 286 (1 billion * 3 KB / 1024 / 1024 / 10). We choose the maximum between the capacity and the size, and we get 286.

How it works...

Behind the scenes, DDB throughput is controlled by the number of partitions that are allocated to your table. It is important to consider how your data will be spread across these partitions to ensure you get the performance you expect *and have paid for*.

We start this recipe by calculating the size of the items in your database, for throughput purposes. DDB has a minimum size it will consider, and even if an operation uses less than this size, it is rounded up in terms of allocated throughput used. The minimum size depends on the type of operation:

- Read operations are calculated in 4-K blocks.
- Write operations are calculated in 1-K blocks.

We then work out what the required RCU and WCU is, based on the expected number of operations. These values are what can then be used to provision the DDB table, as they represent the minimum required throughput (in optimal conditions).

Once you have these values, you can use them to provision your table.

Next, we calculate the throughput per partition key. These calculations rely on knowing what the performance of each partition is expected to be. The numbers 3,000 (for RCUs) and 1,000 (for WCUs) represent the capacity of a single DDB partition. By expressing the capacity in terms of partition performance (reads and writes) and adding them together, we get the minimum number of partitions required from a capacity point of view.

We then do the same calculation for the total data size. Each DDB partition can handle up to 10 GB of data. Any more than that will need to be split between multiple partitions.

 The specific values for partition capacity (for reads, writes, and size) have been stable for a while but may change in the future. Double-check that the current values are the same as used here for complete accuracy.

Once we have the minimum partitions for both capacity and size, we take the highest value and work with that. This ensures we meet both the capacity and size requirements.

Finally, we take the provisioned capacity and divide it by the number of partitions. This gives us the throughput performance for each partition key, which we can then use to confirm against our use case.

There's more...

There are many nuances to using DDB efficiently and effectively. Here are some of the more important/impactful things to note:

- Burst capacity
- Metrics
- Eventually consistent reads

Burst capacity

There is a burst capacity available to tables that go over their allocated capacity. Unused read and write capacity can be retained for up to five minutes (such as 300 seconds, for calculation purposes). Relying on this capacity is not good practice, and it will undoubtedly cause issues at some stage in the future.

Metrics

DDB tables automatically send data to CloudWatch metrics. This is the quickest and easiest way to confirm that your calculations and provision capacity are meeting your needs. It also helps you to keep an eye on your usage to track your throughput needs over time. All metrics appear in the AWS/DynamoDB namespace. Some of the most interesting metrics for throughput calculations are as follows:

- `ConsumedReadCapacityUnits`
- `ConsumedWriteCapacityUnits`
- `ReadThrottleEvents`
- `WriteThrottleEvents`

There are other metrics available; refer to the *Amazon DynamoDB Metrics and Dimensions* documentation at `https://docs.aws.amazon.com/amazondynamodb/latest/developerguide/metrics-dimensions.html` for more details.

Eventually consistent reads

Using eventually consistent reads (as opposed to strongly consistent reads) *halves* the RCU requirements for calculation purposes. In this recipe, we have used strongly consistent reads because it works with all workloads, but you should confirm that your use case actually requires it. Use eventually consistent reads if it does not.

By reducing the required provisioned capacity for reads, you effectively reduce your *cost* for using DDB.

See also

- In `Chapter 10`, *Advanced AWS CloudFormation*, we use DynamoDB in the *Detecting resource drift from templates with drift detection* recipe

AWS Networking Essentials 7

Networking is a foundational component of using other AWS services such as EC2 and RDS. Using constructs such as **Virtual Private Cloud** (**VPC**) and **Network Address Translation** (**NAT**) gateways gives you the capability and confidence to secure your resources at a networking level. Amazon Route 53 is the managed **Domain Name Service** (**DNS**) that allows you to route internet users to your applications in a variety of flexible ways.

Learning the fundamentals of networking on AWS will give you the ability to create flexible architectures for a variety of cloud-native and hybrid scenarios.

In this chapter, we will cover the following recipes:

- Creating a VPC and subnets
- Managing a transit gateway
- Setting up a **Virtual Private Network** (**VPN**)
- Setting up NAT gateways
- Managing domains with Route 53

Creating a VPC and subnets

In this recipe, we're going to build a secure network (VPC) in AWS. This network will consist of two public and private subnets split across two **availability zones** (**AZ**). It will also allow inbound connections to the public subnets for the following protocols:

- SSH (port 22)
- HTTP (port 80)
- HTTPS (port 443):

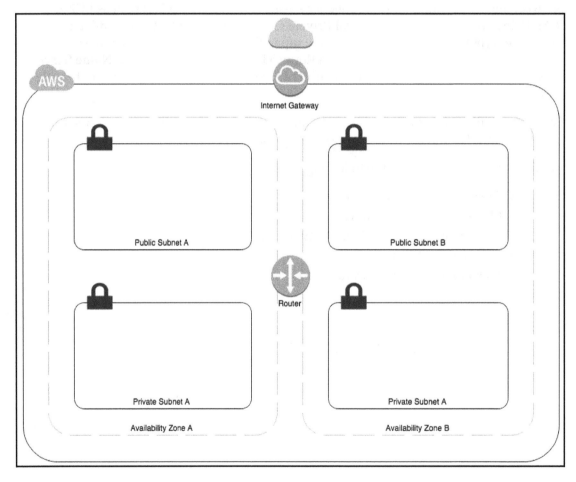

Building a secure network

Getting ready

Before we proceed, you're going to need to know the names of at least two of the AZ in the region we're deploying to. The recipes in this book will typically deploy to us-east-1, so to get things moving, you can just use the following:

- us-east-1a
- us-east-1b

 When you create an AWS account, your zones are randomly allocated. This means that us-east-1a in your account isn't necessarily the same data center as us-east-1a in my account.

How to do it...

Just a heads up: this will be one of the larger templates that we'll create in this book. Let's get started:

1. Go ahead and create a new CloudFormation template for our VPC. Use the filename 07-01-VPC.yaml.

 The entire template can be downloaded from this book's GitHub repository, which can be found at https://github.com/PacktPublishing/AWS-SysOps-Cookbook-Second-Edition.

2. Start with the first two parameters, which correspond to the AZ we discussed previously. We don't provide any default values for these parameters in order to maintain region portability:

```
Parameters:
  AvailabilityZone1:
    Description: Availability zone 1 name (e.g. us-east-1a)
    Type: AWS::EC2::AvailabilityZone::Name
  AvailabilityZone2:
    Description: Availability zone 2 name (e.g. us-east-1b)
    Type: AWS::EC2::AvailabilityZone::Name
```

3. Then, add the remaining parameters to define the IP address ranges for the following:

- The entire VPC
- The public subnets (*A* and *B*)
- The private subnets (*A* and *B*):

```
VPCCIDR:
  Description: CIDR block for VPC
  Type: String
  Default: "172.31.0.0/21" # 2048 IP addresses
PublicSubnetACIDR:
  Description: CIDR block for public subnet A
  Type: String
  Default: "172.31.0.0/23" # 512 IP address
PublicSubnetBCIDR:
  Description: CIDR block for public subnet B
  Type: String
  Default: "172.31.2.0/23" # 512 IP address
PrivateSubnetACIDR:
  Description: CIDR block for private subnet A
  Type: String
  Default: "172.31.4.0/23" # 512 IP address
PrivateSubnetBCIDR:
  Description: CIDR block for private subnet B
  Type: String
  Default: "172.31.6.0/23" # 512 IP address
```

AWS reserves a small number of IP addresses in your IP space for AWS-specific services. The VPC DNS server is one such example of this. It's usually located at the second (*.2) IP address in the block allocated to your VPC.

4. Now, we can start to define Resources. We'll start by defining the VPC itself:

```
Resources:
  # VPC & subnets
  ExampleVPC:
    Type: AWS::EC2::VPC
    Properties:
      CidrBlock: !Ref VPCCIDR
      EnableDnsSupport: true
      EnableDnsHostnames: true
      Tags:
        - { Key: Name, Value: Example VPC }
```

5. Then, we will define the public subnets. Public subnets are defined as subnets with a route to the **Internet Gateway (IGW)**:

```
PublicSubnetA:
    Type: AWS::EC2::Subnet
    Properties:
      AvailabilityZone: !Ref AvailabilityZone1
      CidrBlock: !Ref PublicSubnetACIDR
      MapPublicIpOnLaunch: true
      VpcId: !Ref ExampleVPC
      Tags:
        - { Key: Name, Value: Public Subnet A }
  PublicSubnetB:
    Type: AWS::EC2::Subnet
    Properties:
      AvailabilityZone: !Ref AvailabilityZone2
      CidrBlock: !Ref PublicSubnetBCIDR
      MapPublicIpOnLaunch: true
      VpcId: !Ref ExampleVPC
      Tags:
        - { Key: Name, Value: Public Subnet B }
```

6. Next, we will add the private subnets:

```
PrivateSubnetA:
  Type: AWS::EC2::Subnet
  Properties:
    AvailabilityZone: !Ref AvailabilityZone1
    CidrBlock: !Ref PrivateSubnetACIDR
    VpcId: !Ref ExampleVPC
    Tags:
      - { Key: Name, Value: Private Subnet A }
PrivateSubnetB:
  Type: AWS::EC2::Subnet
  Properties:
    AvailabilityZone: !Ref AvailabilityZone2
    CidrBlock: !Ref PrivateSubnetBCIDR
    VpcId: !Ref ExampleVPC
    Tags:
      - { Key: Name, Value: Private Subnet B }
```

7. Then, we will create the IGW for the VPC:

```
ExampleIGW:
  Type: AWS::EC2::InternetGateway
  Properties:
    Tags:
      - { Key: Name, Value: Example Internet Gateway }
```

```
IGWAttachment:
  Type: AWS::EC2::VPCGatewayAttachment
  DependsOn: ExampleIGW
  Properties:
    VpcId: !Ref ExampleVPC
    InternetGatewayId: !Ref ExampleIGW
```

8. We need to create a couple of route tables. The first one we'll focus on is the public route table. We'll assign this route table to the two public subnets we've created. This route table will have just one route in it, which will direct all internet-bound traffic to the internet gateway we created in the previous step:

```
PublicRouteTable:
  Type: AWS::EC2::RouteTable
  Properties:
    VpcId: !Ref ExampleVPC
    Tags:
      - { Key: Name, Value: Public Route Table }
PublicInternetRoute:
  Type: AWS::EC2::Route
  DependsOn: IGWAttachment
  Properties:
    RouteTableId: !Ref PublicRouteTable
    GatewayId: !Ref ExampleIGW
    DestinationCidrBlock: "0.0.0.0/0"
RouteAssociationPublicA:
  Type: AWS::EC2::SubnetRouteTableAssociation
  Properties:
    RouteTableId: !Ref PublicRouteTable
    SubnetId: !Ref PublicSubnetA
RouteAssociationPublicB:
  Type: AWS::EC2::SubnetRouteTableAssociation
  Properties:
    RouteTableId: !Ref PublicRouteTable
    SubnetId: !Ref PublicSubnetB
```

9. We'll create the private route table in a similar fashion. Since the private subnet is isolated from the internet, we won't add a route to the internet gateway. Note that if you were to follow the NAT gateway recipe in this book, it will require a routing table as an input parameter—this is the routing table you want to add NAT routes to:

```
PrivateRouteTable:
  Type: AWS::EC2::RouteTable
  Properties:
    VpcId: !Ref ExampleVPC
    Tags:
```

```
        - { Key: Name, Value: Private Route Table }
    PrivateSubnetAssociationA:
      Type: AWS::EC2::SubnetRouteTableAssociation
      Properties:
        RouteTableId: !Ref PrivateRouteTable
        SubnetId: !Ref PrivateSubnetA
    PrivateSubnetAssociationB:
      Type: AWS::EC2::SubnetRouteTableAssociation
      Properties:
        RouteTableId: !Ref PrivateRouteTable
        SubnetId: !Ref PrivateSubnetB
```

10. We can now focus on the security aspects of our network. Let's focus on public subnets. These are the subnets you'll add your load balancers to; you'll also add things such as bastion boxes and NAT gateways. For this, we need to add a **Network Access Control List** (**NACL**) with several entries. An NACL is the equivalent of a stateless firewall that is applied to the subnet and allows the following:

    - Allows outbound traffic to all ports. Outbound access is unrestricted from hosts in our public subnets.
    - Allows inbound traffic to ephemeral ports (above `1024`). This ensures that packets that are returned to us from our outbound connections are not dropped.
    - Allows inbound access to low port numbers for SSH, HTTP, and HTTPS (`22`, `80`, and `443`):

```
    PublicNACL:
      Type: AWS::EC2::NetworkAcl
      Properties:
        VpcId: !Ref ExampleVPC
        Tags:
          - { Key: Name, Value: Example Public NACL }
```

11. Allow outbound to everywhere:

```
    NACLRulePublicEgressAllowAll:
      Type: AWS::EC2::NetworkAclEntry
      Properties:
        CidrBlock: "0.0.0.0/0"
        Egress: true
        Protocol: 6
        PortRange: { From: 1, To: 65535 }
        RuleAction: allow
        RuleNumber: 100
        NetworkAclId: !Ref PublicNACL
```

12. Allow outbound to the VPC on all protocols:

```
NACLRulePublicEgressAllowAllToVPC:
    Type: AWS::EC2::NetworkAclEntry
    Properties:
      CidrBlock: !Ref VPCCIDR
      Egress: true
      Protocol: -1
      RuleAction: allow
      RuleNumber: 200
      NetworkAclId: !Ref PublicNACL
```

13. Allow inbound from everywhere to ephemeral ports:

```
NACLRulePublicIngressAllowEphemeral:
    Type: AWS::EC2::NetworkAclEntry
    Properties:
      CidrBlock: "0.0.0.0/0"
      Protocol: 6
      PortRange: { From: 1024, To: 65535 }
      RuleAction: allow
      RuleNumber: 100
      NetworkAclId: !Ref PublicNACL
```

14. Allow inbound from everywhere on port 22 for SSH:

```
NACLRulePublicIngressAllowSSH:
    Type: AWS::EC2::NetworkAclEntry
    Properties:
      CidrBlock: "0.0.0.0/0"
      Protocol: 6
      PortRange: { From: 22, To: 22 }
      RuleAction: allow
      RuleNumber: 200
      NetworkAclId: !Ref PublicNACL
```

15. Allow inbound from everywhere on port 443 for HTTPS:

```
NACLRulePublicIngressAllowHTTPS:
    Type: AWS::EC2::NetworkAclEntry
    Properties:
      CidrBlock: "0.0.0.0/0"
      Protocol: 6
      PortRange: { From: 443, To: 443 }
      RuleAction: allow
      RuleNumber: 300
      NetworkAclId: !Ref PublicNACL
```

16. Allow inbound from everywhere on port 80 for HTTP:

```
NACLRulePublicIngressAllowHTTP:
    Type: AWS::EC2::NetworkAclEntry
    Properties:
      CidrBlock: "0.0.0.0/0"
      Protocol: 6
      PortRange: { From: 80, To: 80 }
      RuleAction: allow
      RuleNumber: 400
      NetworkAclId: !Ref PublicNACL
```

17. Allow inbound from VPC on all protocols:

```
NACLRulePublicIngressAllowFromVPC:
    Type: AWS::EC2::NetworkAclEntry
    Properties:
      CidrBlock: !Ref VPCCIDR
      Protocol: -1
      RuleAction: allow
      RuleNumber: 500
      NetworkAclId: !Ref PublicNACL
```

18. Associate the NACLs with the subnets:

```
NACLAssociationPublicSubnetA:
    Type: AWS::EC2::SubnetNetworkAclAssociation
    Properties:
      NetworkAclId: !Ref PublicNACL
      SubnetId: !Ref PublicSubnetA
  NACLAssociationPublicSubnetB:
    Type: AWS::EC2::SubnetNetworkAclAssociation
    Properties:
      NetworkAclId: !Ref PublicNACL
      SubnetId: !Ref PublicSubnetB
```

19. We need to do the same for our private subnets. These subnets are somewhat easier to deal with. They should *only* be allowed to talk to hosts within our VPC, so we just need to add some NACLs that allow inbound and outbound traffic in our VPCs IP range:

```
PrivateNACL:
    Type: AWS::EC2::NetworkAcl
    Properties:
      VpcId: !Ref ExampleVPC
      Tags:
        - { Key: Name, Value: Example Private NACL }
```

20. Allow all protocols from the VPC range:

```
NACLRulePrivateIngressAllowVPC:
    Type: AWS::EC2::NetworkAclEntry
    Properties:
      CidrBlock: !Ref VPCCIDR
      Protocol: -1
      RuleAction: allow
      RuleNumber: 100
      NetworkAclId: !Ref PrivateNACL
```

21. Allow TCP responses from everywhere:

```
NACLRulePrivateIngressAllowEphemeral:
    Type: AWS::EC2::NetworkAclEntry
    Properties:
      CidrBlock: "0.0.0.0/0"
      Protocol: 6
      PortRange: { From: 1024, To: 65535 }
      RuleAction: allow
      RuleNumber: 200
      NetworkAclId: !Ref PrivateNACL
```

22. The following code allows outbound traffic to everywhere (all protocols):

```
NACLRulePrivateEgressAllowVPC:
    Type: AWS::EC2::NetworkAclEntry
    Properties:
      CidrBlock: "0.0.0.0/0"
      Egress: true
      Protocol: -1
      RuleAction: allow
      RuleNumber: 100
      NetworkAclId: !Ref PrivateNACL
```

23. Associate the NACLs with the subnets:

```
NACLAssociationPrivateSubnetA:
    Type: AWS::EC2::SubnetNetworkAclAssociation
    Properties:
      NetworkAclId: !Ref PrivateNACL
      SubnetId: !Ref PrivateSubnetA
  NACLAssociationPrivateSubnetB:
    Type: AWS::EC2::SubnetNetworkAclAssociation
    Properties:
      NetworkAclId: !Ref PrivateNACL
      SubnetId: !Ref PrivateSubnetB
```

24. Finally, we'll add some `Outputs` to our template. These outputs are usually candidates that we can feed into other templates or components of automation:

```
Outputs:
  ExampleVPC:
    Value: !Ref ExampleVPC
  PublicSubnetA:
    Value: !Ref PublicSubnetA
  PublicSubnetB:
    Value: !Ref PublicSubnetB
  PrivateRouteTable:
    Value: !Ref PrivateRouteTable
  PublicRouteTable:
    Value: !Ref PublicRouteTable
  PrivateSubnetA:
    Value: !Ref PrivateSubnetA
  PrivateSubnetB:
    Value: !Ref PrivateSubnetB
```

25. You can go ahead and create your VPC in the web console or via the CLI using the following command:

```
aws cloudformation create-stack \
  --stack-name secure-vpc \
  --template-body file://07-01-VPC.yaml \
  --parameters \
  ParameterKey=AvailabilityZone1,ParameterValue=<az-1> \
  ParameterKey=AvailabilityZone2,ParameterValue=<az-2>
```

You can fine-tune this template for your own use, or if you don't need it after completing the recipe, delete it to avoid any future charges associated with the VPC.

How it works...

When you run this template, AWS will create an isolated, secure network just for you. While it contains a number of resources and concepts that will be familiar to network administrators, it's essentially an empty shell, which you can now go ahead and populate.

For example, each VPC contains a virtual router. You can't see it and you can't log into it to perform any special configuration, but you can customize its behavior by modifying the route tables in this template.

The NACLs we've deployed are not stateful and should *not* be considered a substitution for security groups. NACLs are *complementary* to security groups, which are stateful and frankly much easier to change and manage than NACLs. While the NACLs in our recipe allow everywhere (0.0.0.0/0) to make inbound connections to port 22, you'll want to use security groups to lock this down to a specific IP range (your corporate data center, for example).

There's more...

Actually, there's a *lot* more. Despite the amount of code in this recipe, we've really only covered the basics of what's possible with VPCs and networking in AWS. Here are some of the main VPC topics you'll encounter as you progress with your VPC usage:

- Direct Connect is a method of connecting DC to your VPC using a private, dedicated pipe. Doing this often provides better network performance, and may also be cheaper than a VPN connection over the internet.
- You can configure your VPC to connect to your corporate DC over the internet via VPN. This requires that you run supported VPN hardware in your DC.
- IPv6 is an advanced option that greatly expands the number of available addresses. We've left it out to keep things simple.
- The VPC endpoints feature exposes AWS endpoints inside your VPC so that you don't have to route traffic over the public internet to consume them.
- In VPC peering, you can peer a VPC to one or more VPCs so that (unencrypted) traffic can flow between them. The IP ranges must not clash and, while the peering is free, you will still need to pay for traffic between VPCs. Transitive peering isn't supported, so if you need the traffic to traverse VPCs, you'll require a VPN/routing appliance of some kind. Alternatively, you can use the Transit Gateway service.
- VPC sizing:
  - For IPv4, you can deploy networks between sizes /28 and /16.
  - For IPv6, your VPCs will be fixed in size at /56.
  - A VPC can be resized after creation.

- Regarding VPC flow logs, you will want to enable VPC flow logs in order to monitor traffic and do any kind of network debugging.
- Multicast traffic isn't supported.

- Subnets must reside in a single AZ; they can't span AZs.
- **Elastic load balancers** (**ELBs**) can scale out to use a lot of private IP addresses if you are sending a large amount of traffic through them. Keep this in mind when you're sizing your subnets.
- The number of VPCs you can deploy is limited to five per region, per account. You can request to increase this limit if necessary. Internet gateways have the same limit, and increasing one limit increases the other.
- The *default* VPC:
    - First and foremost, the default VPC is created automatically for you when you create your account. It has some different properties and behaviors to the VPCs you create for yourself.
    - If you try to launch an EC2 instance without specifying a subnet ID, AWS will attempt to launch it in your default VPC.
    - It consists of only public subnets. These subnets are configured to provide a public IP address to all instances by default.
    - It's possible to delete the default VPC in a region.

See also

- Check out the AWS VPC quick start for another best practice example of a VPC that you can install with a single click: `https://aws.amazon.com/quickstart/architecture/vpc/`

Managing a transit gateway

A transit gateway is a brand new service, as of 2019, and it solves a problem that's faced by many architects who want to create complex environments spanning several networks. To understand the need for transit gateways, first, you need to understand the non-transitive nature of an AWS VPC.

A VPC can peer with other VPCs, which sets up a bi-directional route between those VPCs. However, what's not supported is transitive routing via an intermediate VPC, as shown in the following diagram:

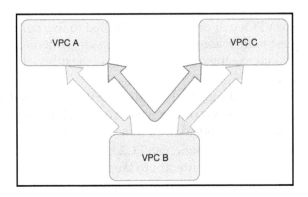

VPC peering

VPC A and **VPC B** have a peering relationship. **VPC B** and **VPC C** also have a peering relationship. Network traffic can be routed successfully (indicated by the green arrows) from **A** to **B** and from **B** to **C**, but not from **A** to **C** via **B** (indicated by the red arrow).

Before Transit Gateway was introduced, a complex setup involving a Cisco **Cloud Services Router** (**CSR**) was required. While this did enable the creation of a transit VPC (which would allow traffic via the red arrow in the preceding diagram), it was costly and difficult to configure. Transit Gateway solves this problem in an AWS-native way.

Getting ready

To complete this recipe, you will need to create two new EC2 instances in two separate VPCs:

- Follow the *Creating a VPC and subnets* recipe in this chapter to create VPCs with non-overlapping CIDR blocks.
- Follow the *Launching an instance* recipe in `Chapter 4`, *AWS Compute*, to create an EC2 instance in each VPC.

How to do it...

Follow these steps to configure a transit gateway to communicate between two VPCs that do not have a direct peering relationship:

1. Log in to your account and go to the VPC management console.
2. Scroll down to the bottom of the menu on the left-hand side of the screen and click **Transit Gateways**:

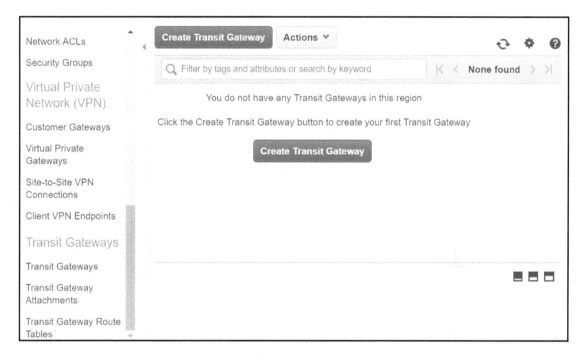

Create Transit Gateway

3. Click **Create Transit Gateway**.

4. Fill out the **Name tag** and **Description** for the transit gateway:

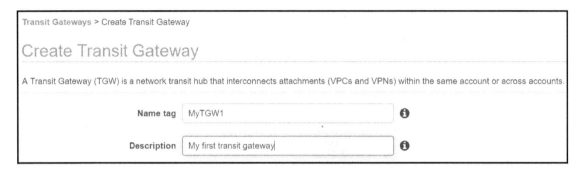

Transit Gateway name and description

5. In the **Configure the Transit Gateway** section, leave the defaults as they are:

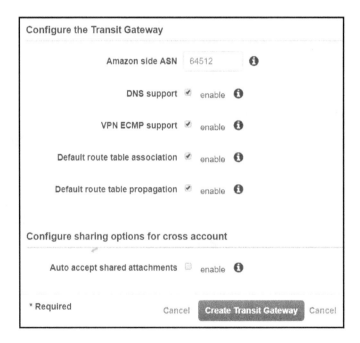

Configure the Transit Gateway screen

6. Click **Create Transit Gateway**.

7. Immediately after creation, the gateway will be in a pending state:

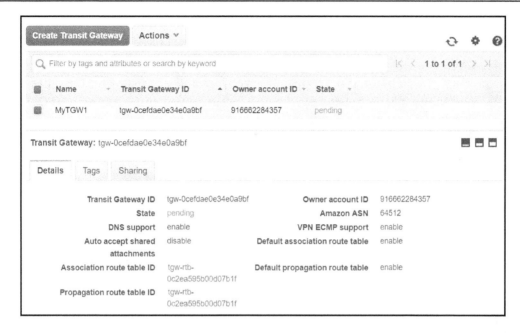

Gateway pending

8. Once the gateway is available, select **Transit Gateway Attachments** from the left-hand menu and click **Create Transit Gateway Attachment**:

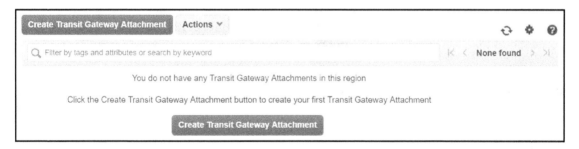

Create Transit Gateway Attachment screen

9. On the following screen, select the transit gateway from the **Transit Gateway ID** dropdown.
10. Give the attachment an **Attachment name tag**.
11. Select one of your VPCs in the **VPC ID** dropdown.
12. Select the subnets from that VPC.

13. Click **Create Attachment** and then repeat *steps 9-12* for the other VPC.
14. Go to **Route Tables** under the **Virtual Private Cloud** menu.
15. Choose one of the VPC route tables and add a route for the IP addresses in the other VPC to point to the transit gateway target. Do the same for the other VPC.
16. Test the connectivity between the EC2 instances you created in each VPC. Note that the `ping` command will be blocked by NACL firewall rules that prevent ICMP traffic.
17. Once you've finished, delete the Transit Gateway to avoid any future charges.

How it works...

Transit gateway operates at layer 3 of the **Open Systems Interconnection** (**OSI**) model. Layer 3 is the network layer, which sits between the data link layer (layer 2) and the transport layer (layer 4). This layer handles the forwarding of packets and communication with routers along the network path from the origin to the destination.

Transit Gateway greatly simplifies connecting multiple VPCs by allowing you to configure your network as a hub and spoke design, where each VPC (a spoke) only needs to be connected to the gateway (the hub). VPN connections can also be connected to the hub to enable hybrid connectivity scenarios with on-premises networks.

The Transit Gateway default route table is automatically configured with the routes that are needed to connect your VPCs. VPN connection routes are propagated to the network in your data center by means of the **Border Gateway Protocol** (**BGP**). You can also create route tables manually in order to segment network traffic.

Using AWS **Resource Access Manager** (**RAM**), you can share your Transit Gateway with other accounts so that the VPCs in that account can connect to your networks.

Creating a Virtual Private Network (VPN)

A VPN allows you to create a secure tunnel for network traffic between your on-premises data center and your AWS account using the **Internet Security Protocol** (**IpSec**). AWS VPN functionality comes in several distinct flavors, as follows:

- A managed VPN service to enable clients to connect to your AWS VPC and on-premises environments. Users connect to the VPN using a client based on the OpenVPN standard.

- CloudHub, which an AWS service that allows you to create a secure network route between remote office locations.
- Site-to-Site VPN, which is a secure connection between your data center and your VPC.

In this recipe, we will show you how to set up a VPN connection between your data center and your VPC. The benefit of creating a link like this is that all the data transfers between the two sites are sent through a secure IPSec tunnel, instead of traveling over the public internet. This kind of locked down communication is often an absolute requirement for complying with industry-specific rules and regulations.

How to do it...

Follow these steps to create a virtual private gateway and a customer gateway:

1. Log in to your AWS account, go to the VPC dashboard, and select **Virtual Private Gateways**. Click **Create Virtual Private Gateway**:

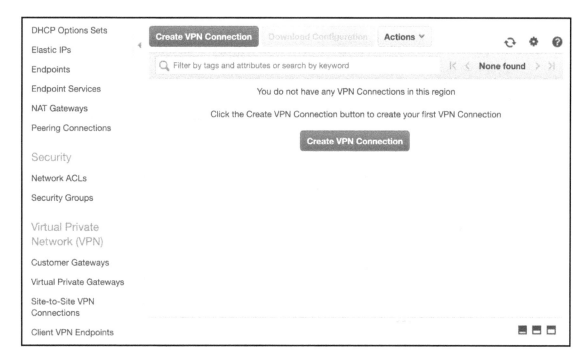

Create Virtual Private Gateway screen

2. Give the VPG a **Name** tag and leave **ASN** in its default state. Click **Create Virtual Private Gateway**.

3. Go back to the left-hand menu and select **Site-to-Site VPN Connections**. Click **Create VPN Connection**:

Create VPN Connection screen

4. Give the VPN a **Name** tag and select the **VPG** from the drop-down menu.

5. Select **New** from the **Customer Gateway** radio buttons and specify the IP address of your customer gateway device.

6. If you have a BGP ASN, enter it here; otherwise, use the default private **Autonomous System Number** (**ASN**).

7. Click **Create VPN Connection**. Once it becomes available, you will be able to download the configuration needed for the device in your data center:

Downloading the device configuration

8. Go to **Route Tables** under the VPC menu. Select the **Route Propagation** tab and configure your route table to allow propagation from the **Virtual Private Gateway** (**VPG**):

Route propagation

You now have a secure network route from your data center into your AWS VPC.

How it works...

The VPN connection from your data center into your AWS account uses IPSec to create secure tunnels using the latest generation encryption to ensure the secrecy of your communications traffic.

You can create as many as five VPGs per region, and as many as 50 customer gateways. Each of the VPGs can support up to 10 IPSec connections.

The customer gateway is a virtual representation of the hardware device in your data center that implements the client side of the VPN connection. AWS provides the configuration information you need to set up your device when you set up the Site-to-Site VPN in the console.

There's more...

A VPG is highly available, with endpoints in two separate AZs so that you can failover from the primary tunnel to the secondary in the case of a temporary outage. You can also configure CloudWatch metrics and alarms to keep you informed about the health of your VPN connection.

You might be wondering about a few of the terms you encountered in this recipe, such as BGP and ASN. We will cover these in the following subsections.

BGP

The BGP is the standard protocol that's used between internet systems to enable routing and determine reachability between autonomous systems. BGP operates over TCP on port 179, directly connecting edge routers that are controlled by large enterprises and service providers. The route tables maintained by these edge routers are what enable traffic on the internet to find an alternate route to the destination in case a segment of the network is unavailable.

ASN

Autonomous System Numbers are closely related to BGP. Each of the autonomous systems that make up the global network that constitutes the internet has a unique identifier, that is, the ASN. Edge routers are configured manually with a combination of the ASN and IP address of peer routers. In many of the recipes in this book, we use the default private ASN (usually 65,000), but if your organization has a public ASN, you will want to make sure you configure your VPN using that number.

Setting up NAT gateways

Unless required, your instances should not be publicly exposed to the internet. When your instances are on the internet, you have to assume they will be attacked at some stage.

This means most of your workloads should run on instances in private subnets. Private subnets are those that are not connected directly to the internet.

To give your private instances access to the internet, you use NAT. A NAT gateway allows your instances to initiate a connection *to* the internet, without allowing connections *from* the internet.

Getting ready

For this recipe, you must have the following existing resources:

- A VPC with an IGW
- A public subnet
- A private subnet route table

You will need the IDs for the public subnet and private subnet route table. Both of these resources should be in the same AZ.

How to do it...

In this recipe, you will create a new CloudFormation that creates a stack with a NAT gateway. Let's get started:

1. Start with the usual CloudFormation template version and description:

    ```
    AWSTemplateFormatVersion: "2010-09-09"
    Description: Create NAT Gateway and associated route.
    ```

2. The template must take the following required parameters:

    ```
    Parameters:
      PublicSubnetId:
        Description: Public Subnet ID to add the NAT Gateway to
        Type: AWS::EC2::Subnet::Id
      RouteTableId:
        Description: The private subnet route table to add the NAT
        Gateway route to
        Type: String
    ```

3. In the `Resources` section, define an **Elastic IP (EIP)** that will be assigned to the NAT gateway:

    ```
    Resources:
      EIP:
        Type: AWS::EC2::EIP
        Properties:
          Domain: vpc
    ```

4. Create the NAT gateway resource, assigning it the EIP you just defined in the public subnet:

    ```
    NatGateway:
      Type: AWS::EC2::NatGateway
      Properties:
        AllocationId: !GetAtt EIP.AllocationId
        SubnetId: !Ref PublicSubnetId
    ```

5. Finally, define the route to the NAT gateway and associate it with the private subnet's route table:

```
Route:
  Type: AWS::EC2::Route
  Properties:
    RouteTableId: !Ref RouteTableId
    DestinationCidrBlock: 0.0.0.0/0
    NatGatewayId: !Ref NatGateway
```

6. Save the template with a known filename, for example, `07-02-NATGateway.yaml`.

7. Launch the template with the following CLI command:

```
aws cloudformation create-stack \
  --stack-name nat-gateway \
  --template-body file://07-02-NATGateway.yaml \
  --parameters \
  ParameterKey=RouteTableId,ParameterValue=<route-table-id> \
  ParameterKey=PublicSubnetId,ParameterValue=<public-subnet-id>
```

How it works...

The parameters that are required for this recipe are as follows:

- A public subnet ID
- A private subnet route table ID

The public subnet ID is needed to host the NAT gateway, which must have internet access. The private subnet route table will be updated with a route to the NAT gateway.

Using the AWS NAT gateway service means that AWS takes care of hosting and securing the service for you. The service will be hosted redundantly in a single AZ.

 You can use this recipe multiple times to deploy NAT gateways in each of your private subnets. Just make sure the public subnet and the private subnet are in the same AZ.

In the unlikely (but possible) event of an AZ outage, you should deploy a NAT gateway per subnet. This means that if one NAT gateway goes offline, instances in the other AZ can continue to access the internet as normal. You are deploying your application in multiple subnets, aren't you?

This recipe will only work if you have created your own private subnets, as the default subnets in a new AWS account are all *public*. Instances in a public subnet have direct access to the internet (via an IGW), so they do not need a NAT gateway.

See also

- The *Creating a VPC and subnets* recipe

Managing domains with Route 53

In this recipe, we'll show you how to host a domain in Route 53 and add some records to it:

Hosting a domain

Getting ready

You technically don't need to have registered a domain name in order to proceed with this recipe, but it helps if you have a real domain that you can use.

How to do it...

Follow these steps to create a hosted zone:

1. Create a new CloudFormation template and add the following parameters to it:

```
Parameters:
  DomainName:
    Description: Your domain name (example.org)
    Type: String
```

2. Next, we need to add a HostedZone resource to our template, as follows:

```
Resources:
  DNSHostedZone:
    Type: AWS::Route53::HostedZone
    Properties:
      Name: !Ref DomainName
```

3. You're now ready to go ahead and create your hosted zone in Route 53. You can do so via the CloudFormation web console or by using the following CLI command:

```
aws cloudformation create-stack \
  --stack-name example-hosted-zone \
  --template-body file://07-03-Route53.yaml \
  --parameters \
  ParameterKey=DomainName,ParameterValue=<your-domain-name>
```

This will create a hosted zone in Route 53. Once the stack has been created, go and find it in the web console. You'll see that there are a number of name servers associated with it. These are the name servers to use if you wish to proceed with delegating your domain name to AWS's Route 53 servers using your domain name registrar's control panel.

How it works...

Amazon Route 53 acts as a traditional registrar, where you can claim a domain and then configure the DNS entries for that domain. But Route 53 takes routing functionality much further, integrating closely with AWS services to allow you to configure complex scenarios for routing traffic to a global collection of regional and edge locations. Users can be routed based on geographic location by the latency of the connection to your regional resources, or according to the health of the target servers, which can provide a robust failover mechanism. Integration with services such as S3 and CloudFront allows you to easily host a website without setting up any servers.

There's more...

A hosted zone with no DNS records will be of limited use to you. Here are some examples of records that you may wish to add to your template:

```
DNSRecords:
  Type: AWS::Route53::RecordSetGroup
  Properties:
    HostedZoneId:
      Ref: DNSHostedZone
    RecordSets:
    - Name: !Ref DomainName
      Type: A
      TTL: 60
      ResourceRecords:
        - "127.0.0.1"
    - Name: !Ref DomainName
      Type: MX
      TTL: 60
      ResourceRecords:
        - "10 smtp.example.org"
        - "20 smtp.example.org"
    - Name: !Ref DomainName
      Type: TXT
      TTL: 60
      ResourceRecords:
        - '"v=spf1 include:spf.example.org ?all"'
```

Some items of note:

For the priority in MX records, add the number at the start of the record, followed by a space.

For TXT records such as spf entries, which typically need to be quoted, you can surround double quotes with single quotes.

Here's how this looks in the Route 53 web console:

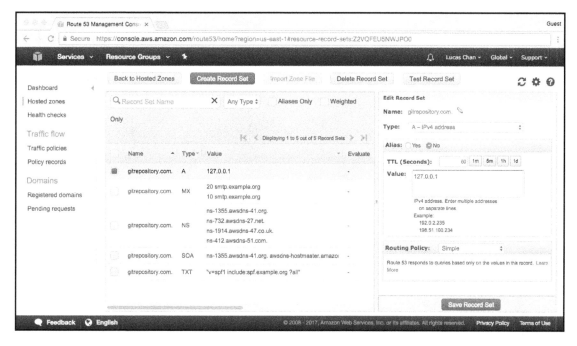

Hosting a domain

See also

- The *Hosting a static website* recipe in Chapter 3, *AWS Storage and Content Delivery*

AWS Account Security and Identity

8

Security is one of the most critical areas of using the cloud, and it should always be your top priority! It's important to get it right, because good security practices reinforce themselves, leading to a virtuous cycle of capabilities and control.

There are many tools and AWS services to ensure that your cloud-based infrastructure is even more secure than the resources in your own data center. Some administrators might be skeptical about that statement, but consider the fact that AWS employs thousands of security experts to make sure that all avenues of attack have been carefully considered. The scrutiny that AWS gets from large enterprises and governments is much more attention than is ever paid to individual data centers, so you can rest assured that it is possible to create extremely secure environments on AWS.

That said, it is equally possible to create architectures that are wide open to the public if you aren't careful, so it pays to spend a healthy amount of time studying the subjects that will be introduced in this chapter. Don't be the administrator that leaves customer data lying around in a public S3 bucket, or the developer who checks the password into a source code repository!

AWS **Identity and Access Management (IAM)** is the backbone of security in AWS. It provides incredibly granular levels of permissions to allow (and deny) specific users access to your resources, so many of our discussions about security revolve around IAM.

In this chapter, we will cover the following topics:

- Administering users with IAM
- Deploying Simple Active Directory service
- Creating instance roles
- Using cross-account roles
- Storing secrets

- Protecting applications from DDoS
- Configuring AWS WAF
- Setting up intrusion detection

By mastering these topics, you will have a solid foundation with which to move forward, creating secure applications in the cloud that guarantee the privacy of your customer data.

Administering users with IAM

Before we introduce this recipe, we need to talk briefly about IAM. It's free, and is enabled on every account. It allows you to create groups and users, and allows you to control exactly what they can and can't do, through the use of a policy statement.

By default, groups, users and roles will have no permissions until you assign them either an *AWS Managed Policy* or a *Customer-Managed Policy* (one which you manage). You may want to use AWS Managed Policies as a starting point in order to avoid having to create and maintain your own, but it's good practice to refine your requirements, and scope down access privileges with custom policies.

 There's a third kind of policy, called an **Inline Policy**. Use this sparingly. In fact, the only time we typically see it is in CloudFormation templates.

You pretty much never want to assign a policy directly to a user. If you go down this path, you'll create a lot of work for yourself in the future, when you have a large number of users that need to be administered separately. Instead, you want to apply policies to groups, and then assign users to those groups. Fortunately, it's a pretty easy process, and we're about to walk you through it.

The IAM dashboard provides a URL that your IAM users can use to log in to the web console (if you've assigned them a password and given them access to do so). You can also customize this *IAM sign-in link* if necessary. Don't forget to give this URL to any IAM users that you create, so they know where to go to sign in.

It will look something like the following, until you customize it: `https://<account-id>.signin.aws.amazon.com/console`.

Now, jump right in. There's no excuse for not using IAM. Start today!

Getting ready

All you need to proceed is the CLI tool installed with a profile that can call the AWS IAM API. If you don't have this, you can follow along with the recipe steps using the AWS web console instead, as the process is the same.

How to do it...

Follow these steps to use the CLI to create a new IAM user:

1. Create a new group by running this CLI command:

```
aws iam create-group --group-name <group-name>
```

2. The output looks like this:

```
{
    "Group": {
      "Path": "/",
      "GroupId": "AGPAIHM2XJ2ELQTNYBFQQ",
      "Arn": "arn:aws:iam::067180688831:group/PowerUsers",
      "GroupName": "PowerUsers"
    }
}
```

3. The group doesn't have permissions to do anything yet, so you'll need to attach a policy to it. You can do it with this command (which, unfortunately, doesn't provide any feedback if it successfully runs):

```
aws iam attach-group-policy \
  --group-name <group-name> \
  --policy-arn <policy-arn>
```

4. You can find the **Amazon Resource Name** (**ARN**) for the policy that you'd like to attach to the AWS IAM web console. You can also run the following CLI command in order to get a list of policies:

```
aws iam list-policies
```

5. In this example, we're dealing with `PowerUsers`, so we want to attach the following ARN, which maps to the AWS Managed Policy for power users:

```
arn:aws:iam::aws:policy/PowerUserAccess
```

6. Now, we can go ahead and create a new user, by running this CLI command:

```
aws iam create-user --user-name <new-username>
```

7. You'll get a response that looks like this:

```
{
   "User": {
      "UserName": "lucille.bluth",
      "Path": "/",
      "CreateDate": "2017-02-19T06:16:50.558Z",
      "UserId": "AIDAIU5P6ESCGYTVGACFE",
      "Arn": "arn:aws:iam::07180688831:user/lucille.bluth"
   }
}
```

8. If you wish to give this user access to the web console, you'll need to create a login profile for them. You can do it like so:

```
aws iam create-login-profile --user-name <username> \
   --password <password> \
   --password-reset-required
```

9. Forcing a password reset here is probably good practice. The API should respond to you like so:

```
{
   "LoginProfile": {
      "UserName": "lucille.bluth",
      "CreateDate": "2017-02-19T06:29:06.244Z",
      "PasswordResetRequired": true
   }
}
```

10. To give the API access to the user, they'll need a set of API keys. Generate them with this command:

```
aws iam create-access-key --user-name <username>
```

11. The output will look something like this:

```
{
    "AccessKey": {
      "UserName": "lucille.bluth",
      "Status": "Active",
      "CreateDate": "2017-02-19T06:59:45.273Z",
      "SecretAccessKey": "abcdefghijklmnopqrstuvwxyz",
      "AccessKeyId": "AAAAAAAAAAAAAAAAAAAA"
    }
}
```

12. Access keys can only be retrieved once. There is no way to fetch them again after they've been generated and shown to you. If you lose your access keys, you'll have to regenerate a new set of keys.

13. This user still doesn't have any permission to do anything; this is because they don't yet belong to a group. Let's add them to the group that we created in step 1:

```
aws iam add-user-to-group \
  --group-name <group-name> \
  --user-name <username>
```

> Unfortunately, this command doesn't return any output, either. You can verify whether or not this worked by running this command:
> `aws iam list-groups-for-user --user-name <username>`.

14. You should see something like this:

```
{
    "Groups": [
        {
            "Path": "/",
            "CreateDate": "2017-02-19T07:24:46Z",
            "GroupId": "AGPAIHM2XJ2ELQTNYBFQQ",
            "Arn": "arn:aws:iam::067180688831:group/PowerUsers",
            "GroupName": "PowerUsers"
        }
    ]
}
```

Be sure to delete this user account if you no longer need it once you have completed the recipe.

There's more...

This pretty much covers the basics of how to create IAM groups and users, and how to assign policies to them. Here are some of the IAM tips and gotchas that we've run into over the years:

- Users can exist in more than one group. Use this to your advantage.
- Groups, however, cannot exist within other groups.
- Users can have more than one set of API keys. This is necessary when they need to perform key rotation.
- You can (and should) define a strong password policy for your IAM users.
- The `PowerUserAccess` policy is good, but it does not allow IAM access. At first, this might not seem to be a problem; however, if you are bound by this policy, you will encounter issues when running CloudFormation stacks that create IAM roles for EC2 instances, for example.
- IAM is a global service, meaning that users and groups are global, not region-specific. By default, a user can use AWS services in any region.
- EC2 key pairs are region-specific, and not specific to an IAM user. In other words, IAM users don't have SSH keys associated with them.
- Your IAM username and password (and access keys) won't provide you with SSH or **RDP** (short for **Remote Desktop Protocol**) access to running instances. Credentials for these services are managed separately.
- You can assign up to 10 policies to a group or user.
- You should also enable **multi-factor authentication** (**MFA**) on IAM user accounts for added security. This is used primarily for accessing the web console, but you can also configure your policies so that MFA will be required for API calls, too. You can choose between hardware and software tokens. A good rule of thumb is to use software tokens for IAM users, and hardware tokens for root logins.

See also

- The *Using cross-account roles* recipe

Deploying Simple Active Directory service

This recipe will show you how to deploy an AWS **Simple Active Directory** (**Simple AD**) service.

Simple AD is powered by Samba 4, and is a Microsoft AD-compatible, managed service. It will work with many applications that require AD support, and provides a large range of the commonly used AD features, including the following:

- User accounts
- Single sign-on (Kerberos)
- Group memberships
- Domain joining

It also integrates with other services provided by AWS, such as the following:

- AWS Management Console
- WorkMail
- WorkDocs
- WorkSpaces and WorkSpaces Application Manager

AWS manages the backup and restoration of the directory for you, in the form of daily snapshots, and through its ability to perform point-in-time recovery.

Features that aren't supported include the following:

- Trust relationships with other AD domains
- DNS dynamic updates
- Schema extensions
- MFA
- **LDAPS** (short for **Lightweight Directory Application Protocol Secure**)
- PowerShell AD cmdlets
- Transfer of FSMO roles

The ideal scenario for Simple AD usage, is when you don't require advanced AD features and you're supporting less than 5,000 users. If either of these isn't true, you will want to look at the full-featured Microsoft AD service. However, brace yourself for some added complexity and much higher costs if you choose this path.

Getting ready

Before going ahead, we'll need the following pieces of info:

- The **Fully Qualified Domain Name (FQDN)** for your directory (for example, `megacorp.com`).
- A password for administering your directory. This password corresponds to the administrator user that will be created on your behalf. Note that the password needs to be between 8-64 characters, and will also need to contain one character from three of the following four groups:
    - Lowercase letters
    - Uppercase letters
    - Numbers
    - Non-alphanumeric characters
- The ID of the VPC that we're deploying to.
- The IDs of two subnets in this VPC. These subnets need to be in different availability zones.
- The size of the directory that you'd like to deploy. You can choose between small and large.

A domain controller is going to be deployed in each of the two subnets that you've chosen. They'll be communicating with each other on a fairly large number of ports. Ideally, these subnets would exist in the same *tier* in your VPC, and by extension, would not have any **NACLs** (short for **Network Access Control Lists**), which would stop the controllers from talking with each other.

 If for some reason, you're restricting traffic from using NACLs within your VPC tiers, you will want to refer to the AWS docs for a list of which ports to allow. For more details, visit `http://docs.aws.amazon.com/directoryservice/latest/admin-guide/prereq_simple.html`.

How to do it...

1. Create a new CloudFormation template file. We'll start by populating it with `Parameters` that correspond to all the requirements that we previously mentioned:

```
AWSTemplateFormatVersion: '2010-09-09'
Parameters:
```

```
FullyQualifiedName:
  Description: The fully qualified name for the directory
    (e.g. megacorp.com)
  Type: String
  AllowedPattern: '^([a-zA-Z0-9]+[\\.-])+([a-zA-Z0-9])+$'
Password:
  Description: The password for the directory Administrator
  Type: String
  NoEcho: true
```

2. Then, we add parameters for the VPC, subnets, and directory size:

```
VpcId:
  Description: The ID of the VPC to deploy to
  Type: AWS::EC2::VPC::Id
SubnetIds:
  Description: Subnets where the directory will be deployed to
    (pick at least 2)
  Type: List<AWS::EC2::Subnet::Id>
DirectorySize:
  Description: The size of the directory to deploy
  Type: String
  AllowedValues:
    - Small
    - Large
```

3. Next, we define our `Resources`. Even though two Simple AD domain controllers are being deployed, we only need to create one resource here:

```
Resources:
  ExampleDirectory:
    Type: AWS::DirectoryService::SimpleAD
    Properties:
      Name: !Ref FullyQualifiedName
      Password: !Ref Password
      Size: !Ref DirectorySize
      VpcSettings:
        SubnetIds:
          - !Select [ 0, Ref: SubnetIds ]
          - !Select [ 1, Ref: SubnetIds ]
        VpcId: !Ref VpcId
```

4. You can now go ahead and run this template in the CloudFormation web console, or via the CLI, like this:

```
aws cloudformation create-stack \
  --stack-name example-directory \
  --template-body file://08-active-directory-as-a-service.yaml \
  --parameters \
  ParameterKey=FullyQualifiedName,ParameterValue=<fqdn> \
  ParameterKey=Password,ParameterValue=<password> \
  ParameterKey=VpcId,ParameterValue=<vpd-id> \
  "ParameterKey=SubnetIds,ParameterValue='<subnet-1>,<subnet-2>'" \
  ParameterKey=DirectorySize,ParameterValue=<Small/Large>
```

How it works...

It will take several minutes to create the directory. Once the status becomes active, you may proceed with further setup and integration tasks. Your directory listing page will eventually show a directory listing that looks similar to this:

Simple AD details

There's more...

- The password for the administrator account can't be retrieved or reset. Be sure to keep this password somewhere safe.
- You may notice an additional security group appear in your EC2 console. This group is necessary for the directory controllers (although you won't see these appear as EC2 instances in your console).
- The directory will contain an account with the `AWSAdminD-` prefix. This account is necessary for AWS to perform maintenance tasks, such as backup and FSMO role transfers. Removing this account or changing its password is almost certainly a bad idea.

See also

- The *Building a secure network* recipe in `Chapter 7`, *AWS Networking Essentials*

Creating instance roles

This recipe is reasonably short, but it contains a really important concept to anyone who is new to the AWS platform. Understanding and utilizing IAM roles for the EC2 will significantly reduce your exposure to lost credentials, and will probably help you sleep a little better at night, too. In a nutshell, instance roles help you to get AWS credentials off your servers and out of your code base(s).

Roles contain one or more policies. We're going to create a role that has some AWS Managed Policies, as well as an Inline Policy. As the name would suggest, an AWS Managed Policy is a policy that is created and fully controlled by AWS. The Inline Policy is going to be created by us, and will be embedded in our role definition.

The AWS Managed Policies that we'll use will allow read-only access to the S3 and EC2 APIs. The Inline Policy that we'll create will allow writing access to CloudWatch Logs. We'll talk through why you would or wouldn't choose a Managed Policy later in this recipe.

How to do it...

Follow these steps in order to use CloudFormation to create an instance role:

1. Create a new CloudFormation template file, and add the first `Resource` parameter. This is going to be our role that contains references to the Managed Policies, and also to our Inline Policy:

```
AWSTemplateFormatVersion: '2010-09-09'
Resources:
  ExampleRole:
    Type: AWS::IAM::Role
    Properties:
      AssumeRolePolicyDocument:
        Version: "2012-10-17"
        Statement:
          -
            Effect: Allow
            Principal:
              Service:
                - ec2.amazonaws.com
            Action:
              - sts:AssumeRole
```

2. Complete the definition of the role by adding policies:

```
ManagedPolicyArns:
  - arn:aws:iam::aws:policy/AmazonS3ReadOnlyAccess
  - arn:aws:iam::aws:policy/AmazonEC2ReadOnlyAccess
Path: /
Policies:
  -
    PolicyName: WriteToCloudWatchLogs
    PolicyDocument:
      Version: "2012-10-17"
      Statement:
        -
          Effect: Allow
          Action:
            - logs:CreateLogGroup
            - logs:CreateLogStream
            - logs:PutLogEvents
            - logs:DescribeLogStreams
          Resource: "*"
```

3. We now need to create an `InstanceProfile` resource. A profile encapsulates a single IAM role and, roughly speaking, that's all it's used for. A profile can contain only a single IAM role, so it's not clear why AWS has built this extra layer of abstraction; presumably, they have plans to give profiles of other properties aside from roles:

```
ExampleInstanceProfile:
    Type: AWS::IAM::InstanceProfile
    Properties:
      Roles:
        - !Ref ExampleRole
      Path: /
```

4. For convenience, we'll add some `Outputs` parameters, which will provide the profile name and ARN to us, after the stack has been created:

```
Outputs:
  ExampleInstanceProfile:
    Value: !Ref ExampleInstanceProfile
  ExampleInstanceProfileArn:
    Value: !GetAtt ExampleInstanceProfile.Arn
```

5. You can now create your instance role using CloudFormation via the web console:

```
aws cloudformation create-stack \
  --stack-name example-instance-profile \
  --template-body file://08-creating-instance-roles.yaml \
  --capabilities CAPABILITY_IAM
```

This role can now be assigned to your EC2 instances.

How it works...

How on earth does this solve the problem of hardcoded AWS API keys? Well, something really interesting happens when you assign a role to an EC2 instance. The metadata for that instance will return a set of short-lived API keys. You can retrieve these keys by sending an HTTP request to the metadata URL (this is a service that EC2 instances can use to fetch information about themselves): `http://169.254.169.254/latest/meta-data/iam/security-credentials/<role name>`.

The output of a curl request to this URL will look something like this:

```
{
  "Code" : "Success",
  "LastUpdated" : "2017-02-17T11:14:23Z",
  "Type" : "AWS-HMAC",
  "AccessKeyId" : "AAAAAAAAAAAAAAAAAAAA",
  "SecretAccessKey" : "zzzzzzzzzzzzzzzzzzzzzzzzzzzzzzzzzzzzzzzz",
  "Token" : "token",
  "Expiration" : "2017-02-17T12:14:23Z"
}
```

If you take `AccessKeyId` and `SecretAccessKey`, which are returned in the response, you can use them to query the AWS API. The policies applied to the instance, based on the role assigned to it, will determine exactly what API actions the instance is able to perform using these keys.

The really fun part is that you don't have to worry too much about handling these keys at all (although, it's really useful to know how all this works under the hood). For example, the AWS CLI tools will automatically fetch these keys for you prior to running any CLI commands. The same goes for the AWS SDKs.

Take a scenario where your developers are building an application that needs to fetch files from S3. As long as they are using the AWS SDK to do this, and the application is running on an EC2 instance that has been assigned a role that contains a policy that allows files to be fetched from S3, then no credentials are required by the application whatsoever! The SDK will take care of the queries to the metadata service for you.

The AWS SDKs are available for almost every widely used language, so there's no excuse for keeping hardcoded AWS credentials in config files or source code.

You will see your instances roles listed in the IAM console under the **Roles** section. Clicking on the role will reveal further details, such as the policies that have been assigned to it.

There's more...

Here are some more facts to keep in mind about IAM:

- IAM is a global service. This means that the roles and policies that you create will be available in every region.
- You'll find all the available AWS Managed Policies in the AWS web console. There's quite a few of them, so don't be afraid to use the search bar.

- There's another kind of policy, called a Customer-Managed Policy. These are policies that are managed by you, and they will appear in the AWS console, amongst the AWS Managed Policies.
- It is possible to attach an IAM role to an existing/running EC2 instance. This previously wasn't the case, and the role could only be assigned at the time that the instance launched.
- AWS automatically and periodically rotates the credentials that are returned by the metadata service.
- It's not always appropriate to use an AWS Managed Policy. For example, if a server needs to write to CloudWatch Logs, it may be tempting to assign it to the AWS Managed Policy that provides full access. If you do this, however, you'll also be giving the server access to delete log groups and streams. This is almost certainly undesirable. You'll want to inspect the policies before you apply them, and defer to an Inline or Customer-Managed Policy, where appropriate. The principle of least privilege applies here.

Using cross-account roles

Using multiple accounts to provision your resources (for example, development and production environments) provides a form of *blast radius* protection—even in the worst-case scenario, any issues or damages are limited to the account in which they occur, and not your entire AWS presence.

Creating and assuming roles across accounts is the best way to manage access to multiple accounts. Specific roles provide a clear and explicit declaration of permissions that can be easily reviewed, and revoked if needed. Resist the temptation to create new IAM users in each account, or to utilize IAM accounts in scenarios where you need to provide access to your account to someone from a different organization, such as a consultant.

This recipe provides a way to scale your access across many accounts, without compromising your security.

Getting ready

This recipe assumes you already have two AWS accounts created and ready to go.

In one account (the source account, referred to as account *A*) you will need an IAM user.

While you will need to use your account's root credentials to set up the first role in an account, *do not* use them on a day-to-day basis. The root account has permissions to do anything in your account, and should only be used when necessary.

How to do it...

Follow these steps in order to create a cross-account role:

1. Start a new template with a version and description:

```
AWSTemplateFormatVersion: "2010-09-09"
Description: This template creates a role that can be assumed from
another account.
```

2. The template will take one parameter—the source account that can assume the role:

```
Parameters:
  SourceAccountNumber:
    Type: String
    Description: The AWS account number to grant access to assume
      the role.
    AllowedPattern: "[0-9]+"
    MaxLength: "12"
    MinLength: "12"
```

3. The role itself will consist of the trust role and a sample policy:

```
Resources:
  CrossAccountRole:
    Type: "AWS::IAM::Role"
    Properties:
      Path: "/"
      AssumeRolePolicyDocument:
        Version: "2012-10-17"
        Statement:
          - Sid: ""
            Action: "sts:AssumeRole"
            Effect: Allow
            Principal:
              AWS: !Sub "arn:aws:iam::${SourceAccountNumber}:root"
      Policies:
        - PolicyName: DoEverything
          PolicyDocument:
            Version: "2012-10-17"
```

```
Statement:
  - Action:
    - "*"
    Effect: Allow
    Resource: "*"
    Sid: DoEverything
```

This role has full access to the target account.

4. Finally, we create an output that will make it easy to retrieve the target role ARN:

```
Outputs:
  RoleARN:
    Description: The Role ARN that can be assumed by the
      other account.
    Value: !GetAtt CrossAccountRole.Arn
```

5. Save the template with a known name, for example, `08-03-CrossAccountRoles.yaml`.

6. Deploy the role to the target account (that is, account *B*), by using the CLI tool:

```
aws cloudformation create-stack \
  --stack-name CrossAccountRole \
  --template-body file://src/08-03-CrossAccountRoles.yaml \
  --parameters \
  ParameterKey=SourceAccountNumber, \
  ParameterValue=<your-source-account-number> \
  --capabilities CAPABILITY_IAM
```

7. Get (just) the target role ARN from the outputs of your CloudFormation stack:

```
aws cloudformation describe-stacks \
  --stack-name CrossAccountRole \
  --query 'Stacks[0].Outputs[0].OutputValue' \
  --output text
```

8. In your source account (that is, account *A*) confirm that you can assume the target role, by manually invoking the CLI tool:

```
aws sts assume-role \
  --role-arn <your-target-role-arn> \
  --role-session-name CrossAccountRole
```

How it works...

While cross-account roles are extremely useful for administering multiple AWS accounts, they're not the most intuitive thing to configure. Here's a diagram that illustrates the resources and their interactions:

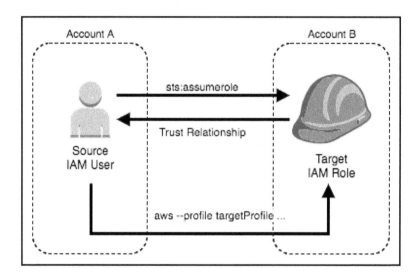

Multiple cross-account roles and their interactions

The first few steps of this recipe are simply creating the target IAM role in a clear and repeatable way, using CloudFormation.

You must explicitly call out the AWS account number that will be allowed to assume this role. If you want to allow multiple accounts to assume the role, simply add more statements to the AssumeRolePolicyDocument property of the role.

The sample policy that is created in this template gives full access to the target account (because Action and Resource are both set to *). You should adjust this as appropriate, according to your needs.

Defining an output value that returns the IAM role's ARN will make it easier to get the generated ID later in the recipe.

We then launch the template in the target account. As this template creates IAM resources, you must supply the --capabilities CAPABILITY_IAM argument. If you don't have any existing IAM users that can launch it, use the AWS web console (after logging in with your root credentials). This means that you don't need to bother creating IAM users in the target account.

Once you have deployed the template, you will no longer need to log in to the account manually—you can just assume the newly created role from the trusted (source) account. Using an IAM role in the target account means that your day-to-day access does not require multiple passwords, which takes work to manage and store securely. You only need to have one password—the password of your source IAM user.

After the stack has finished creating (which shouldn't take long, as it's only creating one resource), you can quickly extract the target role's ARN with a `describe-stacks` call, combined with a specifically crafted `--query` argument. The JMESPath `Stacks[0].Outputs[0].OutputValue` query gets the `OutputValue` property of the first output in the first stack returned, which we know will be the target role ARN, because there is only one output in the template.

Finally, the sample `assume-role` command will return the credentials for the target role (that is, `ACCESS_KEY_ID` and `SECRET_ACCESS_KEY`). You can then use this in an API call, via the CLI tool, or one of the SDKs. Keep in mind that these tokens will be short-lived.

See the next section for a more convenient way to use the credentials with the CLI tool, by creating profiles.

There's more...

Just as there are multiple ways to use roles, there are multiple ways to utilize cross-account roles.

AWS CLI profiles

One of the easiest ways to use a cross-account role, is to configure it as a profile for the AWS CLI tool to use. This means that you can quickly and easily switch accounts, just by changing the profile you use when executing your commands.

To do this, you must define the target role in the CLI configuration file. With this configuration, it is assumed that your `default` profile is in the source account (that is, account *A*).

Add the following snippet to the ~/.aws/config file on Linux and macOS computers, and to the C:\Users\[USERNAME]\.aws\config file on Windows:

```
[profile accountb]
role_arn = <your-target-account-role-arn>
source_profile = default
```

To use switch roles, all you need to do is pass the --profile argument along with your command:

```
aws --profile accountb ...
```

Storing secrets

A common mistake that new administrators make when getting started with Infrastructure-as-Code is committing secrets (passwords, access keys, and so on) into their repositories. While this makes their infrastructure repeatable, it also makes it much more likely that their credentials will be compromised. Once something is in version control, it's hard and annoying to remove it (that's the point of version control!). Even if you do remove it, it's almost impossible to know if it has already been viewed/copied by someone unintended.

AWS makes it easy to avoid the use of passwords altogether, by assigning roles to resources such as EC2 instances or lambda functions, but there are some instances where you have no other choice but to store credentials somewhere. This is where AWS Secrets Manager comes in. You can store credentials—usernames and password or access keys and secret keys—and then retrieve them later in a secure way. You can also automatically handle rotating those credentials on a regular schedule.

How to do it...

Follow these steps in order to learn how to store a username and password in AWS Secrets Manager:

1. Log in to your AWS account, and go to the **AWS Secrets Manager** dashboard.
2. Click **Store a new secret**.

3. Select **Other types of secrets**:

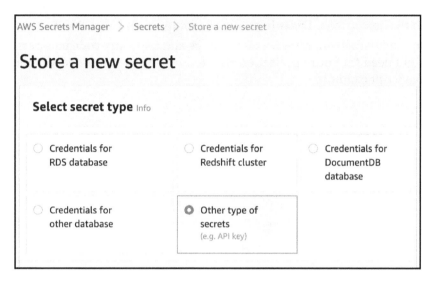

Store a new secret

4. Add your secret key/value pair in the **Plaintext** box. Go with the default for the encryption key:

Specify key/value pairs

5. Click **Next.**
6. Give the secret a **Name**, optional **Description** and **Tags**, and click **Next.**
7. On the next screen, **Disable automatic rotation**, and click **Next.**
8. On the final screen, review your settings and copy any code snippets that you might need for your application. The following is a simplified version of the JavaScript example:

```
var AWS = require('aws-sdk'),
    region = "us-east-1",
    secretName = "MySecret",
    secret,
    decodedBinarySecret;

var client = new AWS.SecretsManager({region: region});

client.getSecretValue({SecretId: secretName}, function(err, data) {
    if (err) {
        throw err;
    }
    else {
        if ('SecretString' in data) {
            secret = data.SecretString;
        } else {
            let buff = new Buffer(data.SecretBinary, 'base64');
            decodedBinarySecret = buff.toString('ascii');
        }
    }
    // Your code goes here.
});
```

9. Click **Store** to complete the process.

You now have a secret that is securely stored and encrypted using the **Key Management Service (KMS)**. If you already have a **Relation Database Service (RDS)** database created in your account, experiment with secrets that are automatically integrated with RDS. This is a huge improvement over storing usernames and passwords in configuration files or environment variables!

How it works...

AWS Secrets Manager uses the AWS KMS to encrypt and store your secrets safely and securely. Any application that needs a secret to access a resource, such as a relational database, makes an API call into AWS Secrets Manager—the API call is subject to all of the normal authentication and authorization mechanisms that come into play when interacting with the AWS API. A decrypted secret is returned to the client application, which then uses it to access the resource.

Automatic key rotation is accomplished by tight integration with AWS services such as AWS RDS. There is no need to manually rotate your credentials, which might require application changes or downtime. AWS Secrets Manager handles it all for you.

There's more...

AWS Secrets Manager also allows you to:

- Set up policies that prevent developers from accessing production credentials
- Audit changes to secrets with CloudTrail
- Tag secrets in order to manage them with tag-level permissions
- Automate the rotation of credentials with direct RDS integration
- Use VPC endpoints to keep the transmission of secrets on your private network

Protecting applications from DDoS

A **distributed denial of service** (**DDoS**) attack can be a real nightmare for network administrators. Attackers send malicious commands to an application from a huge number of sources, often compromised computers all over the world, in an attempt to disable the application. Individually, the requests might seem innocuous, as it might be something like asking for the contents of a single web page. But, on aggregate, the requests can put enough of a strain on servers to bring an application to its knees.

Since the requests originate from so many sources all over the world, it's not as simple as configuring an **access control list** (**ACL**) to block the traffic. To mitigate these types of attacks, you need a much more intelligent and reactive service. AWS Shield does this job for you, and comes in two varieties—AWS Shield Standard and Advanced.

How to do it...

Luckily for you, there is nothing that you have to do in order to enable AWS Shield Standard, if you are using Amazon Route 53 and Amazon CloudFront to publish your content on the web. Basic DDoS protection is built into those services by default.

How it works...

AWS Shield Standard works in combination with Amazon CloudFront and Amazon Route 53, in order to protect against attacks at Layers 3 and 4 of the **Open Systems Interconnection** (**OSI**) stack. At the application layer, AWS **Web Application Firewall** (**WAF**) can be used, by writing custom rules to handle these kinds of attacks.

AWS Shield Advanced extends protection to individual elastic IP addresses, without any need to make changes to your application's routing. It can also automatically mitigate things, such as HTTP and DNS query floods, at the application level. AWS Shield Advanced is another good reason to have at least Business-level support on your AWS account. With Business or Enterprise support, you get quick access to the AWS **DDoS Response Team** (**DRT**), which will help you to deal with sudden, large-scale attacks.

AWS Shield Advanced also gives you detailed visibility into attacks as they happen, either via the console or CloudWatch.

There's more...

AWS Shield Advanced also comes with a potentially huge cost-savings benefit. If your resources scale up in response to a DDoS attack, you are eligible for credits to offset the costs that you incur during the scale-out.

At the time of writing, AWS Shield Advanced costs $3,000 per month, in addition to support contract fees. For a large application or enterprise running on AWS, this fee pales in comparison to the damage that can be done by an extended outage due to a DDoS attack. If you are managing any mission-critical application that might attract the attention of malicious users who are intent on taking you down, you should give AWS Shield Advanced some serious consideration.

Configuring AWS WAF

Web application firewalls are a critical component to any secure web application. AWS WAF allows you to easily set up protection for your applications that are running on a variety of AWS services, including the following:

- Amazon CloudFront
- Amazon EC2
- Amazon Elastic Load Balancer
- Amazon API Gateway

AWS WAF protects you from a wide variety of common exploits that plague web applications, allowing you to configure rules by IP address and HTTP headers. It is even capable of detecting and stopping SQL injection attacks, which are some of the most common ways that data is exfiltrated from an application that is running on the internet.

How to do it...

In this recipe, you will configure WAF to run on top of a lambda function that publishes an endpoint via an API Gateway:

1. Log in to your AWS account, and go to the **Lambd**a dashboard.
2. Create a new lambda function, and choose **Author from scratch**. Give it a name and click **Create function**:

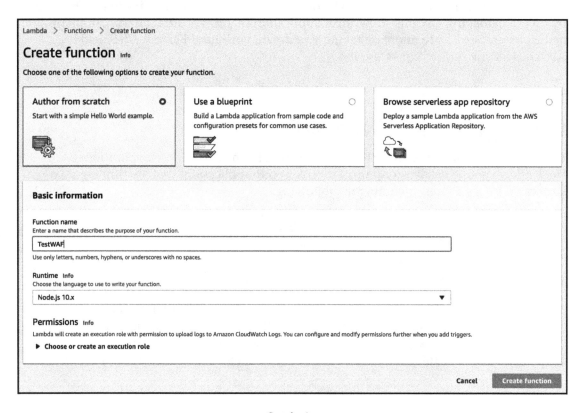

Create function

3. Add an API Gateway integration trigger:

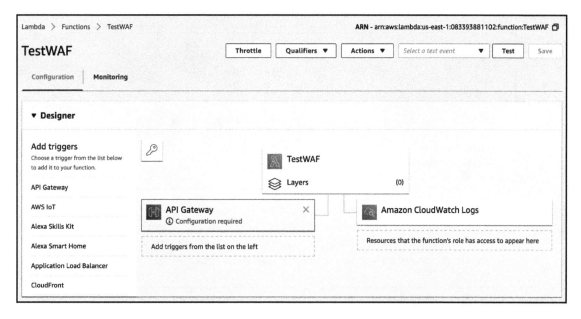

Add API Gateway trigger

4. Select **Create a new API**, and then **Save** the lambda function:

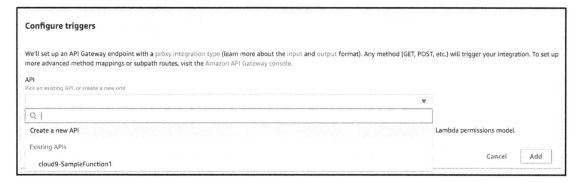

Configure the trigger

5. Click the endpoint URL in the API Gateway configuration summary, and you should see **Hello from Lambda**, if you left the default function code alone:

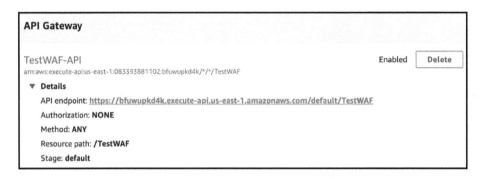

The API Gateway stage URL for your new function

6. Go to the API Gateway dashboard, select the new gateway you just created, and then select the **default** stage. Click **Create Web ACL**:

The API Gateway stage editor

7. In the WAF console, create a new web ACL. Review the concepts overview and click **Next**.

8. Give the ACL a name, select your region, then select your new API Gateway stage. Click **Next**:

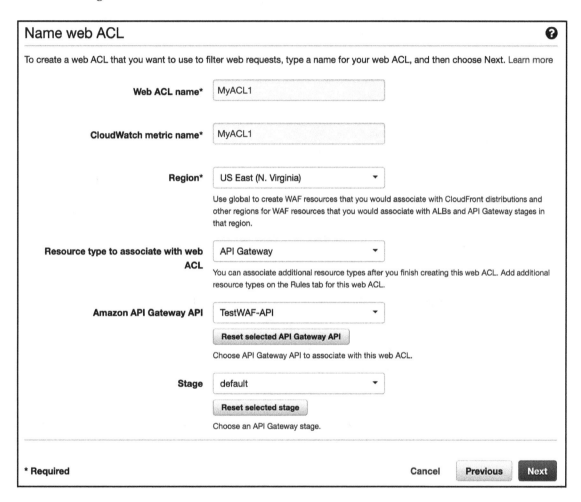

Web ACL configuration

9. Create an IP match condition and add you current IP address. If you aren't sure what your IP is, visit a site such as `https://www.whatismyip.com/`, and then add `/32` to the address, in order to make it comply with CIDR (short for **Classless Inter-Domain Routing**) notation:

Add an IP address

10. Create a rule. Give the rule a name, select the IP address that you created in the previous step, and then click **Create**:

Add conditions

11. Click **Review and Create**; then **Confirm and Create**.
12. Go back to the API stage, and select the new ACL that you just created. Save the changes.
13. Refresh the endpoint URL, and you should see `{"message":"Forbidden"}`.

With this recipe, you have successfully integrated AWS WAF with an AWS lambda function. You can apply what you have learned here to other resources, such as EC2 instances sitting behind an application load balancer, and you can create more complex rules in order to meet your needs.

How it works...

AWS WAF works by applying web ACLs to resources such as API Gateway stages. Web ACLs consist of conditions, such as traffic originating from a certain IP address, and rules, which specify what happens when a certain condition is met.

Examples of conditions are as follows:

- Scripts
- IP addresses
- Geographic locations
- Request length
- SQL code in the request
- Headers

Examples of rules are:

- Regular rules that simply check conditions
- Rate-based rules that only apply if a certain condition is met a number of times

Web ACLs have a default action, such as allowing all traffic, and actions to take when a rule is activated, such as denying traffic from a certain IP.

There's more...

The AWS marketplace features managed rules for AWS WAF, which are provided by AWS Partners, to save you time in writing your own firewall rules. These managed rules, which can be purchased via the marketplace, offer rules such as the following:

- Cyber Security Cloud's OWASP Security Set
- F5's Bot Protection Rules and **Common Vulnerabilities and Exposures** (**CVE**)
- Fortinet's SQLi/XSS rules
- TrendMicro's WordPress protection

Setting up intrusion detection

An **intrusion detection system** (**IDS**) is a system that is configured to monitor a network, or specific resources, in order to watch for policy violations that might indicate that a bad actor has infiltrated the network. Unusual user activity, odd patterns in data flows throughout a network, or changes to critical operating system files can indicate an intrusion.

An IDS is often integrated with a **Security Information and Event Management (SIEM)** system, to collect and analyze all of the information reported by an IDS.

Amazon GuardDuty is a service offered by AWS that can act as your cloud IDS. GuardDuty uses machine learning algorithms to monitor log sources, such as AWS CloudTrail and Amazon VPC Flow Logs, for any activity that could indicate unauthorized activity in your account.

How to do it...

This recipe will walk you through the basics of setting up GuardDuty, in order to monitor your resources. There really isn't much to it, beyond enabling the service for your account:

1. Log in to your AWS account and go to the **GuardDuty** dashboard.
2. Click **Get Started**, and then click **Enable GuardDuty**.
3. Click **Settings**, and then click **Generate Sample Findings**.
4. Go back to **Findings** and check out what typical findings might look like:

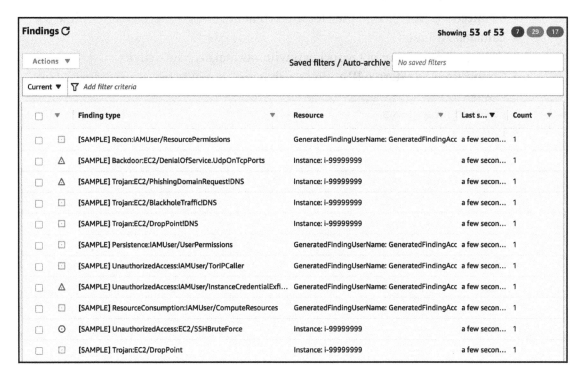

GuardDuty Findings

How it works...

GuardDuty uses threat detection feeds from a variety of sources in order to stay up to date with the latest malicious activity that is common on the internet. It monitors logs and applies machine learning to alert you when something suspicious is happening. Alerts are sent to CloudWatch, so that you can then take action on these alerts, by sending messages to administrators, or even automating responses with AWS Lambda.

GuardDuty can consolidate findings across multiple accounts, and feed them all into a central administrative account, which makes setting up enterprise-wide monitoring quick and easy.

There's more...

Here are some of the things that GuardDuty can detect:

- EC2 instance compromise
- Account compromise
- Connections from geographic locations that are not associated with routine use
- Unusual API calls
- DNS queries that are not associated with normal account activity
- Connections to external IP addresses that are known to be associated with bad actors
- Failed login requests
- Port scanning

Managing Costs

One of the hardest things to get used to when starting with AWS is that you pay for almost everything that you use. One of the biggest benefits of AWS is that you only pay for what you use. This makes it hard to quickly answer the question that often arises when people first start using AWS—*How much is it going to cost?*

In a *traditional* infrastructure or data center setup, many costs are paid during the initial outlay or in annual contracts. AWS has no upfront fees and few long-term commitments, so the usual thought process around costs is turned on its head.

There are a number of helpful tools that can help you to get a better estimate of your AWS usage costs. Don't forget that every AWS service page has a pricing section. While some pricing models can be a bit confusing at the start, it quickly makes sense.

In this chapter, we will cover the following topics:

- Estimating costs with the Simple Monthly Calculator
- Estimating costs with the Total Cost of Ownership Calculator
- Estimating CloudFormation template costs
- Reducing costs by purchasing reserved instances

Estimating costs with the Simple Monthly Calculator

The AWS Simple Monthly Calculator is a web application provided to help you estimate and forecast your AWS costs. By listing the resources you expect to consume, you can calculate your pay-as-you-go costs, which is how AWS bills you. There are no upfront costs involved with AWS usage. The calculator allows you to quickly get an estimate of your monthly bill, and the results can be shared with others via a unique URL.

Getting ready

In order to use the AWS Simple Monthly Calculator effectively, you need to already know the specific services and resources that you will use on a monthly basis.

You also need to know specifics about things such as monthly data transfer and the amount of data that you will need to store. In AWS, you get charged for data flowing out of AWS (for example, visitors to your website), but not for data flowing between AWS services within the same region (for example, EC2 instances to **Relational Database Service** (**RDS**) databases). Data ingress from outside of AWS into your account is free.

How to do it...

In this recipe, you will use the Simple Monthly Calculator to estimate your monthly charges:

1. Go to the calculator website,
   `http://calculator.s3.amazonaws.com/index.html`:

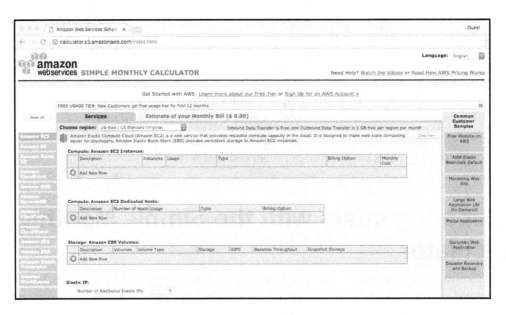

The Simple Monthly Calculator

2. Select/deselect the free usage tier option as is relevant for your account—if the account is less than 12 months old, you are eligible for the free usage tier:

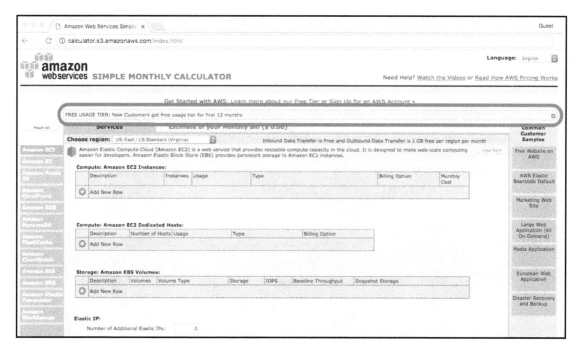

The FREE USAGE TIER checkbox

3. Make sure that you have the correct region selected before adding the resources, as they can differ in price from region to region:

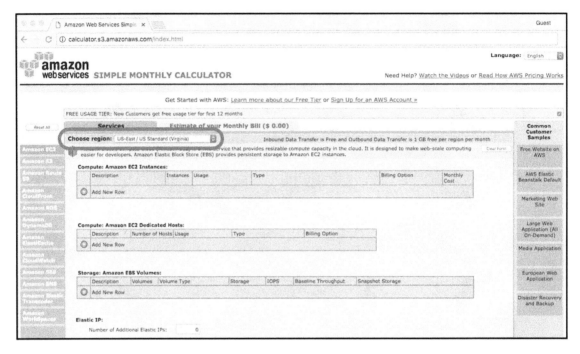

Region selection

4. Add your resources by selecting the relevant service from the left-hand menu, and filling in your details:

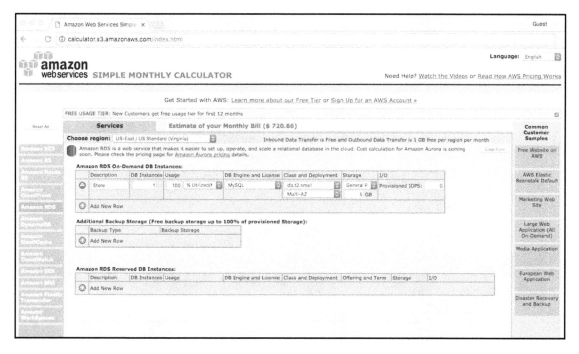

Service selection

5. Continue to add resources as necessary:

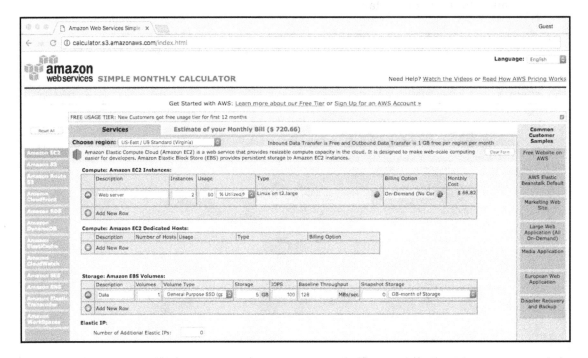

Adding resources to the calculator

6. Once you've added all your resources, view the estimated monthly bill on the **Estimate of your Monthly Bill** tab:

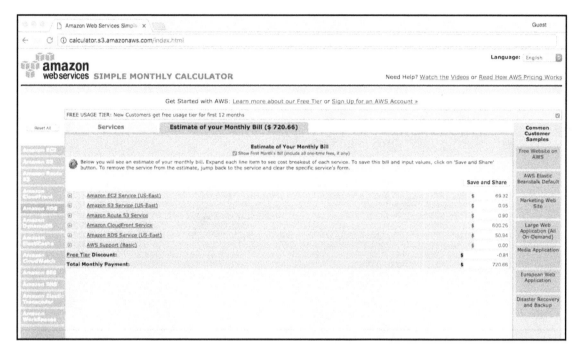

Estimate your monthly bill

7. After confirming the estimate's detail, click on the **Save and Share** button to add some additional metadata about your report. All the fields are optional:

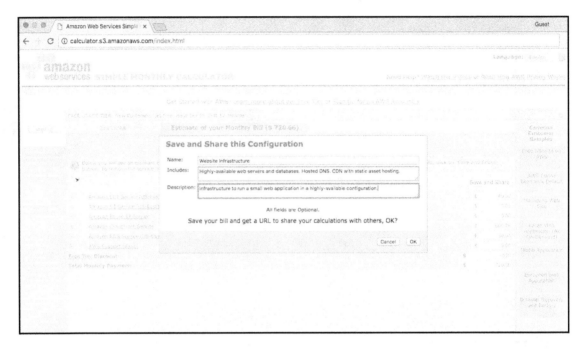

Save and share the report

8. A specific, one-time URL will be generated for your report, which you can then share with others:

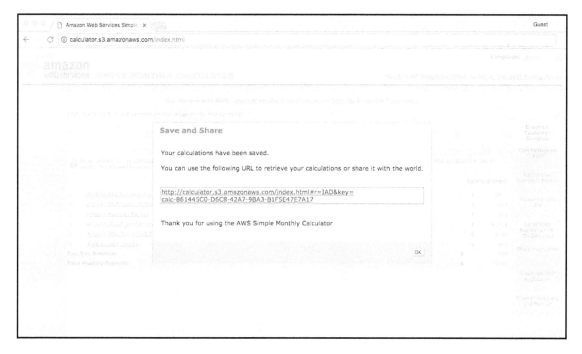

The calculations can be viewed by anyone who has this link

The generated URL can be used to share the results, but keep in mind that this URL is not locked down with any security.

How it works...

The accuracy of the calculator is completely dependent on your ability to forecast your requirements and usage—not an easy thing to do when you first start using AWS!

Unfortunately, not all AWS services are present in the calculator (a notable omission is AWS Lambda). For those services, you will have to do your own calculations based on the service-specific pricing pages.

The cost of services and resources can vary from region to region. In general, the us-east-1 region is the cheapest, and also has the most services (not all services are available in all regions), so use that if you want to know the lowest-cost option. Other regions' prices vary due to supply and demand, the cost of operations, and undoubtedly many other reasons that AWS doesn't go into.

Some services (for example, DynamoDB, Lambda, and so on) have a free tier that applies even if your account does not qualify for the *standard* free tier (that is, the account is more than 12 months old). These services will have a note on their specific calculator page, detailing the inclusions:

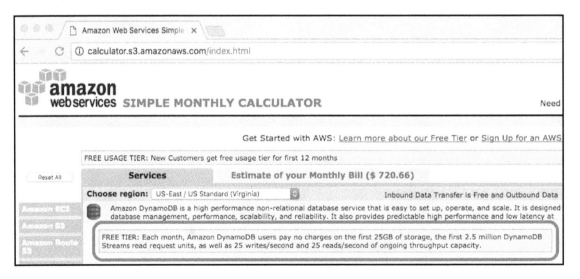

AWS Simple Monthly Calculator—FREE TIER

Keep in mind the expiration date of the free tier when calculating your total annual costs.

See also

- The *Estimating CloudFormation template costs* recipe

Estimating costs with the Total Cost of Ownership Calculator

The AWS **Total Cost of Ownership** or **TCO** Calculator is designed to provide you with a ballpark view of how much it will cost you to run an equivalent infrastructure on AWS in comparison to your co-located or on-premises data center.

The calculator has been audited by an independent third party, but you should, of course, check its output against your own calculations before you make any purchasing decisions.

Getting ready

In this example, we're going to describe a typical three-tier rails image processing application that is running with a modest amount of hardware. You can use our example configuration, or follow along with your own hardware requirements.

How to do it...

1. Navigate to `https://awstcocalculator.com/`.
2. Choose your currency, location, AWS region, and workload type. In our case we're going to choose the following:
   - **Australian dollar**
   - **Colocation**
   - **Asia Pacific (Sydney)**
   - **General**

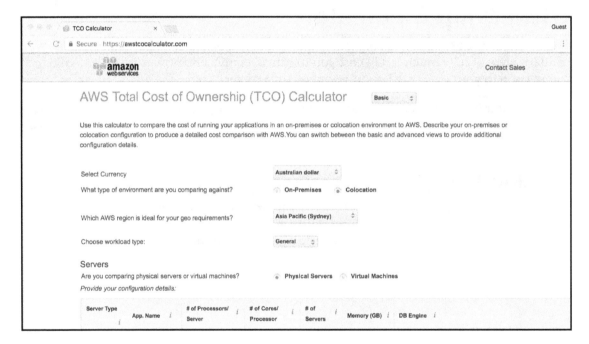

TCO calculator—workload

3. Now we need to describe our server requirements. We're going to specify that our app is running on physical servers with tiers that look like this:

- An nginx application with two servers, two processors and two cores per processor, and 16 GB RAM.
- A rails application with four servers, two processors and four cores per server, and 32 GB RAM.
- A MySQL database with two servers, two processors and eight cores per server, and 64 GB RAM.

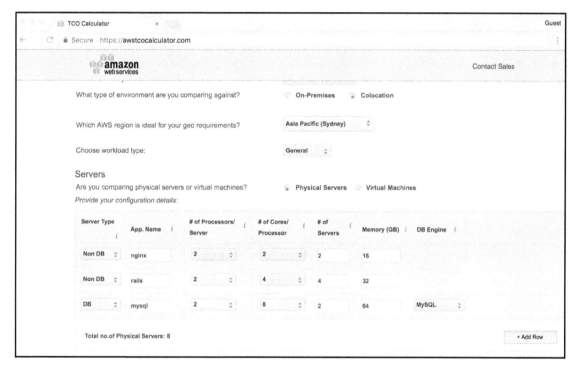

TCO calculator—Servers

4. Lastly, we need to input our storage requirements. For our example, the rails application, we need the following:

- **Storage Type: Object**
- **Raw Storage Capacity**: 2
- **% Accessed Infrequently**: 90

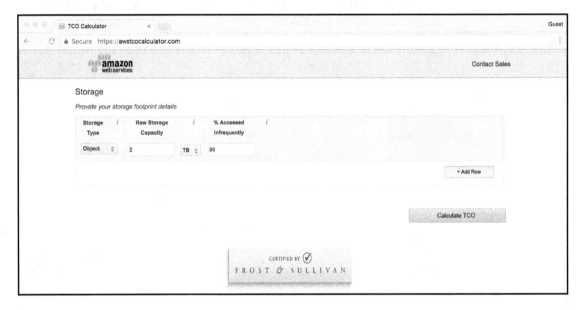

TCO calculator—Storage

5. Go ahead and click **Calculate TCO**.

6. The 3 year cost breakdown graphs provide a high-level view of your potential cost savings. You can see that, in our example, AWS estimates that we'll save 68% on our infrastructure costs over the next 3 years. That's pretty impressive!

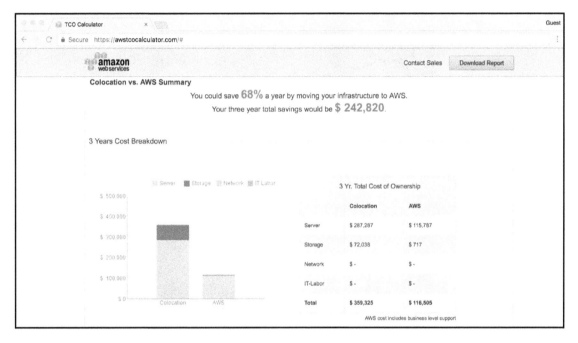

TCO Calculator—summary

7. Scroll further through the report to see cost breakdowns categorized by resource type:

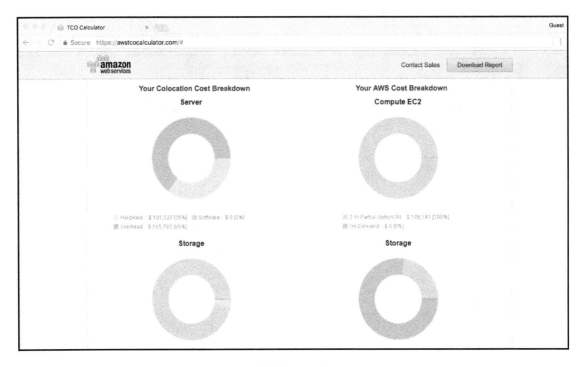

TCO Calculator—graphs

The TCO calculator can be an invaluable tool when convincing executive decision-makers of the long-term value of cloud migration.

How it works...

The calculator will take your server requirements and map them to EC2 instances of an appropriate size. Since we've been specific that we need an object store for our storage, it will calculate our storage costs based on the price for S3 storage in our region.

There's more...

Let's take a look under the hood and see how we're able to save so much money on AWS:

- The prices for our EC2 instances are based on a 3 year reserved instance price with a partial upfront payment. Is this a fair comparison? Yes and no. You would probably be locked in to a fixed hardware contract with your on-premises or co-located solution, so it makes sense to apply similar contract terms to your AWS pricing model. In reality, you'd probably want to think about purchasing reserved instances *after* you've moved to AWS and performed some fine-tuning around which instance types to use. On the flip side, the AWS costs could be reduced even further if your servers ran under **All Upfront** instance reservations.

- The comparison of object storage systems may or may not be fair, depending on the feature set of your on-premises or co-located solution. For example, S3 has the ability to apply an *infrequently accessed* storage class on stored objects, which reduces their cost if they are not frequently accessed. You'd probably not have this feature in your on-premises or co-located storage.

- The 3 year cost for storage in our on-premises/co-located facility is AU $69,660, of which a whopping 97% is the *monthly cost to operate a rack*. This includes rental of space, cooling, power, and so on.

- While the cost calculator is taking a pure infrastructure view, it also does factor in support costs. If you are new to AWS, you will probably be leaning on AWS support a little bit to get up and running.

- You'll also want to factor in some costs around training and potentially hiring staff who are skilled in deploying and migrating systems to AWS. Your developers are also going to start thinking differently about how to build and deploy their applications. Make sure to factor this in, too.

- If you aren't totally happy with the on-premises or co-location estimates, you can go ahead and change the figures used in the calculation. Scroll to the top of the page and click **Modify Assumptions** to input your own hardware prices:

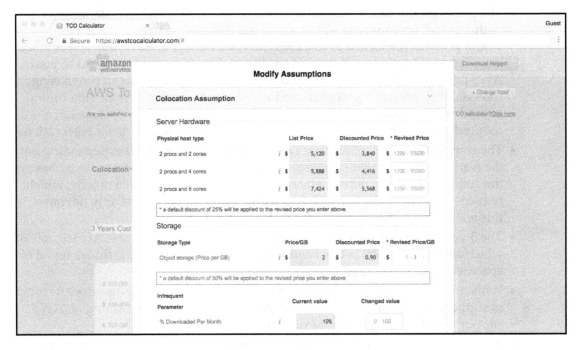

TCO Calculator—Modify Assumptions

See also

- The *Reducing costs by purchasing reserved instances* recipe

Estimating CloudFormation template costs

Most of the recipes in this book have been managed and launched using CloudFormation, the AWS Infrastructure as Code service. CloudFormation has a convenient feature that allows you to directly plug in the resources from the template into the Simple Monthly Calculator.

Getting ready

For this recipe, you will need an existing CloudFormation template. The template does not need to be deployed as a stack; just the file is required.

In this example, we will use the template from Chapter 6, *Managing AWS Databases*: 06-01-RDS.yaml.

How to do it...

Follow these steps to use a CloudFormation template as the basis for cost estimation:

1. Run the following command to generate the report:

```
aws cloudformation estimate-template-cost \
  --template-body \
  file://06-01-RDS.yaml \
  --parameters ParameterKey=VPCId,ParameterValue=test \
  ParameterKey=SubnetIds,ParameterValue=\"test,test\" \
  ParameterKey=DBUsername,ParameterValue=test \
  ParameterKey=DBPassword,ParameterValue=test \
  --query Url \
  --output text
```

2. Click or copy and paste the URL into a browser to see the report:

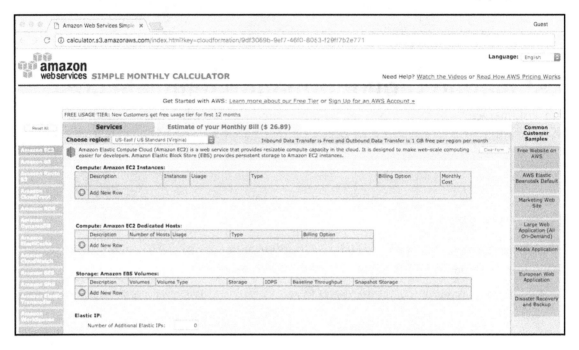

AWS Simple Monthly Calculator

3. Click on **Amazon RDS** in the left-hand menu to see the individual service page details:

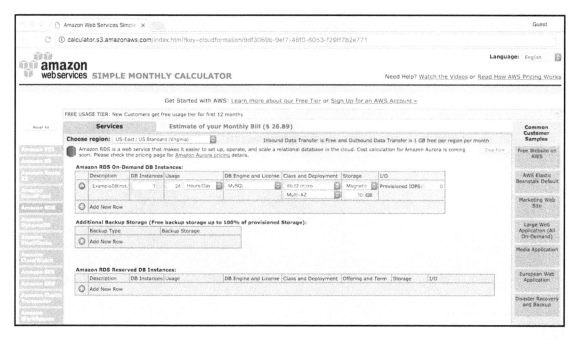

AWS Simple Monthly Calculator—RDS

4. Click on **Estimate of your Monthly Bill** to see a total summary of the template resources:

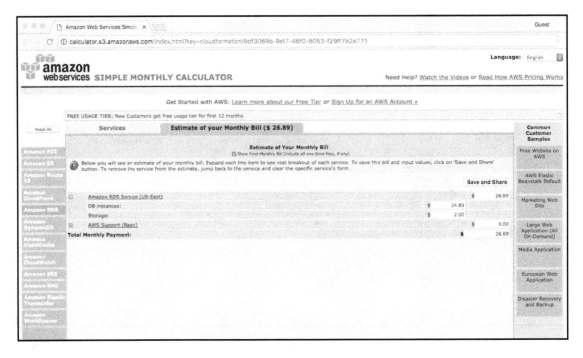

AWS Simple Monthly Calculator—total monthly payment

Using a CloudFormation template can save you a lot of time with the AWS Simple Monthly Calculator.

How it works...

The `estimate-template-cost` command requires all the parameters of your template. As you can see in the first step, the actual values aren't important, because the template won't actually be launched. You simply need to make sure that the type of value you give matches the required type for that parameter (for example, the `SubnetIds` value must be a list of values in this template).

> The region that you specify is important! Some services (but not all) can cost different amounts depending on the region they are in. Generally, the us-east-1 region is the cheapest.

At the end of the command, we limit the output to just the report URL via the `--query` argument.

 You can share the generated URL with others, but you will not be able to retrieve earlier reports unless you keep track of the URL yourself.

On the calculator website, the template's resources will be pre-populated, even if you can't immediately see them. The report always defaults to the Amazon EC2 service page, so you will have to go to the relevant service page via the left-hand menu (in this case, Amazon RDS).

Finally, you can see a complete report of your template's monthly cost on the **Estimate of your Monthly Bill** tab. If your template contains many different types of resources/services, you will see them summarized here.

See also

- The *Estimating costs with the Simple Monthly Calculator* recipe

Reducing costs by purchasing reserved instances

Reserved instances allow for deep cost savings, and have various models to give you a balance between flexibility and cost savings. Here are a few pointers to get you going down the right path:

- Reserved instances have no distinguishing technical features compared to regular on-demand instances.
- Reserved instances are not a specific EC2 resource; rather, they are a billing construct that gives you a discount for continuous usage that matches the subscription.

- Put simply, purchasing a reserved instance entitles you to a discounted hourly rate on an on-demand instance that matches the properties of the reserved instance.
- The discounted hourly rate will be of varying size, depending on how much you pay up front. As a general rule, the more you pay up front, the higher the discount.

When you purchase a reserved instance, you're required to specify the following properties:

- **Platform**: **Linux/Windows**
- **Scope**: **Region** or **Availability Zone**
- **Instance Type**: For example, **m5.large**
- **Tenancy**: Shared or dedicated
- **Offering Class**: Standard or convertible
- **Term**: 1-12 months or 1-3 years
- **Payment Option**: No upfront, partial upfront, all upfront

We'll explore the ins and outs a little later in this section. For now, let's dive in and see how to make a purchase.

Getting ready

You'll need an AWS account and some idea of which instance types you wish to reserve and for how long. Refer to the reserved instance properties that were mentioned previously for the exact information you'll need to proceed.

The **Payment Option** you choose will dramatically affect the price you pay when purchasing the reservation:

- **No Upfront**: This means you pay nothing now, but you will be charged the discounted hourly rate for the entire term, whether or not you have an instance that matches the reservation. Also, note that choosing this option limits you to one year for **Standard** reservations and three years for **Convertible** reservations.

- **Partial Upfront**: These reservations mean that you pay a smaller upfront fee, and then you are charged a discounted hourly rate only for the instance hours you use.
- **All Upfront**: As the name suggests, you'll be required to pay the full cost of the instance for the entire term. An effective 100% discount is applied to the hourly rate of your matching instances for that term.

Once you know all the properties of the instance reservation, you can go ahead and make a purchase.

How to do it...

Follow these steps to purchase a reserved instance:

1. Go to the EC2 web console, select **Reserved Instances**, then **Purchase Reserved Instances:**

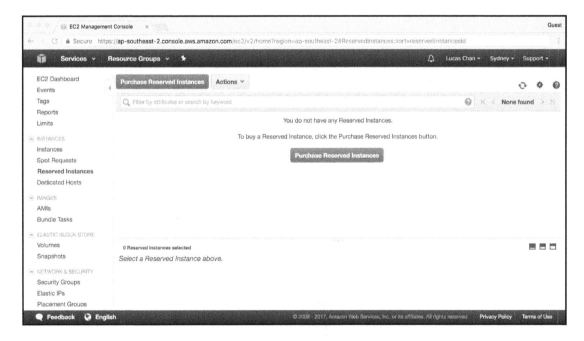

Purchase Reserved Instances

2. We now need to perform a search for the instance type that you wish to purchase. In this example, we're going to choose the following:
   - **Platform**: **Linux/Unix**
   - **Tenancy**: **Default**
   - **Offering Class**: **Standard**
   - **Instance Type**: **t2.micro**
   - **Term**: **1 months-12 months**
   - **Payment Option**: **All Upfront**

3. Obviously, choose the options that best match your workload. You almost certainly want to choose **Default** as **Tenancy** here. Dedicated tenancy/instances are run on hardware that will be occupied by only one customer (you) and are a lot more expensive:

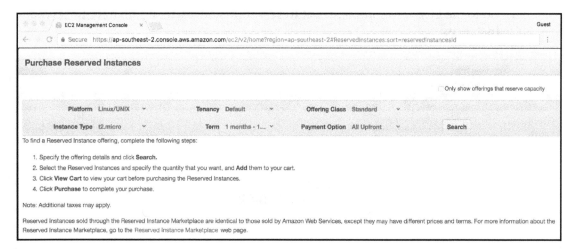

Purchase Reserved Instances—Search

4. The console will return a price for the instance reservation. Note that because we didn't select **Only show offerings that reserve capacity**, what we are seeing is a single result, that is, a reservation that applies to the region we're currently viewing in the console. Think of this as a *region-level* reservation:

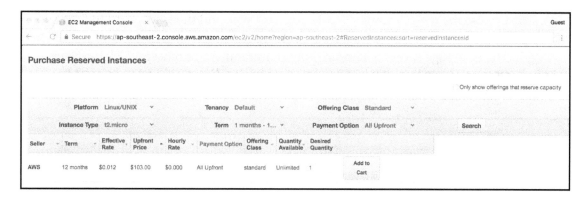

Purchase Reserved Instances—Add to Cart

5. Now try selecting **Only show offerings that reserve capacity** and note that all availability zones are showing for the current region. You can think of these as *AZ-level* reservations. Choosing one of these options obviously locks you in to a specific availability zone; however, you also get a *capacity reservation*:

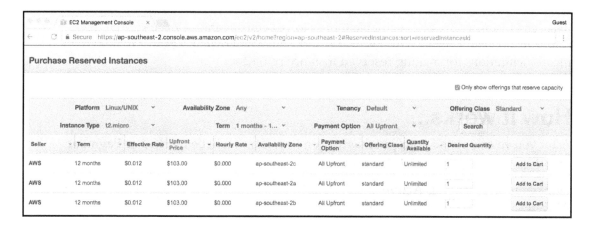

Purchase Reserved Instances—Capacity Reservations

6. Choose the reservation that looks right for you, and then click **Add to Cart** and then **View Cart**.

7. The next page shows a summary of your imminent purchase. Click **Purchase** to proceed. Note that this is the point of no return. Reserved instances can't be canceled. Choose wisely!

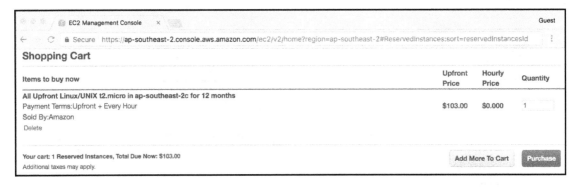

Purchase Reserved Instances—Cart

Reserved instances are an invaluable tool to lower your overall AWS usage charges. Carefully analyze your EC2 usage, or use a tool such as Trusted Advisor to help with recommendations for making reserved instance purchases.

How it works...

After you've completed your purchase, your reservation will be marked as **Payment Pending**, and then soon after, **Active** (there's a third possible status, which is **Retired**).

Once your reservation is **Active**, the discount will automatically apply to match instances. AWS refers to this hourly discount as a *billing benefit*.

Choosing a **Convertible** reservation class immediately rules out anything but a 3 year term. In return, you get a little more flexibility than the **Standard** reservations, because if you decide the reservation no longer meets your needs, you can *convert* it to a reservation that is of equal or higher value, paying the difference, of course.

If you made a reservation for a specific availability zone, AWS also provides you with a *capacity reservation*, which will give you some guarantees around the availability of instances in that zone. This is something you might want to consider if your workload needs to maintain a certain amount of capacity in the event of an entire availability zone outage, for example. An event such as this tends to cause a rush of new instance requests in the unaffected zones; however, customers without a capacity reservation may find that their new instance requests can't be fulfilled, because of a lack of capacity (this is not unheard of), causing them to miss out or forcing them to issue new instance requests for a different zone and/or instance type while at the same time crossing their fingers.

Unlike the *billing benefit* (hourly discount), which is applied immediately after purchase, a capacity reservation is used by the first instance you launch in the zone matching the properties of your reservation.

There's more...

Here are a few more tips to help with your cost-optimization efforts:

- Services that launch instances on your behalf (auto scaling, Elastic Beanstalk, and so on) are also eligible to have hourly discounts applied to them.
- **Standard** reservations can be made for either 1 or 3 years. As mentioned before, **Convertible** reservations are fixed at 3 years.
- Under a consolidated billing model, reserved instance discounts are applied across all your subaccounts. For example, if you purchase a reserved instance intended for account *A* but there is no server matching its properties, the reservation will automatically apply to matching instances in account *B*. This only applies to the billing benefit and not the capacity benefit. Note that this behavior can be disabled.
- Reserved instances can be sold in the AWS marketplace. This is useful if the reservation no longer suits your needs. Note that you will need a US bank account for this.
- If reserved instances don't seem to match your type of workload, you might consider a scheduled instance or a spot instance instead.

10
Advanced AWS CloudFormation

In Chapter 1, *AWS Fundamentals*, you were given a basic introduction to AWS CloudFormation fundamentals. What you learned is definitely enough to get you started with the basic administration of your account but, as you start to tackle more challenging projects, you will want to learn a few advanced techniques. In this chapter, you will follow recipes that will allow you to customize the behavior of CloudFormation, and apply your templates across multiple regions and accounts.

In this chapter, we will introduce some advanced techniques, which you can use to take your CloudFormation skills to the next level. The following topics will be covered:

- Creating and populating an S3 bucket with custom resources
- Using a macro to create an S3 bucket for CloudTrail logs
- Using mappings to specify regional AMI IDs
- Using StackSets to deploy resources to multiple regions
- Detecting resource drift from templates with drift detection

Creating and populating an S3 bucket with custom resources

As discussed in the introduction to CloudFormation in `Chapter 1`, *AWS Fundamentals*, it's common for there to be cases where you need more advanced behavior than what is available by default in CloudFormation. Before custom resources, this led AWS developers down the path of doing most of their automation in CloudFormation, and then running some **command-line interface** (**CLIs**) commands to fill in the gaps.

Fast forward to today, and the emerging pattern is to use a custom resource to delegate to an AWS Lambda function. Lambda can fill in the gaps by making API calls on your behalf. While it's also possible to create a custom resource that communicates with your custom code via a **Simple Notification Service** (**SNS**), and a compute resource such as an **Elastic Compute Cloud** (**EC2**) instance, Lambda should be your first choice.

In this section, you will learn how to build a custom resource that creates an Amazon **Simple Storage Service** (**S3**) bucket, and then populates that bucket with test data. It's a simple example that might not be terribly useful, but it serves to demonstrate the basic concepts. Once you have mastered the technique, you will surely come up with some more creative uses for custom resources.

How to do it...

Follow these steps to create a lambda function, and a custom resource that makes use of that function, in order to create an S3 bucket:

1. Log in to your account, and go to the **Lambda** console.
2. Click **Create function**, and choose the **Author from scratch**.
3. Give your function a unique, descriptive name.
4. Choose **Node.js 8.10** as the **Runtime**:

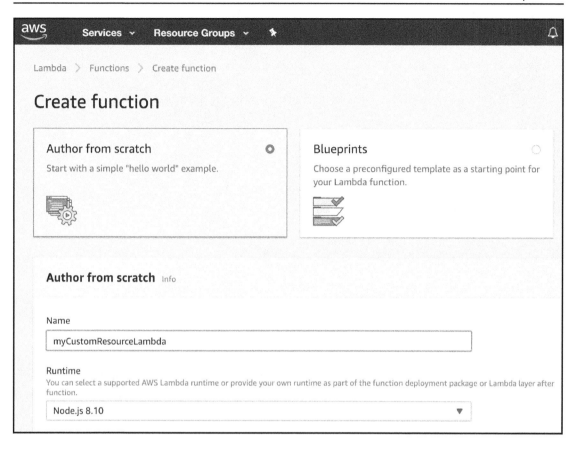

The Lambda console allows you to author a function from scratch, or choose from a variety of templates

5. Create a custom role by clicking on the IAM console link. A new screen opens, where you can create the role that will be associated with the lambda function. Give it a descriptive name.

6. Click **Edit** to customize the policy. You need to give the lambda function permissions to write to CloudWatch logs, and also give it permission to administer the S3 bucket. Paste in the following code:

```
{
    "Version": "2012-10-17",
    "Statement": [
        {
            "Effect": "Allow",
            "Action": [
                "logs:CreateLogGroup",
                "logs:CreateLogStream",
```

```
                              "logs:PutLogEvents"
                ],
                "Resource": "arn:aws:logs:*:*:*"
            },
```

7. Continue with the statement that provides the S3 permissions:

```
    {
        "Effect": "Allow",
        "Resource": [
            "arn:aws:s3:::*",
            "arn:aws:s3:::*/*"
        ],
        "Action": [
            "s3:CreateBucket",
            "s3:DeleteBucket",
            "s3:PutObject",
            "s3:DeleteObject"
        ]
    }
    ]
}
```

8. Click **Allow**, in order to associate the new role with the lambda function.

9. Back on the **Lambda** console, click **Create function**, and paste the following code into the function code editor for index.js. This code sample continues over several blocks. Start with the required imports and constants:

```
/**
 * This is a custom resource handler that creates an S3 bucket
 * and then populates it with test data.
 */

var aws = require("aws-sdk");
var s3 = new aws.S3();

const SUCCESS = 'SUCCESS';
const FAILED = 'FAILED';
const KEY = 'test_data.csv';
```

10. Continue with the definition of the handler function:

```
exports.handler = function(event, context) {

    console.info('mycrlambda event', event);
    // When CloudFormation requests a delete,
    // remove the object and the bucket.
    if (event.RequestType == "Delete") {
```

```
        let params = {
            Bucket: event.ResourceProperties.BucketName,
            Key: KEY
        };
```

11. Continue with the code that implements a delete request:

```
s3.deleteObject(params, function(err, data) {
        if (err) {
            console.log(err, err.stack);
            sendResponse(event, context, FAILED);
        } else {
            console.log('Deleted object', data);
            let params = {
                Bucket: event.ResourceProperties.BucketName
            };
            s3.deleteBucket(params, function(err, data) {
                if (err) {
                    console.log(err, err.stack);
                    sendResponse(event, context, FAILED);
                } else {
                    console.log("Deleted bucket", data);
                    sendResponse(event, context, SUCCESS);
                }
            });
        }
    });
    return;
}
```

12. We don't take any action for an update:

```
if (event.RequestType == "Update") {
    // Nothing to do here
    sendResponse(event, context, SUCCESS);
    return;
}

var params = {
    Bucket: event.ResourceProperties.BucketName
};
```

13. Create the bucket in response to a create request:

```
s3.createBucket(params, function(err, data) {
    if (err) {
        console.log(err, err.stack);
        sendResponse(event, context, FAILED, data);
```

```
            } else {
                console.log('Created bucket ' +
                    event.ResourceProperties.BucketName);
                // Now that we have created the bucket, populate it with test
data
                params = {
                    Body: '1,\"A\"\n2,\"B\"\n3,\"C\"',
                    Bucket: event.ResourceProperties.BucketName,
                    Key: KEY
                };
                s3.putObject(params, function(err, data) {
                    if (err) {
                        console.log(err, err.stack);
                        sendResponse(event, context, FAILED, data);
                    } else {
                        console.log('Created object test_data.csv');
                        sendResponse(event, context, SUCCESS, data);
                    }
                });
            }
        });
};
```

14. Declare the following function to send responses back to the S3 signed URL, which is monitored by CloudFormation:

```
/**
 * Send a response to the signed URL provided by CloudFormation.
 */
function sendResponse(event, context, status, data) {

    var body = JSON.stringify({
        Status: status,
        Reason: "",
        PhysicalResourceId: context.logStreamName,
        StackId: event.StackId,
        RequestId: event.RequestId,
        LogicalResourceId: event.LogicalResourceId,
        Data: data
    });
```

15. Continue the sendResponse function:

```
console.log("body:\n", body);

var https = require("https");
var url = require("url");
```

```
var parsedUrl = url.parse(event.ResponseURL);
var options = {
    hostname: parsedUrl.hostname,
    port: 443,
    path: parsedUrl.path,
    method: "PUT",
    headers: {
        "content-type": "",
        "content-length": body.length
    }
};
```

16. End the function by making the HTTPS request:

```
var request = https.request(options, function(response) {
        console.log("response.statusCode: " +
            response.statusCode);
        console.log("response.headers: " +
            JSON.stringify(response.headers));
        context.done();
    });
    request.on("error", function(error) {
        console.log("sendResponse Error:" + error);
        context.done();
    });
    request.write(body);
    request.end();
}
```

17. Click **Save** to the function. Copy the **Amazon Resource Name** (**ARN**) at the top right of the screen:

Copy the function ARN

18. Now that you have created a lambda function that will execute your custom logic, go to the **CloudFormation** console.

19. Create a file on your filesystem (the name doesn't matter, but you should give it a .yaml extension) with the following content:

```
AWSTemplateFormatVersion: "2010-09-09"
Parameters:
    MyFunctionArn:
      Type: String
      Description: The ARN of the lambda function
    MyBucketName:
      Type: String
      Description: The name of the bucket to create
Resources:
  MyCustomResource:
      Type: Custom::CreateBucketWithData
      Version: "1.0"
      Properties:
        ServiceToken: !Ref MyFunctionArn
        BucketName: !Ref MyBucketName
```

20. In the **CloudFormation** console, click **Create Stack**. Select **Upload a template to Amazon S3**, and upload the file.

21. Give the stack a unique name, and paste the ARN from the function that you created earlier into the **MyFunctionArn** parameter textbox. In the **MyBucketName** parameter textbox, enter a globally unique name for the bucket that is to be created by your lambda function:

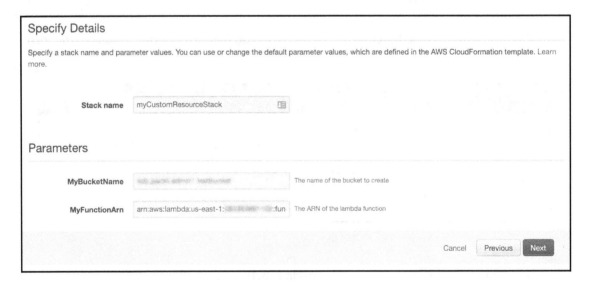

Stack details

22. Click through the next two screens, and then click **Create**. It might take a few minutes for the stack to finish. You can watch its progress on the **CloudFormation** console.

23. Once the stack is complete, go to the **S3** console to confirm that the custom resource has successfully created the bucket, and the test data file within the bucket:

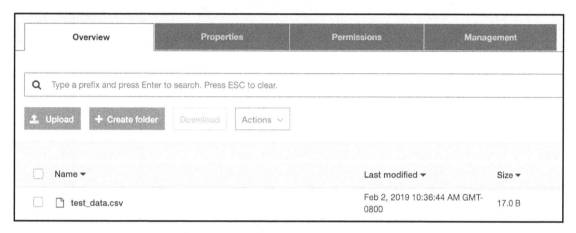

Bucket overview screen

24. Delete the stack and the lambda function, so that you are left with a clean environment. This will avoid any unexpected costs in the future.

How it works...

Whenever you create, update, or delete a stack with an embedded custom resource, CloudFormation uses the ARN that you supply as a parameter to communicate with your lambda function. This ARN is referred to as the service token. The execution of the stack waits for a response from your code, but that response is asynchronous, so CloudFormation needs a way to poll for the result of the operation.

This is where S3 comes into the picture.

In your custom lambda code, when you have determined that the operation has succeeded or failed, you must report the status back to CloudFormation via a signed S3 URL, or your stack will be stuck with a CREATE_IN_PROGRESS status:

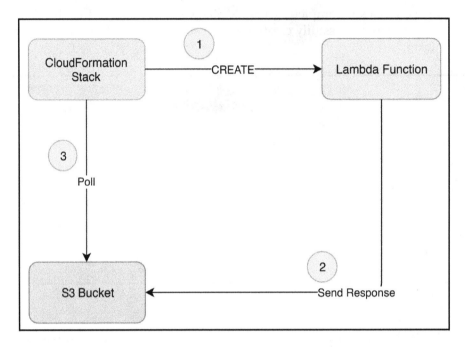

The process flow between CloudFormation, Lambda, and S3

When CloudFormation receives the response status back from Lambda, it can then continue with the stack creation if your operation succeeded, or start a rollback if your operation failed. Note that the S3 bucket in the previous diagram is the bucket that is managed by CloudFormation, not a bucket that we created ourselves. The CloudFormation management bucket serves as an **inter-process communication (IPC)** mechanism.

There's more...

In this recipe, we entered our code directly into the **Lambda** console. While this is OK for learning exercises, for production code, you should investigate the **Serverless Application Model** (**SAM**), and AWS CodeCommit. SAM provides a simplified template syntax for creating applications that are based on lambda functions, and CodeCommit is a Git-compatible distributed version control system. It's best practice to always store your code in version control, so that you can easily compare revisions, and share code with your peers.

 SAM is an open source project that is documented here: `https://docs.aws.amazon.com/serverless-application-model/latest/developerguide/what-is-sam.html`.

Using a macro to create an S3 bucket for CloudTrail logs

A CloudFormation macro is a transformation that allows you to create your own shorthand, in order to inject snippets into your templates. You probably already know a little bit about macros—`AWS::Include` and `AWS::Serverless` are both macros that are hosted by CloudFormation. Now, you have the ability to write your own macros, and with some creativity, you will find that this can be a very powerful tool to add to your arsenal as an AWS administration guru.

In this recipe, you will create a simple macro that allows you to configure an AWS CloudTrail auditing trail, and a bucket to hold the audit logs, all in just a few short lines of YAML. Similar to the last recipe on custom resources, you will create a lambda function in order to implement the macro transformation.

How to do it...

Follow these steps in order to create a lambda function, and a macro that uses that function to transform your template, before launching the stack:

1. Log in to your AWS account, and go to the **Lambda** console.
2. Click **Create function** and **Author from scratch**.
3. Give the function a descriptive name.
4. Choose **Python 3.6** as the **Runtime**.
5. Choose to **Create a Custom Role**. A new screen opens, where you can create the role that will be associated with the lambda function. Give it a descriptive name:

Edit the policy document for the new Lambda execution role

6. Click **Edit** to customize the policy. You need to give the lambda function permissions to write to CloudWatch logs, and to create a CloudTrail, and also give it permission to administer the S3 bucket. Paste in the following code:

```
{
    "Version": "2012-10-17",
    "Statement": [
        {
            "Effect": "Allow",
            "Action": [
                "logs:CreateLogGroup",
                "logs:CreateLogStream",
                "logs:PutLogEvents"
            ],
            "Resource": "arn:aws:logs:*:*:*"
        },
```

7. Continue with the S3 permissions:

```
{
    "Effect": "Allow",
    "Resource": [
        "arn:aws:s3:::*",
        "arn:aws:s3:::*/*"
    ],
    "Action": [
        "s3:CreateBucket",
        "s3:DeleteBucket",
        "s3:PutObject",
        "s3:DeleteObject"
    ]
},
```

8. And finally, add CloudTrail permissions to the policy:

```
{
    "Effect": "Allow",
    "Resource": "*",
    "Action": [
        "cloudtrail:*"
    ]
}
    ]
}
```

9. Click **Allow** in order to associate the new role with the lambda function.
10. Back on the **Lambda** console, click **Create function**:

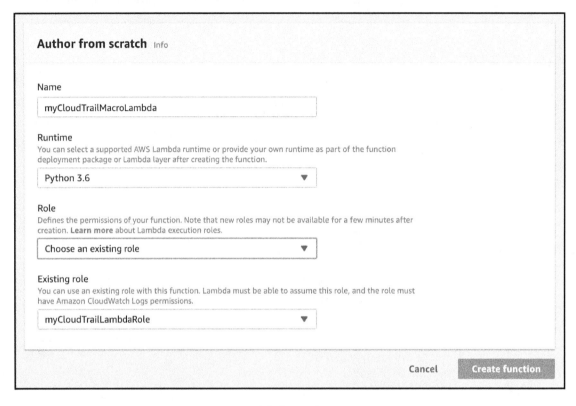

Author from scratch

11. Paste the following code into the function code editor for `index.js`. Note that this code sample continues over several blocks:

```
"""
Lambda Handler for the CloudTrailBucket macro.

This macro transforms a resource with type "CloudTrailBucket" into
a bucket, a bucket policy, and a CloudTrail configuration that logs
activity to that bucket.
"""

def lambda_handler(event, _):
    "Lambda handler function for the macro"

    print(event)
```

12. Continue by inspecting the fragment for the bucket name:

```
# Get the template fragment, which is the entire
# starting template
fragment = event['fragment']

bucket_name = None

# Look through resources to find one with type CloudTrailBucket
for k, r in fragment['Resources'].items():
    if r['Type'] == 'CloudTrailBucket':
        r['Type'] = 'AWS::S3::Bucket'
        r['DeletionPolicy'] = 'Retain'
        bucket_name = k
```

13. Create the policy for the bucket (note that this code fragment is broken up over several entries):

```
bucket_policy = {
    "Type" : "AWS::S3::BucketPolicy",
    "Properties" : {
        "Bucket" : {"Ref" : bucket_name},
        "PolicyDocument" : {
            "Version": "2012-10-17",
            "Statement": [
                {
                    "Sid": "AWSCloudTrailAclCheck",
                    "Effect": "Allow",
                    "Principal": {
                        "Service":"cloudtrail.amazonaws.com"
                    },
```

14. Continue with the following code:

```
                    "Action": "s3:GetBucketAcl",
                    "Resource": {
                        "Fn::Join" : [
                            "", [
                                "arn:aws:s3:::", {
                                    "Ref": bucket_name
                                }
                            ]
                        ]
                    }
                },
```

15. Continue with the following code:

```
    {
        "Sid": "AWSCloudTrailWrite",
        "Effect": "Allow",
        "Principal": {
            "Service":"cloudtrail.amazonaws.com"
        },
        "Action": "s3:PutObject",
        "Resource": {
            "Fn::Join" : [
                "", [
                    "arn:aws:s3:::", {
                        "Ref": bucket_name
                    },
                    "/AWSLogs/",
                    {
                        "Ref":"AWS::AccountId"
                    }, "/*"
                ]
            ]
        },
```

16. Finish the policy with this code:

```
        "Condition": {
            "StringEquals": {
                "s3:x-amz-acl": "bucket-owner-full-control"
            }
        }
    }
            ]
        }
    }
}
```

17. Complete the transformation of the fragment and return it:

```
if bucket_name:
    # Add the policy to the fragment
    fragment['Resources'][bucket_name + 'BucketPolicy'] = bucket_policy

    # Create the trail and add it to the fragment
    trail = {
        'DependsOn' : [bucket_name + 'BucketPolicy'],
        'Type' : 'AWS::CloudTrail::Trail',
        'Properties' : {
            'S3BucketName' : {'Ref': bucket_name},
```

```
            'IsLogging' : True
        }
    }
    fragment['Resources'][bucket_name + 'Trail'] = trail

# Return the transformed fragment
return {
    "requestId": event["requestId"],
    "status": "success",
    "fragment": fragment,
}
```

18. Go to the **CloudFormation** console, where you will create two new stacks. The first stack creates the macro as a named resource in your account, and this can be used in any future template.

19. Paste the following code into a file on your filesystem:

```
AWSTemplateFormatVersion: "2010-09-09"
Description: "This template creates the macro"
Parameters:
  FunctionArn:
    Type: String
Resources:
  CloudTrailBucketMacro:
    Type: AWS::CloudFormation::Macro
    Properties:
      Name: CloudTrailBucket
      FunctionName: !Ref FunctionArn
```

20. Select **Upload a template to Amazon S3**, and choose the file that you just created. Click **Next**, and give the stack a name.

21. Paste in the function ARN of the Lambda function that you created earlier in this recipe.

22. Click **Next**, and then **Next** on the following screen.

23. Click **Create**. It may take a few minutes for the stack to be created. Wait until the status is **CREATE_COMPLETE**, before continuing.

24. Now you will create a new (second) stack that makes use of the macro. Go back to the **CloudFormation** console, and click **Create stack**.

25. Paste the following code into a file on your filesystem:

```
AWSTemplateFormatVersion: "2010-09-09"
Transform: CloudTrailBucket
Description: "This template will be transformed by the macro"
Resources:
  MyCloudTrailBucket:
    Type: CloudTrailBucket
```

26. Select **Upload a template to Amazon S3**, and choose the file that you just created. Click **Next**, and give the stack a name.

27. Click **Next**, and **Next** on the following screen.

28. You will notice that the final confirmation screen is different than what you normally see when you create a stack. Since a macro is transforming your template, you will, instead, be creating and executing a change set:

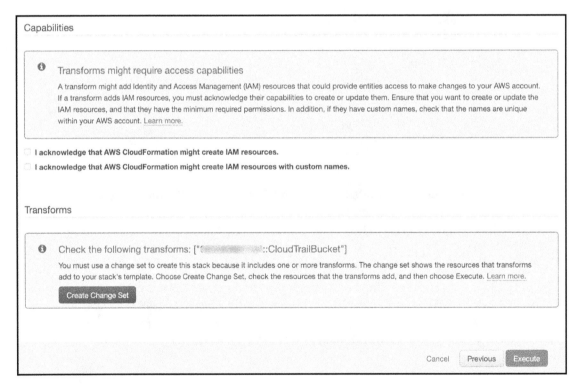

Stack confirmation screen

29. Check the boxes in order to acknowledge that IAM resources will be created in this stack.

30. Click **Create Change Set**. You will get a summary of the resources that will be created:

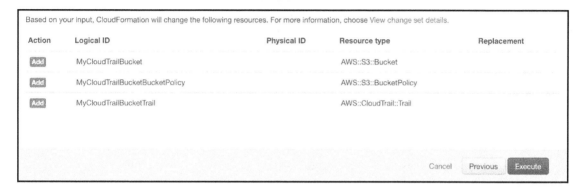

Based on your input, CloudFormation will change the following resources. For more information, choose View change set details.

Action	Logical ID	Physical ID	Resource type	Replacement
Add	MyCloudTrailBucket		AWS::S3::Bucket	
Add	MyCloudTrailBucketBucketPolicy		AWS::S3::BucketPolicy	
Add	MyCloudTrailBucketTrail		AWS::CloudTrail::Trail	

Cancel   Previous   Execute

Create a change set

31. Click **Execute** in order to launch the stack.

32. Once the stack is complete, go to the **CloudTrail** dashboard, and click **View Trails**. You should see your new trail, along with the newly created bucket name:

Trails

Deliver logs to an Amazon S3 bucket. CloudTrail events can be processed by one trail for free. There is a charge for processing events with additional trails. For more information, see AWS CloudTrail Pricing.

Create trail

Name	Region	Organization trail	S3 bucket	Log file prefix	CloudWatch Logs Log group	Status
myCloudTrailBucketStack -MyCloudTrailBucketTrail- 1XQQS51YN5968	US East (N. Virginia)	No	mycloudtrailbucketst ack-mycloudtrailbuc ket-bf8yqwecopwv			✓

CloudTrail dashboard

33. Click through to the S3 bucket, and inspect the contents. It may take a few minutes for the new audit logs to show up.

34. Delete the stack to clean up the resources from this recipe.

How it works...

Macros are actually a very simple concept—take the contents of a template, pass them to a lambda function as a string, and do string manipulation on the contents in order to replace or add elements. Then, the Lambda function passes the altered contents back to CloudFormation, and the stack is executed as if it had been originally written with the new content.

You created a global resource in your account by using the `AWS::CloudFormation::Macro` resource, which you linked to a custom lambda function. You then created a stack that makes use of that macro in order to expand a very short and simple template into a much more complex set of resources.

In this recipe, what we have done is to replace this code:

```
AWSTemplateFormatVersion: "2010-09-09"
Transform: CloudTrailBucket
Description: "This template will be transformed by the macro"
Resources:
  MyCloudTrailBucket:
  Type: CloudTrailBucket
```

We replaced it with this:

```
AWSTemplateFormatVersion: '2010-09-09'
Resources:
  MyCloudTrailBucket:
    Type: AWS::S3::Bucket
    DeletionPolicy: Retain
  MyCloudTrailBucketBucketPolicy:
    Type: AWS::S3::BucketPolicy
    Properties:
      Bucket:
        Ref: MyCloudTrailBucket
      PolicyDocument:
        Version: '2012-10-17'
        Statement:
        - Sid: AWSCloudTrailAclCheck
          Effect: Allow
          Principal:
            Service: cloudtrail.amazonaws.com
          Action: s3:GetBucketAcl
          Resource:
            Fn::Join:
            - ''
            - - 'arn:aws:s3:::'
              - Ref: MyCloudTrailBucket
```

```
    - Sid: AWSCloudTrailWrite
      Effect: Allow
      Principal:
        Service: cloudtrail.amazonaws.com
      Action: s3:PutObject
      Resource:
        Fn::Join:
        - ''
        - - 'arn:aws:s3:::'
          - Ref: MyCloudTrailBucket
          - "/AWSLogs/"
          - Ref: AWS::AccountId
          - "/*"
      Condition:
        StringEquals:
          s3:x-amz-acl: bucket-owner-full-control
MyCloudTrailBucketTrail:
  DependsOn:
  - MyCloudTrailBucketBucketPolicy
  Type: AWS::CloudTrail::Trail
  Properties:
    S3BucketName:
      Ref: MyCloudTrailBucket
    IsLogging: true
```

There's more...

Once you grasp the concept of a CloudFormation macro, you will start to see all of the many ways that macros can be used in order to simplify and standardize the templates that you create in your AWS account.

Here are a few ideas to get you started:

- Create a macro that allows you to embed custom Python or JavaScript code directly into a template.
- Create a shorthand library of resources that are easier to type when authoring templates.
- Standardize the creation of resources, such as S3 buckets, so that your compliance guidelines are met with little extra effort.

- Expand on the built-in functions, such as `Fn::Join` and `Fn::Sub`, in order to create a rich library of string manipulation for use in your templates.
- Combine several resources, with complex dependencies, into a single easy-to-use macro resource. For example, create a private S3 bucket to host a static website, configure an Amazon CloudFront distribution to make the content public, and add a custom domain in Amazon Route 53.

See also

- See the AWS documentation on macros for more details: `https://docs.aws.amazon.com/AWSCloudFormation/latest/UserGuide/template-macros.html`

Using mappings to specify regional AMI IDs

The mappings section is used to define a set of key/value pairs. If you require any kind of AWS region portability, perhaps for **disaster recovery** (**DR**) or availability purposes, or simply to get your application closer to your end user, you'll almost certainly need to specify some mappings in your template. This is particularly necessary if you are referencing anything in your template that is region specific.

The canonical example would be to specify a map of EC2 AMI IDs in your template. This is because AMIs are a region-specific resource, so a reference to a valid **Amazon Machine Image** (**AMI**) ID in one region, will be invalid in another. In this recipe, you will create a CloudFormation stack that allows a user to choose between an instance with Linux or Windows.

How to do it...

Follow these steps to launch an EC2 instance with an AMI ID that matches your region:

1. Go to the **CloudFormation** console, and click **Create stack**.
2. Save the following code to a file on your filesystem:

```
AWSTemplateFormatVersion: "2010-09-09"
Description: Demonstrate CloudFormation Mappings
Parameters:
  OperatingSystem:
    Description: The operating system to run for the instance
    Type: String
```

```
         Default: Linux
         AllowedValues:
            - Linux
            - Windows
         ConstraintDescription: Must be Linux or Windows
     Mappings:
       RegionMap:
         us-east-1:
            Linux: ami-035be7bafff33b6b6
            Windows: ami-0df43b4f8a07c7c14
         us-west-1:
            Linux: ami-0799ad445b5727125
            Windows: ami-06b499097655a3ab5
     Resources:
       MyEC2Instance:
         Type: AWS::EC2::Instance
         Properties:
            ImageId:
              !FindInMap
                - RegionMap
                - !Ref "AWS::Region"
                - !Ref OperatingSystem
            InstanceType: t2.micro
```

3. Select **Upload a template to Amazon S3**, and choose the file that you just created. Click **Next**, and give the stack a name.

4. Click **Next**, and then **Next** on the following screen.

5. Click **Create**.

6. Go to the **EC2** dashboard to confirm the creation of the EC2 instance with the correct AMI.

7. Delete the stack.

How it works...

Mappings are simply dictionaries of name-value pairs, which allow you to make decisions based on variables such as which region the stack is being created in, or whether the environment is in production or development. You use the `Fn::FindInMap` function to access the contents of the mapping. Mappings have two levels of keys; there is a first level that has keys according to a top-level item, such as regions, and then a second level that allows you to define multiple subkeys, such as the operating system type in our previous example.

There's more...

This recipe creates a simple EC2 instance, but, by default, it does not configure an SSH key, or a security group that would allow you to log in remotely. We will cover these options in a later chapter, but if you are curious, go ahead and investigate the `AWS::EC2::SecurityGroup` resource type, and the `KeyName` property of the `AWS::EC2::Instance` resource. Another option for securely logging in to your EC2 instance is AWS Systems Manager Session Manager, a relatively new service that directly gives you a shell login to Linux instances via the AWS console.

See also

- The *Using StackSets to deploy resources to multiple regions* recipe in this chapter, for one of the most common uses of mappings
- See `Chapter 4`, *AWS Compute*, for a more detailed introduction to EC2 instances

Using StackSets to deploy resources to multiple regions

If you have a CloudFormation template that you have authored in order to create resources in a single region, what happens when you want to deploy those same resources into another region, or even another account? You could manually create the stacks, or you could string together a few CLI scripts to do the job for you; but, there's a better way.

StackSets allow you to deploy a template across multiple regions and accounts, in a way that is fully managed by CloudFormation.

Getting ready

Before you can use StackSets, you must establish an account to be the administrator account, and then you must create roles in the administrator account and in the target accounts. In this recipe, you will deploy to a second region, rather than a second account, but those roles still must exist.

The roles *must* have the following names:

- AWSCloudFormationStackSetAdministrationRole
- AWSCloudFormationStackSetExecutionRole

Consult the AWS documentation for details on how to create these roles: https://docs. aws.amazon.com/AWSCloudFormation/latest/UserGuide/stacksets-prereqs.html.

You can create a stack with the following YAML, in order to create these roles in your account.

```
AWSTemplateFormatVersion: '2010-09-09'
Description: Deploys required roles for Stack Sets
Resources:
    AWSCloudFormationStackSetAdministrationRole:
        Type: AWS::CloudFormation::Stack
        Properties:
            TemplateURL:
https://s3.amazonaws.com/cloudformation-stackset-sample-templates-us-east-1
/AWSCloudFormationStackSetAdministrationRole.yml
            TimeoutInMinutes: '3'
    AWSCloudFormationStackSetExecutionRole:
        Type: AWS::CloudFormation::Stack
        Properties:
            TemplateURL:
https://s3.amazonaws.com/cloudformation-stackset-sample-templates-us-east-1
/AWSCloudFormationStackSetExecutionRole.yml
            TimeoutInMinutes: '3'
            Parameters:
                AdministratorAccountId : !Ref "AWS::AccountId"
```

Make sure that you take the time to fully understand how these roles work, since misconfiguration can allow the cross-account role to have more privileges than intended.

How to do it...

Follow these steps to launch a stack in multiple regions:

1. Log in to the AWS console and select the **N. Virginia (us-east-1)** region.
2. Take note of your account ID in the account dropdown in the menu bar.
3. If you haven't completed the previous recipe, do so now, and retain the YAML file on your filesystem. We will use that same template in the following step.
4. Go to the **CloudFormation** console, and click **StackSets**, then **Create StackSet**.
5. Upload the template file from the previous recipe.
6. Give the stack a descriptive name, and choose an operating system:

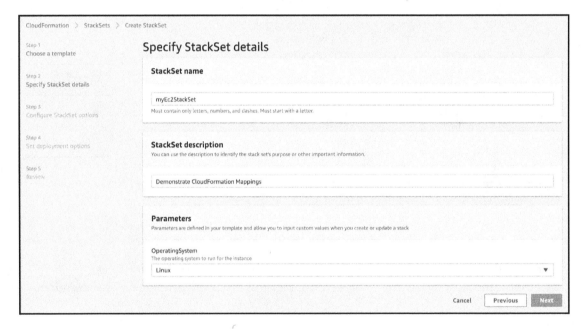

StackSet details

7. Click **Next**, and then select the role that is to be used for the administration of the StackSet:

CloudFormation > StackSets > Create StackSet

Step 1
Choose a template

Step 2
Specify StackSet details

Step 3
Configure StackSet options

Step 4
Set deployment options

Step 5
Review

Configure StackSet options

Tags

You can specify tags (key-value pairs) to apply to resources in your stack. You can add up to 50 unique tags for each stack

Key	Value	Remove

Permissions

Choose an IAM role to explicitly define how CloudFormation will manage your target accounts. If you don't choose a role, CloudFormation uses permissions based on your user credentials. **Learn more.**

IAM admin role ARN - optional
Choose the IAM role for CloudFormation to use for all operations performed on the stack.

| IAM role name ▼ | AWSCloudFormationStackSetAdministrationRole ▼ | Remove |

⚠ AWS CloudFormation will use this role for all stack operations. Other users that have permissions to operate on this stack will be able to use this role, even if they don't have permission to pass it. Ensure that this role grants least privilege.

IAM execution role name

AWSCloudFormationStackSetExecutionRole

IAM execution role name can include letters (A-Z and a-z), numbers (0-9), and select special characters (+=,.@-_) characters. Maximum length is 64 characters.

Cancel   Previous   **Next**

StackSet options

8. Click **Next**. On the following screen, you will configure the deployment options for the StackSet.
9. Select **Deploy stacks** in accounts, and paste in your account number.

10. Under **Specify regions**, select **US East (N. Virginia)** and **US West (N. California)**:

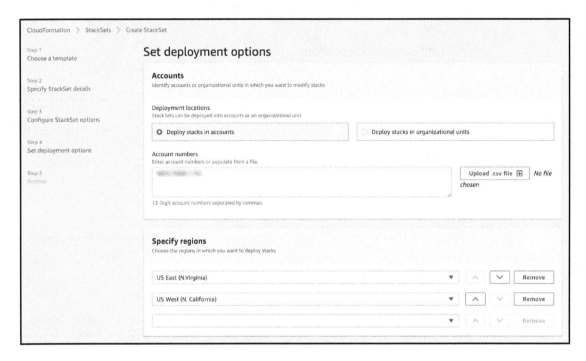

StackSet deployment options

11. Click **Next**, then **Submit**. Wait for the StackSet creation to complete.
12. Go to the **Stack instances** tab in order to see the instances that were created:

Stack instances

13. Go to the **EC2** console in each region in order to confirm that the EC2 instances were created.
14. In order to clean up the resources that were created in this recipe, go back to the **CloudFormation** console, and select the **StackSet**.
15. Select **Delete stacks from StackSet** from the **Actions** drop-down menu.
16. Enter the same configuration information as you did in steps 9-10, in order to specify the account and regions from which to delete stacks.
17. Click **Next**, then **Submit**. Wait until the delete operation finishes.
18. Now that the stacks are deleted, select **Delete StackSet** from the **Actions** drop-down menu.

How it works...

StackSet management is done from an administrator account, and stacks within the StackSet are created in target accounts. The target account, as in this recipe, can be the same as the administrator account. A trust relationship must exist between these accounts, since the administrator account needs the right to create resources in the target accounts. CloudFormation assumes the AWSCloudFormationStackSetAdministrationRole role, which gives it permissions to assume the AWSCloudFormationStackSetExecutionRole role in the target accounts. By default, that role allows all administrative actions, so, in a production setting, you should scope the execution role down to only those actions that are needed in order to create your stack instances. In order to make sure only the administrator account can assume the execution role, an explicit trust relationship is established back to the administrative account.

Check out the AWS documentation for a detailed description of the security prerequisites: `https://docs.aws.amazon.com/AWSCloudFormation/latest/UserGuide/stacksets-prereqs.html`.

There's more...

Here are a few tips to help you to get the most out of the StackSets feature:

- When you design templates that will be used to launch stacks across multiple regions and accounts, keep in mind the specific capabilities of each individual region, since not all services are deployed to all regions. And keep naming conflicts in mind when provisioning resources such as IAM roles or S3 buckets. It's best practice not to give explicit names to resources in templates; rather, you should allow CloudFormation to assign unique names, and then use stack outputs and cross-stack references in order to get the names when you need them.
- Start small with your StackSets, deploying to one region at a time at first, in order to observe whether or not the stacks are successfully created, before deploying to a large number of regions or accounts.
- As with stacks themselves, splitting your StackSets into multiple, smaller templates can make administration much easier. Divide and conquer!

See also

- Chapter 8, *AWS Account Security and Identity*

Detecting resource drift from templates with drift detection

It is best practice to manage your AWS environment using CloudFormation for all new resources, and for all subsequent changes to these resources. If you sidestep CloudFormation, and make a manual change to a resource, then the template and the actual resource have drifted. Drift can cause all manner of problems when you go to make changes to the CloudFormation stack in the future.

In this recipe, you will learn about a new feature of CloudFormation—drift detection.

How to do it...

Follow these steps in order to create a DynamoDB table, and then observe the drift after you have used the console to make a manual configuration change to the table:

1. Paste the following code into a file on your filesystem. Give it a `.yaml` extension:

```yaml
AWSTemplateFormatVersion: "2010-09-09"
Resources:
  SimpleDynamoDBTable:
    Type: AWS::DynamoDB::Table
    Properties:
      AttributeDefinitions:
        -
          AttributeName: "Id"
          AttributeType: "S"
      KeySchema:
        -
          AttributeName: "Id"
          KeyType: "HASH"
      BillingMode: PAY_PER_REQUEST
Outputs:
  TableName:
    Description: Drift Detection Example Table
    Value: !Ref SimpleDynamoDBTable
```

2. Go to the **CloudFormation** console, and click **Create stack**.

3. Select **Upload a template to Amazon S3**, and choose the file that you just created. Click **Next**, and give the stack a name.

4. Click **Next**, and then **Next** on the following screen.

5. Click **Create**.

6. Once the stack has completed, go to the **Outputs** tab, and note the name of the table.

7. Go to the **DynamoDb** dashboard, and view the tables.

8. Select the table that you just created:

A DynamoDB table

9. Now, you are going to introduce drift to your stack, by making a change to the table configuration. Select the **Indexes** tab.

10. Create a new index on an attribute called `Name`:

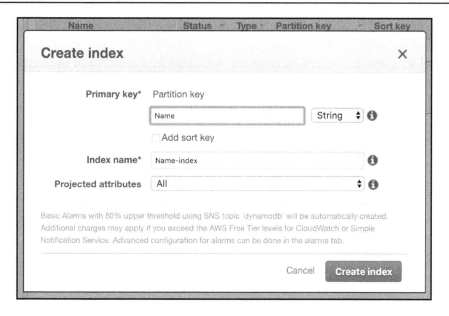

Create a DynamoDB index via the console

11. Once the status on the new **Global Secondary Index** (**GSI**) is active, go back to the **CloudFormation** dashboard, and select the stack.

12. Select **Detect drift** from the **Actions** drop-down menu:

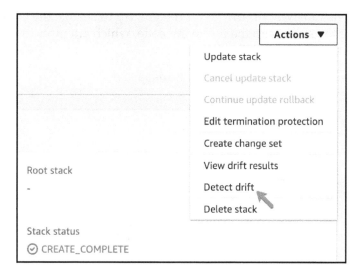

Detect drift

13. You should be able to refresh the page, and see that the stack's **Drift status** has changed to **DRIFTED**.

14. Select **View drifts results** from the **Actions** menu in order to see a report that describes the detected drift:

A drifted stack

15. To demonstrate why the drift is a problem, try to change the billing mode, by updating the stack with the following code, which attempts to add the same index to the table:

```
AWSTemplateFormatVersion: "2010-09-09"
Resources:
 SimpleDynamoDBTable:
 Type: AWS::DynamoDB::Table
 Properties:
 AttributeDefinitions:
 -
 AttributeName: "Id"
 AttributeType: "S"
 - AttributeName: "Name"
 AttributeType: "S"
 KeySchema:
 -
 AttributeName: "Id"
 KeyType: "HASH"
 BillingMode: PAY_PER_REQUEST
```

```
GlobalSecondaryIndexes:
    -
    IndexName: "Name-index"
    KeySchema:
    -
    AttributeName: "Name"
    KeyType: "HASH"
    Projection:
    ProjectionType: "ALL"
Outputs:
    TableName:
    Description: Drift Detection Example Table
    Value: !Ref SimpleDynamoDBTable
```

16. Choose **Actions Update Stack**.
17. Select **Replace the current template**, and upload the new file.
18. Click **Next** until you reach the final confirmation screen, and then click **Update Stack**.
19. After a few moments, the stack will fail:

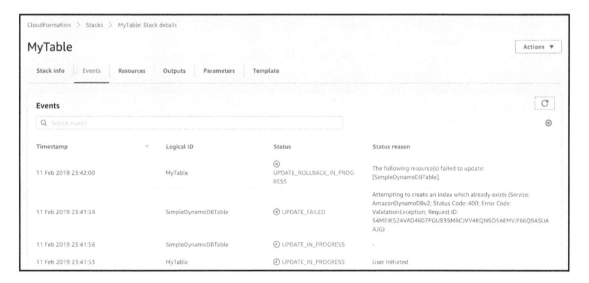

A failed stack update

20. Drift detection will not fix the problem for you. It only points out that there is a problem, and it's up to you to fix it.
21. Go back to the **DynamoDB** console, and delete the index.

22. Go back to the **CloudFormation** dashboard, and repeat steps 16-18.
23. This time, the stack update will succeed, since the table properties match what CloudFormation expects, based on the prior version of the template.

How it works...

CloudFormation does not maintain a two-way connection with underlying resources. When it comes down to it, CloudFormation only concerns itself with the template as it is written. If you make a change to a resource outside of CloudFormation, your next stack update could go badly, since CloudFormation might attempt to re-create a resource that is already there.

The drift detection feature was added in order to make it easier to spot the differences between your template and the actual resources. At this time, there is strictly a visual tool to help you to identify the resources that need to be manually altered back, in order to match the template. Once there is no drift, then you can safely apply the changes in the template in order to reproduce what someone did manually.

But wait. I'm sure that you are wondering, *What if I detect drift in a resource that is not easy to roll back, such as a database?* Well, that's why you should try *really, really hard* never to introduce drift in the first place. CloudFormation may someday support the notion of resource adoption, but for the time being, your only recourse is to roll back, and get things to the way that CloudFormation expects them to be.

There's more...

There are a few more things to keep in mind regarding drift detection:

- Unsupported resources and properties
- Using the CLI

Unsupported resources and properties

Keep in mind that drift detection does not currently support all resources, and, for the resources it does support, not all properties can be successfully identified. If you get in the habit of making all changes via CloudFormation templates, then hopefully you won't need this feature at all. But, if you do need it, it's worth taking some time to read up on its limitations.

Using the CLI

Drift detection can, of course, be viewed from the CLI:

```
  🗐    bash - "ip-172-31 ×    ⊕
$ aws cloudformation detect-stack-drift --stack-name MyTable
{
    "StackDriftDetectionId": "a9501bb0-2e58-11e9-9187-0eee516a945a"
}
$ aws cloudformation describe-stack-drift-detection-status --stack-drift-detection-id a9501bb0-2e58-11e9-9187-0eee516a945a
{
    "StackId": "arn:aws:cloudformation:us-east-1:          :stack/MyTable/b724bec0-2e54-11e9-8402-0e1e9f06bbc4",
    "StackDriftDetectionId": "a9501bb0-2e58-11e9-9187-0eee516a945a",
    "StackDriftStatus": "DRIFTED",
    "Timestamp": "2019-02-11T23:56:34.411Z",
    "DetectionStatus": "DETECTION_COMPLETE",
    "DriftedStackResourceCount": 1
}
$ ▮
```

Drift detection with the CLI

Use the `detect-stack-drift` and `describe-stack-drift-detection-status` commands in order to view the drift status of a stack.

See also

- `Chapter 6`, *Managing AWS Databases*, for more on DynamoDB
- `Chapter 4`, *AWS Compute*, for more on EC2

11
AWS Well-Architected Framework

In this chapter, you will learn about the AWS Well-Architected Framework, which was developed by AWS based on years of working with customers to help them build secure, highly performant, and reliable systems. You will be introduced to the five pillars of the framework: security, operational excellence, performance efficiency, reliability, and cost optimization. You will also learn how to conduct a basic assessment of your technology, and then take your architecture to the next level with the Well-Architected Tool.

The quality of your architecture is ultimately reflected by the experience your customers will have while using your applications and services. No user wants a site that goes down frequently, exposes their private information, or costs them too much money. Use the wisdom that's passed down in the Well-Architected Framework to learn how to follow industry best practices and keep your customers happy.

In this chapter, we will cover the following recipes:

- Understanding the five pillars of the Well-Architected Framework
- Conducting a technology baseline review self-assessment
- Using The Well-Architected Tool to evaluate a production workload

Understanding the five pillars of the Well-Architected Framework

The AWS Well-Architected Framework is divided into five pillars that cover the gamut from security to operations and providing best practice guidelines for all aspects of developing and maintaining a solution in the cloud. Each of the pillars is described at length in a whitepaper that is available to download from the AWS site: `https://aws.amazon.com/architecture/well-architected/`.

Security

Security should be considered *job zero* when designing a cloud architecture. It should be the first consideration you take, not the last – which is unfortunately too often the case. If securing your infrastructure is an inconvenient afterthought, it will be difficult, if not impossible, to keep your customer data safe and private.

The security pillar of the Well-Architected Framework focuses on protecting *systems* and *information*. *Systems* are the physical and virtual resources that you have provisioned in your IT environment, and *information* is the data that flows throughout those systems.

The foundation of any secure platform is **Identity and Access Management (IAM)**. You must be able to reliably authenticate your users, and once you know exactly who they are, you must provide mechanisms to authorize users to limit what they're allowed to do. The same applies to applications that require access.

Never hardcode credentials into your application code or into configuration files! One of the most common causes for data breaches comes from passwords or API keys that are checked into the source code. Use things such as cross-account roles, EC2 instance profiles, and AWS Secrets Manager to work around use cases where you might be tempted to use hardcoded access keys.

A best practice for securing your cloud system is to adopt a policy of zero trust. Zero trust means that even when data is flowing between servers behind your firewall, on your internal network, you still apply stringent security measures. It helps to be a little paranoid and assume that a bad actor is on your network, watching everything that happens, and looking for a way to infiltrate further. An example of zero trust is encrypting communications between your web servers and your database server, regardless of the fact that they are sitting on your internal network.

One exception to this rule is network traffic that is flowing to and from your EC2 instances. Due to the design of the hypervisor, it is impossible for a third party to sniff that traffic. Unlike a traditional network where a sniffer running in promiscuous mode can see everything, the hypervisor prevents the delivery of packets to anywhere but the target. Regardless, many compliance regimes require all traffic to be encrypted, and it's still good practice.

With Amazon CloudTrail, it's possible to leave an audit trail that details every action taken within your account in all regions. If a security event occurs, auditors must have rapid access to log files that can help them find out who the culprit is, and how they broke in.

Always enable CloudTrail and send the logs to an S3 bucket in a *different* account, accessible only to security auditors. Placing the audit trails in a different security domain means that an attacker will have a harder time covering their tracks.

Simulate security events frequently so that your operations team can practice incident response. When you identify patterns in those responses, automate them so that a human is not required to deal with the situation. This will improve consistency and time to response. An example of this is automatically responding to an S3 bucket being made public – instead of simply sending an email to an administrator to alert them to the problem, write a Lambda function that flips the bucket back to private immediately.

 To learn more about the security pillar, read the official whitepaper: `https://d1.awsstatic.com/whitepapers/architecture/ AWS-Security-Pillar.pdf`.

Operational excellence

The operational excellence pillar is often overlooked, and even in companies that have a good grasp of architectural principles, this is an area that needs improvement. The key to operational excellence is to design your systems with operations in mind from day one. Just like with the security pillar, where we must not wait until after the application is built to consider it, we have to make sure what we are constructing is *operable*.

When you add a new feature to your application, ask yourself these questions:

- How will I know if users are using the new feature?
- What are the **Key Performance Indicators** (**KPIs**) that tell me if the feature is working well?
- Are there any alerts that I should send to the operations team if this feature is not working as intended?
- Are there automated tests in place to make sure new code changes do not break this feature?
- Is the feature documented thoroughly for both internal and external users?
- Is the data that's generated by this feature available to a reporting team for detailed analysis?

A feature is not *done* when just the code for the feature itself is complete. All of those aspects must be considered before calling it done and shipping it to production.

Another critical aspect of operational excellence is to adopt **Infrastructure as Code** (**IaC**). In Chapter 1, *AWS Fundamentals*, you were introduced to AWS CloudFormation, which allows you to construct your resources using JSON or YAML files, instead of logging in to the console and creating them manually, or via the **command-line interface** (**CLI**). IaC allows you to rapidly spin up new environments for development, testing, and disaster recovery. Treating infrastructure as code also allows you to adopt best practices from the software development industry, such as revision control and code reviews.

When you experience an operational failure, don't sweep it under the rug and pretend it never happened. Write a detailed report about exactly what happened, why it happened, what the root cause was, and how you solved it. Document the measures you took to make sure it never happens again, and then share that data with everyone in your organization. We all fail at some point. All systems, both human and machine, are fallible. Expect failure, prepare for it, and learn from it.

One of the best ways to prepare for operational events is to conduct what is called a **game day**. Take a copy of your infrastructure, assign your operations team to monitor it, and then purposefully throw them curveballs to see how they react. What happens if you stop a critical EC2 instance? How will they react if you misconfigure a security group and your web servers are no longer accessible? Can they recover from a faulty software release? The only way to know is to test your team frequently, document the results, and make changes to improve your performance.

There will come times when you are facing a problem that you can't solve alone. AWS support is a fantastic resource that you should take advantage of to help you solve problems with your infrastructure.

 At a bare minimum, purchase a Business Support contract on all production accounts!

Business Support gives you full access to AWS Trusted Advisor and is an invaluable resource that can identify cost savings so significant that it more than makes up for the support fees. And even more critical than that, a Business Support contract gives you a very short **service-level agreement** (**SLA**) so that when you need help, you can get someone on the line quickly.

The most common support call you will make is to increase your service limits. AWS sets soft limits on many resources to protect customers from accidentally provisioning too many resources and waking up to a huge bill. When you hit those limits, your application can grind to a halt. Without business support, you might not be able to meet the SLA with your customers to get them back up and running in an acceptable time period.

Operational excellence is the key to providing your customers with a smooth, consistent experience. It's an area where you are never really done – there are always more things to learn and improvements to make, so keep studying the best practices and keep looking for ways to enhance your operational readiness.

 To learn more about the operational excellence pillar, see the official white paper: https://d1.awsstatic.com/whitepapers/architecture/AWS-Operational-Excellence-Pillar.pdf.

Performance efficiency

On its surface, this pillar is all about speed. It's a well-known fact that website performance has a huge impact on user adoption. Just a few milliseconds can be the difference between a happy user and someone who abandons your site for a competitor.

But the performance efficiency pillar of the Well-Architected Framework goes further than that. It covers the efficient use of computing resources, and how to keep your systems performing at their best as the technology landscape changes and as user demand fluctuates. This pillar is closely related to cost optimization because, in some cases, it's possible to be over-provisioned and paying for resources that you don't need. An efficient system does not necessarily have to be as fast as possible; instead, it should be as fast as it needs to be, using the most optimal resources to accomplish the task at hand.

One of the easiest ways to improve your application's performance and take advantage of the latest technologies is simply to make use of cloud services. AWS offers many services directly related to performance, such as Amazon CloudFront, that would be very difficult for a small technical team to implement on their own. Serverless architectures powered by AWS Lambda offer configurable performance rungs and scalable compute resources at a fraction of the cost of self-hosting your own code on machines that you provision.

With AWS, it's easy to choose the perfect tool for the job to maximize performance. For example, you can experiment with a variety of NoSQL databases, such as Amazon DynamoDB, and compare performance to more traditional databases such as PostgreSQL running on Amazon Aurora. CloudWatch dashboards make it easy to chart your performance so that you can make more informed choices.

Performance efficiency is one of those topics that requires a lot of data so that it can inform us of the best decisions we can make. Make sure that your applications are instrumented to log as much data as possible with regard to performance. Automate your responses to applications that are performing poorly. For example, if a cluster of web servers running on EC2 is struggling to keep up with the load, configure an Auto-Scaling Group to automatically provision new servers until performance falls in line with expectations.

There are EC2 instance types to cover almost every possible performance scenario. Since many applications haven't evolved to containers or serverless functions yet, it is very important for an AWS administrator to understand the plethora of options available. The following is a quick summary of the main EC2 instance types:

- **General-purpose**: These are the go-to instance types that can handle most typical workloads, and are as follows:
    - **A1**: ARM-based AWS Graviton processors.
    - **T3**: Next-generation burstable instances for spiky workloads.
    - **M5**: The latest generation of standard, general-purpose instances. This should be the default starting point for most applications.
- **Compute-optimized**: Choose one of these types if your application has excessive CPU requirements:
    - **C5**: The standard instance type for cost-effective compute-intensive workloads
    - **C5n**: Similar to C5, but with up to 100 Gbps networking
- **Memory-optimized**: If your application eats a ton of RAM, choose an instance from this category:
    - **R5**: Configure an instance for up to 768 GiB.
    - **X1e**: These instances are made specifically for high-performance databases with extreme memory requirements and attached solid-state disks.
    - **High memory**: If you run a large SAP HANA installation, choose this instance to configure up to a whopping 12 TiB per machine!
    - **Z1d**: The Z family offers the highest core frequency available at the time of writing, that is, 4.0 GHz.

- **Accelerated computing**: Many machine learning tasks require access to **Graphical Processing Units (GPUs)**:
    - **P3**: The latest generation of GPU instances, offering the best bang for your buck currently offered by any provider.
    - **F1**: A few specific types of machine learning algorithms perform better with the **field-programmable gate arrays (FPGAs)** provided by this instance type.
- **Storage-optimized**: Choose an instance from this category if the main requirement of your application is hard drive space and disk I/O performance:
    - **H1**: Up to 16 TB of local HDD storage for high-throughput use cases that utilize spinning disks.
    - **I3**: This family offers **Non-Volatile Memory Express (NVMe)** drives for high IOPS at a relatively low cost.
    - **D2**: These instances have the best cost-to-throughput ratio for spinning hard drives, with one 48 TB HDD per instance.

Like any architecture, you should conduct extensive experiments with different instance types under production-equivalent loads to make sure you have made the correct choice.

> This is by no means an exhaustive list. See the official AWS documentation for the complete current list of instances, which evolves rapidly: https://aws.amazon.com/ec2/instance-types/.

Of course, there is much more to optimizing performance than choosing the correct instance type, especially if you have moved on to serverless architectures. Evaluate your storage and networking needs, experiment, gather data, and continually refine your choices as the landscape evolves.

> For more information on the performance efficiency pillar, see the official white paper: https://d1.awsstatic.com/whitepapers/architecture/AWS-Performance-Efficiency-Pillar.pdf.

Reliability

The reliability pillar has a number of crossovers with the operational excellence pillar. We live in a 24/7 world, and users expect applications to be available at all hours, running at full capacity. The reliability pillar of the AWS Well-Architected Framework focuses on techniques and practices that can help you achieve a zero-downtime infrastructure.

When we speak of reliability, be it uptime for a web server or the durability of saved data, we usually speak in terms of *nines*. For example, Amazon S3 offers a staggering 11 nines of durability for stored objects. That's 99.999999999% durability, which is made possible by storing redundant copies throughout a region in various **Availability Zones** (**AZs**). Several services offer SLAs that guarantee a certain amount of uptime, such as Amazon DynamoDB, which offers five nines (99.999%) of uptime for global tables.

How exactly does that break down? Let's take five nines and see what this means in terms of time per week. In a single week, we have the following:

*7 Days * 24 = 168 Hours * 60 = 10,080 Minutes * 60 = 604,800 Seconds*

99.999% of 604,800 seconds leaves us with 6 seconds of total downtime each week.

You have probably heard many vendors bragging that their service has five nines or better, but in reality, it is extremely difficult to achieve. It means there are only 6 seconds throughout an entire week, or 5 minutes per year, that a request to your application will fail due to an outage. And this includes scheduled maintenance!

To achieve levels of reliability anywhere close to five nines, it's obvious that you are going to need a lot of redundancy, because software and hardware fail all the time. It's just a fact of life. When you are running thousands of servers, something is almost always broken. The only way to hide that brokenness from your users is to double, and triple-up on everything so that when the inevitable single failure happens, there is always a backup standing by to take its place.

And this brings us to another concept, called **single point of failure**. Many architectures take care to replicate common resources such as web servers, but what about the router? The firewall? The database? A chain is only as strong as its weakest link. Be sure to inspect every component of your system to make sure you haven't forgotten something that doesn't have any redundancy.

Deploying changes to an environment without downtime can be an extremely difficult problem to solve. For most traditional, monolithic applications, users had to get used to scheduled downtime for maintenance, be that a monthly OS patch update or a weekly new software build. The application is taken offline, changes are applied, and everyone crosses their fingers and hopes for the best when it comes back online. Software updates are almost always to blame when a complex software system has unexpected downtime.

Here are a few strategies that can help you to achieve zero-downtime updates:

- **Blue-green deployments**: Spin up a copy of your workload that is behind an alternate URL. The test is thorough, and when it is ready, swap it out with the prior version so that the new copy (blue) is now live and the old copy (green) is no longer in use. If you see errors in the new deployment with live traffic, simply swap them again to roll back.
- **Canary deployments**: Spin up a new copy of your workload and start by sending small amounts of live traffic to it. If there are no errors, ramp up traffic until the new copy has all the traffic.
- **Feature flags**: Deploy hidden features that can be rolled out slowly and rolled back if needed via configuration at runtime.
- **Schema-less databases**: Traditional relational databases often require downtime for significant schema changes, which are inevitable in any evolving application. Using a database with a flexible schema system, such as Amazon DynamoDB, can mitigate this issue.

The key to any reliable system is testing. Test everything, before and after it is put into production. Automate as much of your testing as possible so that your tests can be run quickly and efficiently every time a change is applied.

In the cloud, it's possible to run your tests with production amounts of data and traffic since it's inexpensive to spin up resources for a short-lived test. One of the key principles of the reliability pillar is to stop guessing about your necessary capacity. Use data to inform your decisions about the resources you provision.

Use auto-scaling for any resource that offers it, such as EC2 and DynamoDB. Configure thresholds for expanding and contracting resources so that you are always using exactly as much as you need for the current workload.

Finally, don't forget to analyze your dependencies. It doesn't matter how reliable your system is if it has a dependency on a separate system that is not reliable. If you can't control the reliability of the dependency, implement a queue or a batch so that the dependency is not in real time.

This pillar also crosses over with cost optimization, since a fully redundant system operating at five nines can be quite expensive! You might need to make some trade-offs to supply your users with a system that has acceptable levels of downtime, such as three nines (roughly 8 hours of downtime per year), in exchange for a more affordable service.

As we mentioned in several chapters in this book, service limits are often a surprising way to experience downtime and an excellent reason to maintain a Business Support contract so that you can quickly get someone on the phone to bump up your soft limits in case you reach capacity. Soft limits are there to protect you from accidentally over-provisioning resources and waking up to an expensive bill. But if you forget about them, they will cause downtime. Have a strategy for studying limits, raising them where appropriate, and monitoring your resources so that you know how much ceiling you have left at any given time.

 Refer to the official AWS white paper for more information: `https://d1.` `awsstatic.com/whitepapers/architecture/AWS-Reliability-Pillar.` `pdf.`

Cost optimization

Most conversations about migrating to the cloud start with cost savings. Although, in reality, it's not the most compelling reason to move to the cloud, it's definitely the first thing on the minds of executives who are making the decisions and writing the checks. In an environment where you can spin up thousands of new resources in minutes at the click of a button, you can just as easily run up a high bill if you aren't careful.

Study the cost optimization pillar of the AWS Well-Architected Framework to learn how to be careful.

If you have just started researching a move to the cloud and you have done a few simple back-of-the-napkin calculations, you may be scratching your head and wondering where the reported cost savings of the cloud are coming from. Optimizing an infrastructure for costs is not something that comes easily, just like it's not easy to create a compelling and useful application that users enjoy. It takes continuous effort and diligent study of all the options available to you, and you will need to move beyond simply doing a lift-and-shift of your on-premises applications to EC2 instances by administrators who have only a superficial understanding of AWS.

In the *Performance efficiency* section, we reviewed the different EC2 instance families. As we know, choosing the right one will make a huge difference in your costs. But there are more than 140 services now offered by AWS, and EC2 is only one of them! Learning the service landscape and finding components that you can offload from instances is where the real cost savings start to happen. And for applications that still require EC2, learning about how purchasing reserved instances or bidding on spot instances can save you significant amounts of money is crucial.

When calculating your **Total Cost of Ownership** (**TCO**) in the cloud, don't forget to add human resources to the cloud resources you have provisioned. Some roles change, some go away, and some are replaced by completely new functions that you need to understand in order to paint the entire picture when it comes to the money you are spending to support a workload.

> Use the TCO calculator to compare the costs of on-premises applications to running those applications in the cloud: `https://aws.amazon.com/tco-calculator/`.

Use automation to shut down resources that you don't need, especially if you have parts of your application that are not in use 24 hours per day. A perfect example of this is development environments and servers that are used for testing. When a developer creates a web-based IDE using AWS Cloud9, the environment is configured to automatically hibernate after it has gone unused for a specified amount of time. If you use AWS CodeBuild as your build environment, containers are only in use for the amount of time that it takes to complete the build. This is a huge advantage over on-premises development environments, where all of those resources require a big upfront investment and continuous maintenance.

It's possible to categorize your AWS resources using tags. You can use resource tags to allocate costs to various departments. Ideally, you should implement some sort of chargeback system so that business owners are responsible for their portion of the cloud infrastructure.

Make use of AWS Trusted Advisor to identify areas where you are spending money on underutilized resources. Upgrade to a Business Support contract on all production accounts so that you can enjoy the full benefits that the Trusted Advisor has to offer. Support is one service you definitely don't want to skimp on. The **Cost Optimization** screen in Trusted Advisor is worth its weight in gold. If you don't have a Business Support contract, valuable information is not available to you, as shown in the following screenshot:

Upgrade your support plan!

Do your best to estimate your future charges on AWS, but in the end, the only way to know exactly what an actual, running workload will cost is to test it. With automation features such as **Infrastructure as Code** (**IaC**) offered by AWS CloudFormation, you can quickly spin up a test environment, run it for a short period of time to test your applications and gauge your costs, and then tear it down just as quickly.

To dive into all the many ways you can optimize your costs on AWS, read the official white paper: `https://d1.awsstatic.com/whitepapers/architecture/AWS-Cost-Optimization-Pillar.pdf`.

Conducting a technology baseline review self-assessment

Later in this chapter, we will walk through a full Well-Architected review, which is an extremely beneficial exercise, but the process can seem daunting if you are new to AWS. In this recipe, you will conduct what is known as a **Technology Baseline Review** (**TBR**) – a self-assessment of your technology that is quick and easy to accomplish. You will ask yourself, and your team, a series of basic questions about your architecture that capture the essence of the Well-Architected Framework. These are the most critical elements to have in place, and you should only give yourself a passing score if you end up with 100% affirmative answers.

 Be completely honest when you conduct a self-assessment! You can't improve if you gloss over areas where you are weak and pretend you are in better shape than you actually are.

How to do it...

Ask yourself the following questions, answer honestly, and make it a priority to resolve any questions where the answer is *no*:

1. Do you have Business Support or greater enabled on all production accounts?
2. Do you use IAM users or federated users instead of the root user login for routine access to your account?
3. Do you have IAM users or some sort of user federation in place?
4. Have you enabled **Multi-Factor Authentication** (**MFA**) on the root account?
5. Have you enabled AWS CloudTrail on all accounts and in all regions?
6. Are you storing all CloudTrail logs in a separate administrative domain (a separate AWS account or equivalent)?
7. Is the CloudTrail log storage tamper-resistant?
8. Have you enabled MFA on all interactive IAM accounts?

9. Are you rotating all IAM user credentials regularly?
10. Have you configured a strong password policy for your users?
11. Does each user have their own dedicated IAM or federated user account?
12. Are IAM policies for users and applications scoped down to the least privilege?
13. Do you have any hardcoded credentials?
14. Are all stored credentials encrypted at rest?
15. Are you regularly backing up your data?
16. Are you testing data recovery on a regular schedule, and after any significant application changes?
17. Do you have a **Recovery Point Objective (RPO)** and **Recovery Time Objective (RTO)** defined for your services?
18. Is your RTO less than 1 day for all critical services?
19. Is your **Disaster Recovery (DR)** plan tested regularly, and after all significant application changes?
20. If any of your S3 buckets have public access, has this access been reviewed to make sure it is necessary, and are controls in place to limit access to data that should not be public?
21. Are your buckets that should not be public configured correctly to prevent public access?
22. Do you have monitoring in place to alert you if a bucket is made public?
23. If you require access to customer accounts, do you use cross-account roles instead of IAM users?

Did you answer *no* to any of those questions? If so, you could be placing your business and your customers at risk.

How it works...

These questions were pulled from the AWS Well-Architected Framework and are considered the absolute minimum threshold for what is considered secure, reliable, performant, cost-efficient, and operationally excellent.

This list is based on years of experience working with customers and partners, and each of the questions represents the possibility of serious consequences if you don't pay attention to it. The history of the internet is rife with examples of companies that have gone out of business overnight due to a hacker gaining access to cloud resources, or a failed database resulting in a complete loss of customer data.

Here's one scenario to consider regarding the disaster recovery questions: what would happen to your company if a hacker gained access to your root access credentials, logged in to your production account, and proceeded to delete everything? What if your backups and audit logs were deleted from that account? Even a robust multi-AZ database setup with cross-region replication of backup files is not going to help you if every resource in the account is deleted. If you wake up one morning and find that your account is simply destroyed, can you recover? Will you still be in business the next day?

The answer to that question should be a confident *yes*!

The response to that absolute worst-case scenario should not only be rehearsed, but it should also be fully automated. By the way, I didn't just make up that scenario to scare you. It has happened many times, both on-premises and on cloud systems. More often than not, it's a disgruntled employee with administrator privileges who has gone rogue, but whether it's an employee or a hacker, the results are the same.

By following the recommendations of the technology baseline review, you can make that scenario much less likely, and even if it does happen, you can be confident in your ability to recover from it.

Once you have made the necessary changes to pass this review with a 100% score, you are ready to dive deeper into the Well-Architected Framework to make even more improvements to your cloud-based applications.

There's more...

The baseline technology review process is an integral part of the **AWS Partner Network (APN)**. If your company aspires to become a member of the APN as a technology partner, you will need to pass a baseline review as part of advancement through the APN tiers and as part of achieving designations such as technical competencies.

If you want to learn more about the APN, check it out at the following URL: `https://aws.amazon.com/partners/`. For more information about the baseline process, see `https://aws.amazon.com/partners/technical-baseline-review/`. Also, you can see the author in a video series about baseline reviews here: `https://www.youtube.com/watch?v=oCkcOxx96-Y`.

If your company provides a SaaS solution on top of AWS, creates **Amazon Machine Images (AMIs)** for commercial purposes, or provides consulting services to companies building on AWS, then you should definitely look into joining the APN!

Using the Well-Architected Tool to evaluate a production workload

AWS recently added the Well-Architected Tool to the AWS console. This is a tool that has been used for years behind the scenes at AWS by solutions architects to conduct detailed reviews with customers and partners. It is now available directly to you, and if you take the time to walk your team through a careful and honest assessment, it can provide valuable insights into ways you can improve your architecture.

How to do it...

Follow these steps to conduct a review on one of your workloads:

1. Gather executives, architects, senior developers, and/or any other key personnel who have knowledge about the workload under review.
2. Log in to your AWS account, select the **AWS Well-Architected Tool** from the **Management Tools** category, and then click **Define workload**:

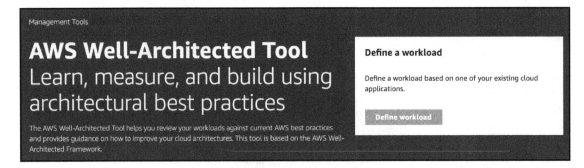

AWS Well-Architected Tool

3. On the next screen, define the properties of the workload:
   - Workload name
   - Description
   - Industry type
   - Environment
   - Regions
   - Account IDs

A workload is an application or a closely related set of components that work together to create some sort of business value. It's up to you to decide how to separate one workload from another for the purposes of a well-architected review.

4. Click **Define workload**, and on the next screen, click **Start review**.
5. Each pillar is divided into a set of questions by topic. Each topic has a list of statements and resources to help you evaluate those statements, as follows:

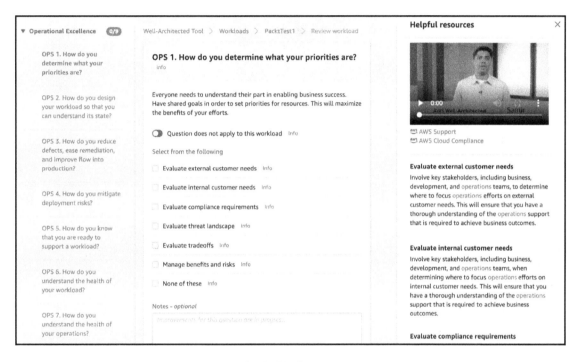

Operational Excellence topic 1

6. Each of the checkboxes represents various facets of the question that's being asked in the current topic. Check the boxes that apply to your workload. Be wary about simply clicking **Question does not apply to this workload** if you are unsure about the answers. Most topics do apply to all workloads in some way, and there is a big difference between *does not apply* and *I don't know*. If you don't know, check **None of these** so that the topic can be flagged as an area for improvement.

7. Click the **Info** link next to each statement if you are not sure how to respond. Keep the Well-Architected white papers handy for reference.

8. Use the **Notes** box to document the details about your workload as it pertains to this topic. The notes can help provide context for anyone who receives a copy of the completed review.

9. Click **Next** to move on to the next topic.

10. When you reach the last topic of the last pillar, click **Save and exit**.

11. Back on the **Review Summary** screen, click the **Save milestone** to save the results of the review at this point in time. You will be able to make changes to the workload review as you improve your architecture:

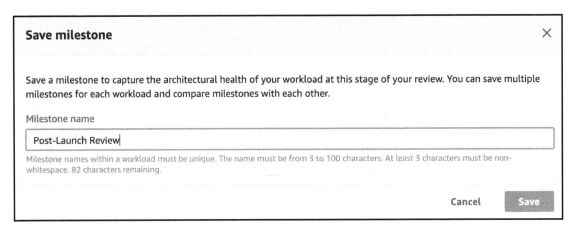

Save milestone screen

12. Click the **Improvement plan** tab to see a summary of areas that need improvement:

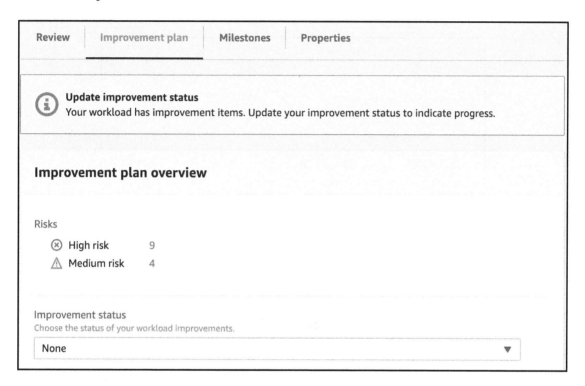

Improvement plan overview screen

13. Scroll down the page to drill into the details for the areas for improvement. As you can see in the following screenshot, the tool has flagged **OPS 7** as a critical remediation item:

OPS 7. How do you understand the health of your operations?

⊗ High risk

▼ Recommended improvement items

- **Identify key performance indicators**
- **Define operations metrics**
- **Collect and analyze operations metrics**
- **Establish baselines for operations metrics**
- **Learn expected patterns of activity for operations**
- **Alert when operations outcomes are at risk**
- **Alert when operations anomalies are detected**
- **Validate the achievement of outcomes and the effectiveness of KPIs and metrics**
- **Resources from partners**

A high-risk topic

14. Click one of the links under **Recommended improvement items** to get more information about it:

Define operations metrics

Define operations metrics to measure the achievement of KPIs. Define operations metrics to measure the health of operations and its activities. Evaluate metrics to determine if operations are achieving desired outcomes, and to understand the health of the operations.

🗎 Publish custom metrics
🗎 Searching and filtering log data
🗎 Amazon CloudWatch metrics and dimensions reference

Collect and analyze operations metrics

Perform regular proactive reviews of metrics to identify trends and determine where appropriate responses are needed.

🗎 Using Amazon CloudWatch metrics
🗎 Amazon CloudWatch metrics and dimensions reference
🗎 Collect metrics and logs from Amazon EC2 instances and on-premises servers with the CloudWatch Agent

Links to more in-depth documentation

15. Go to the **Review** tab and click **Generate report**. Open the PDF after it finishes downloading to see a complete review of your responses.

How it works...

The AWS Well-Architected Tool pulls information together from the official white papers and from AWS documentation to provide a single place where you can catalog the architectural state of your workloads. The recommendations that are given are based on years of experience helping AWS customers to follow best practices while building systems that *their* customers can depend on.

A Well-Architected review that is all green, with no critical red flags or orange flags for recommended improvements, is the pinnacle of architectural prowess. It's not easy to get there, but with determination and persistence, it's absolutely possible.

There's more...

A few technology categories have what is known as a **Well-Architected Lens**, which is an additional white paper that gives details on best practices that are specific to that category. Some of them are as follows:

- **Serverless applications**: Learn how to optimize your serverless architectures that provide access to RESTful APIs, mobile backends, streaming, and other functionality that can be implemented using services such as AWS Lambda.
- **High-performance computing**: This lens covers applications that are deployed to high-throughput instances in clusters that provide access to tremendous amounts of computing power.
- **IoT (short for Internet of Things)**: Apply best practices when you deploy fleets of devices that interact with your cloud resources.

If your company is an AWS partner, and you have a high degree of proficiency with delivering Well-Architected reviews, you can apply to be a part of the Well-Architected Partner program. Your solutions architects will be called upon to conduct reviews of customer workloads as a supplement to the architects employed by AWS. This program gives partners a wealth of opportunities to help customers build secure, reliable, and performant products, and also acts as a solid foot in the door for consulting partners to gain trust with prospective clients. For more information about AWS Well-Architected Partner Program go to `https://aws.amazon.com/partners/well-architected-program/`.

12
Working with Business Applications

AWS offers a suite of products that can assist with routine office productivity tasks, such as document sharing, remote desktops, chat, and email. In this chapter, you will learn the basics of these services so that you can replace expensive on-premises resources with cloud-based alternatives.

In this chapter, we will cover the following recipes:

- Creating a place for employees to share files with WorkDocs
- Hosting desktops in the cloud and allowing users to connect remotely using WorkSpaces
- Giving your users a place to chat and conduct video calls with Chime
- Exploring the use of Alexa for Business
- Hosting your company's email with WorkMail

After completing the recipes in this chapter, you will be ready to move more of your important business applications to a consolidated cloud environment.

Creating a place for employees to share files with WorkDocs

Amazon WorkDocs is a cloud-based document storage service that integrates seamlessly with your operating system's file explorer. It allows you to share files and folders with coworkers, enables collaboration with inline feedback, and saves each version of your documents so you can retrieve old content that was inadvertently deleted.

How to do it...

Follow these steps to set up a WorkDocs site:

1. Log in to your AWS account and go to the WorkDocs dashboard.
2. Click **Get Started Now**, as shown in the following screenshot:

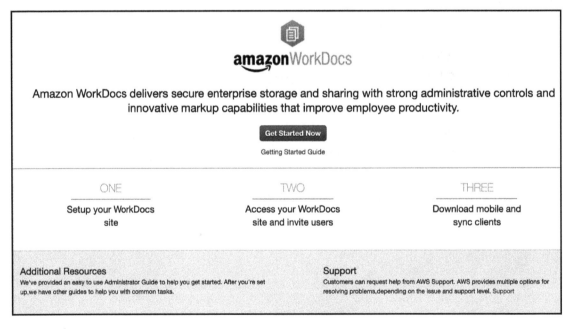

Amazon WorkDocs

3. Click on the **Launch** button to launch the **Quick Start**, as shown in the following screenshot:

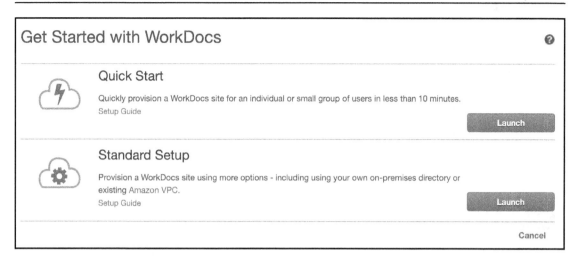

Get started with WorkDocs

4. Fill out the administrative details. Use a globally unique name for the **Site URL**. Do not include any special characters in the URL.

WorkDocs Access Point and Administrator

5. Click **Complete Setup**.

6. It will take up to 10 minutes for the site to be provisioned.

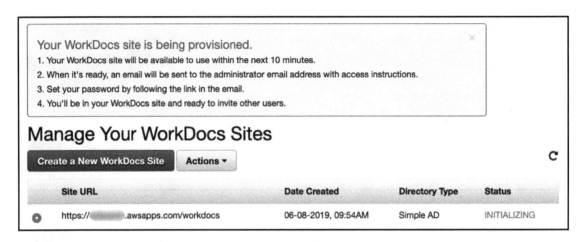

WorkDocs site initializing

7. When initialization is complete, you will receive an email from AWS, as shown in the following screenshot. Click the **Get Started!** button in the email:

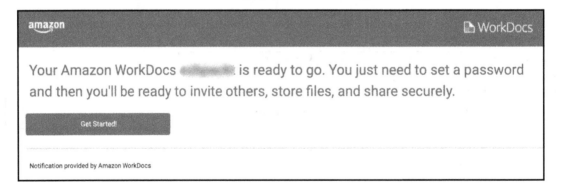

WorkDocs Get Started email

8. You will be redirected to a password creation screen. Set your password and click **Update User**.

9. The next screen you see will be the WorkDocs web interface:

WorkDocs welcome screen

10. Click the **Support** link in the upper-right corner and select **Apps**.
11. Under **DRIVE APP**, select your operating system to install a client that will present your WorkDocs drive as a folder on your machine.
12. Follow the installation instructions, start the application, and enter your WorkDocs **Site URL**. Log in with the credentials you created earlier and the drive should appear. If you are using macOS, you may need to make a security exception to allow the drive to be mounted.
13. Open the drive to see two folders, one for your documents and one for documents that are shared with you:

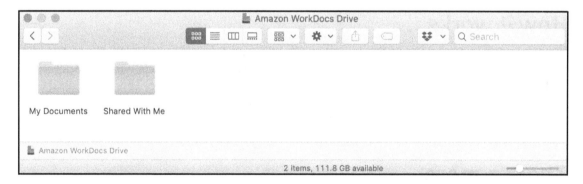

Amazon WorkDocs Drive

14. Go back to the WorkDocs web application, click the user icon in the upper-right corner, then click **Open admin control panel**.
15. Scroll to the bottom of the control panel and click **Invite users**.

16. Invite any additional users to the site by adding their email addresses, as shown in the following screenshot:

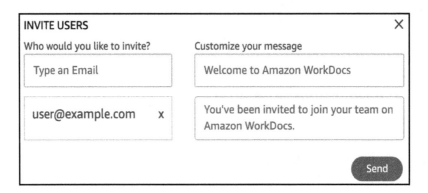

Invite WorkDocs users

At this point, you know the basics of how to create and administer a WorkDocs site to allow employees to easily collaborate and securely store their documents in the cloud. Be sure to delete the site if you no longer need it, to avoid future charges.

How it works...

WorkDocs takes advantage of the security, reliability, and durability of AWS cloud-based resources to provide its functionality. The installed drive client interacts with the operating system's filesystem API to mimic the look and feel of a mounted drive. This client sends files to and receives files from AWS in an asynchronous manner, usually within a few seconds of a file being created or changed.

There's more...

WorkDocs can be set up to integrate with your on-premises directory via AD Connector. You can also set it up with an AWS managed Microsoft Active Directory, which can be an important part of complying with security programs such as **Personal Credit Information (PCI)** or FedRAMP.

Users also have the ability to log in using **single sign-on** (**SSO**).

Multi-Factor Authentication (**MFA**) is also an option that can be used with WorkDocs. MFA is always a recommended option to increase the security of your user files.

Hosting desktops in the cloud and allowing users to connect remotely using WorkSpaces

You might find yourself in a situation where you need to equip a large group of new employees with specialized software, and the costs of installing and maintaining the software on local workstations are too high. This is a perfect use case for Amazon WorkSpaces. Instead of acquiring expensive hardware with high-end CPUs and lots of RAM, all you need is a basic desktop with an internet connection. WorkSpaces allows you to host desktops, with all of the necessary software, in the cloud. Users connect to a remote desktop that is managed for you by AWS and runs at a lower cost than on-premises.

How to do it...

1. Log in to your AWS account and go to the WorkSpaces dashboard.
2. Click **Get Started Now:**

Amazon WorkSpaces

3. Click on the **Launch** button to launch **Quick Setup**, as shown in the following screenshot:

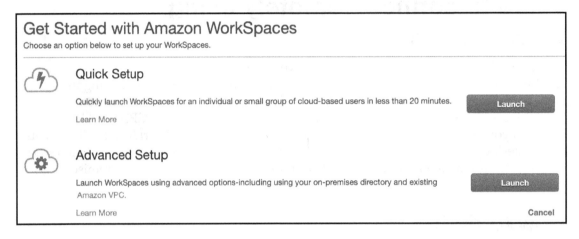

WorkSpaces Quick Setup

4. Select a **Bundle** that is in the free tier, such as **Standard with Amazon Linux 2**:

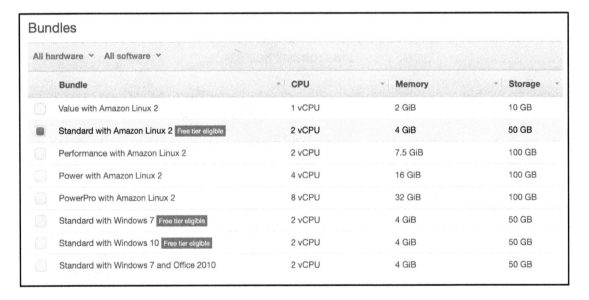

WorkSpaces Bundles

5. Enter the user details and then click **Launch WorkSpaces**:

Launch WorkSpaces

6. The WorkSpace will take a few minutes to initialize:

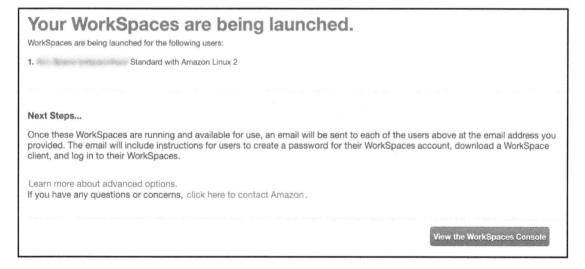

WorkSpaces being launched

7. Click **View the WorkSpaces console**:

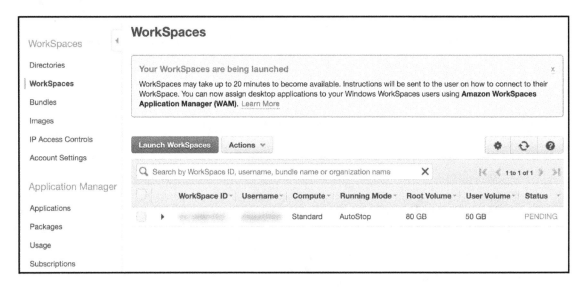

WorkSpaces Console

8. Under **Application Manager**, click **Applications**. You will be redirected to the Amazon **WorkSpaces Application Manager** (**WAM**) console.
9. Click **Get started building your catalog**.
10. Select the **WAM Lite** subscription plan:

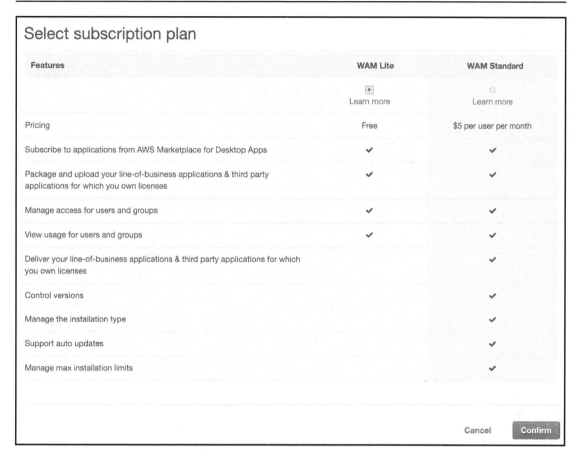

Features	WAM Lite	WAM Standard
	⦿ Learn more	○ Learn more
Pricing	Free	$5 per user per month
Subscribe to applications from AWS Marketplace for Desktop Apps	✔	✔
Package and upload your line-of-business applications & third party applications for which you own licenses	✔	✔
Manage access for users and groups	✔	✔
View usage for users and groups	✔	✔
Deliver your line-of-business applications & third party applications for which you own licenses		✔
Control versions		✔
Manage the installation type		✔
Support auto updates		✔
Manage max installation limits		✔

Select subscription plan

11. You will be redirected to the Marketplace, where you can select applications to be installed on your hosted desktops.
12. Check your email for the WorkSpaces welcome email. Once you have received it, follow the instructions to set a password and download the client.

13. Log in to the WorkSpaces client to launch your cloud desktop.

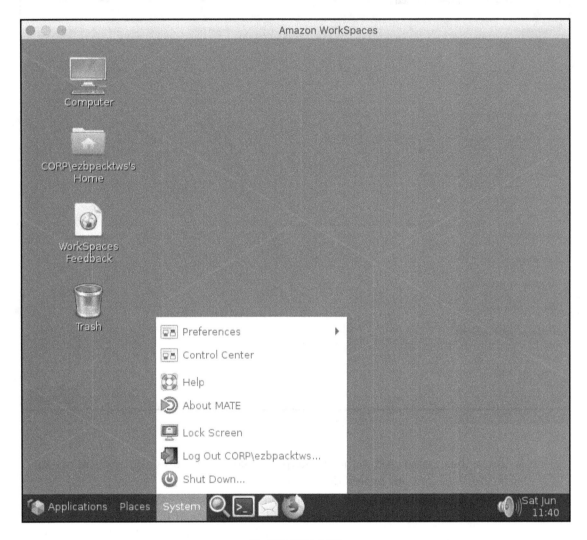

Amazon WorkSpaces desktop

At this point, you should be comfortable with the basics of Amazon WorkSpaces. Don't forget to delete the WorkSpace and any related resources, such as the user directory, in order to avoid future charges.

How it works...

WorkSpaces allows you to provision either Windows or Linux instances with a variety of software bundles available from the Marketplace. These desktops run on a cloud virtual machine so that users can disconnect and reconnect to the desktop without losing any data. Users are managed with a directory service, such as Simple AD or AWS managed Microsoft AD.

There's more...

There are a few more features that you should keep in mind:

- User logins can be secured with MFA.
- User data can be encrypted at rest with AWS **Key Management Service** (**KMS**) keys.
- User logins can be restricted to a specific IP range.
- Each WorkSpace has two **Elastic Network Interfaces** (**ENIs**), one of which is in your VPC to allow easy access to resources in that VPC.

Giving your users a place to chat and conduct video calls with Chime

Amazon Chime offers chat, instant messaging, and voice and video calling for employees on teams or across an entire organization. It has a web client, native applications for macOS and Windows, and mobile clients so that your team members can stay connected wherever they are. During video calls, users can share their screen to display presentations or any other applications running on their desktops.

How to do it...

In this recipe, you will learn how to create a new Chime account, configure a team, and add users to it:

1. Log in to your AWS account and go to the Chime dashboard.
2. Select **Accounts** from the left-hand menu:

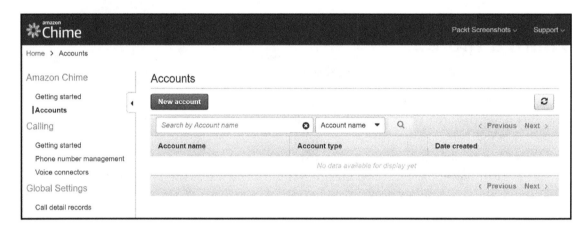

Chime Accounts

3. Click **New account**. Give the account a name—keep in mind that this name will be visible to your users.
4. Once the account is created, click the account name link:

Chime Team Users

5. At this point, you have created a team account. If you were to click on the **Domains** link on the left and configure a unique domain for your account, it would be automatically upgraded to an enterprise account with extra features. For the purposes of this recipe, we will continue with a team account.
6. Click **Invite users**, and add the email addresses for any users you want to invite to the team. Separate email addresses with semicolons:

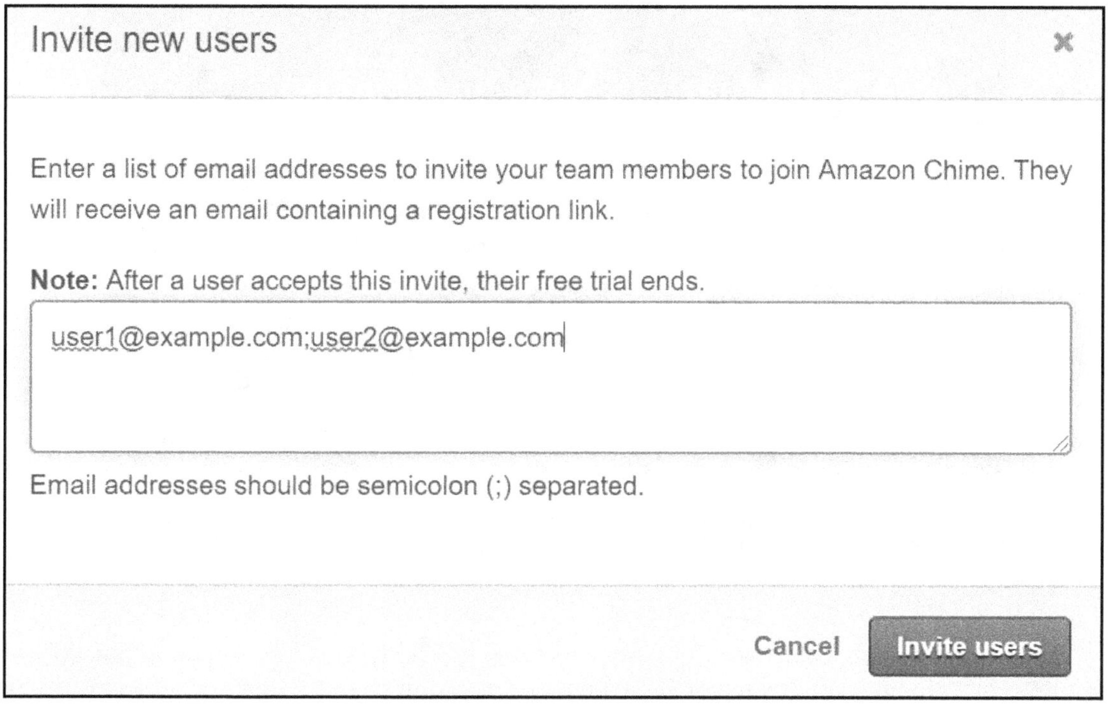

Invite new users   ✖

Enter a list of email addresses to invite your team members to join Amazon Chime. They will receive an email containing a registration link.

Note: After a user accepts this invite, their free trial ends.

```
user1@example.com;user2@example.com
```

Email addresses should be semicolon (;) separated.

Cancel   Invite users

Invite users

7. The invited users will receive an email that redirects them to the web version of Chime, as shown in the following screenshot. Send an invite to yourself so that you can experiment with the interface:

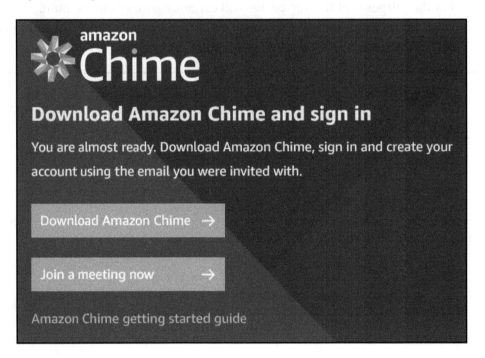

Chime invite

 Note that the login for Chime uses a login with Amazon, so you will need to have, or create, an Amazon account, using the invited email address.

8. You can create chat rooms and meetings, invite new contacts, start instant messages, and join meetings using this interface:

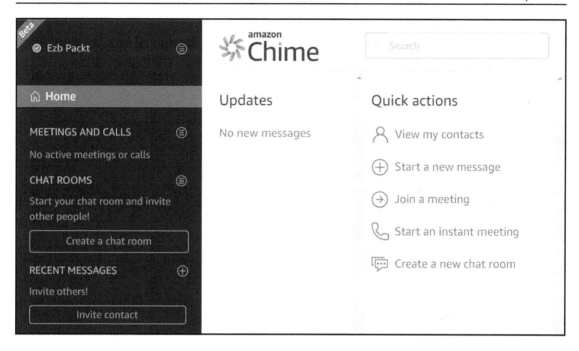

Chime interface

9. Once you are done exploring Chime features and if you don't plan to use the account in the future, go back to the Chime console and delete the account to avoid any future charges.

At this point, you should have a good understanding of what Chime has to offer. It is a stable cost-effective option for your company's communication needs.

How it works...

Chime integrates with email clients such as Outlook to allow you to add a Chime conference to your meetings. By adding `meet@chime.aws` to the invite, Chime will auto-call attendees when the meeting starts. Users can call in with their mobile phones or landlines, or they can use the audio and microphone on their computer.

When attending a Chime meeting, you can see a virtual roster of all attendees. The attendee list shows you who is present, who is running late, and who has declined the meeting. The meeting organizer can record the entire meeting, including video content, for later playback. Chime supports up to 16 desktop users on a single video call, and integrates with many popular conferencing systems.

Chime is well equipped to handle your security and compliance concerns. Chime encrypts all incoming and outgoing traffic using AES-256. This includes instant messages, voice calls, and video content. As Chime is built on top of AWS, it makes use of the security inherent with services such as **Identity and Access Management (IAM)**. CloudTrail and S3 can be used to audit all activities associated with Chime. One handy security-related feature is the ability to force logout for a user across all devices.

Chime can be a very cost-effective option as all of its basic features are free. See the Chime documentation for up-to-date details on costs for pro features, which, at the time of writing, range from $3 to $15 per month. Business Calling and Voice Connector also have pay-as-you-go pricing.

Use the calculator at `https://aws.amazon.com/chime/pricing/` to get an idea of what your monthly bill will be.

There's more...

Chime also allows you to make business calls using **voice over IP (VoIP)** with Voice Connector. Voice Connector allows you to terminate calls to regular phone lines, and allows regular phone calls to be directed into Chime. This service is often used in combination with AWS Direct Connect, which is a physical connection from your network into the AWS network, providing a very reliable connection from your **private branch exchange (PBX)**.

Chime also has integration with Alexa, so starting a conference call can be as simple as saying "Alexa, start my meeting."

Exploring the use of Alexa for Business

Alexa for Business allows you to integrate voice recognition devices, such as the Amazon Echo, into your corporate office environment in many creative ways. As someone who has experienced this personally, I can tell you that walking into a conference room, saying "Alexa, start my meeting," and watching the video conferencing equipment turn on and automatically configure itself is a real joy. It's a huge improvement over the usual 5-10 minutes of wasted time at the beginning of every meeting spent troubleshooting the conference phone or the camera on top of the TV. Alexa for Business integrates with your calendaring system, conferencing software such as Chime, and the hardware that sits in the conference room, turning what was once a hassle into a quick, intuitive interaction.

The capabilities of Alexa for Business go beyond just configuring A/V equipment. Custom skills can be developed to interact with just about any business system, such as your **customer relationship manager** (**CRM**) or **enterprise resource planning** (**ERP**) tool. Employees can configure their personal **Alexa Voice System** (**AVS**) devices at home to interact with the work environment, to enable scenarios such as checking their schedule for the day.

How to do it...

In this recipe, you have to execute the following:

1. Log in to your AWS account and go to the Alexa for Business dashboard.
2. Click the **Get Started** button.
3. You might be presented with a survey, which you can skip.

4. Scroll down on the left-hand menu and select **User Invitations**. Edit the template to add your company name and contact email and save it:

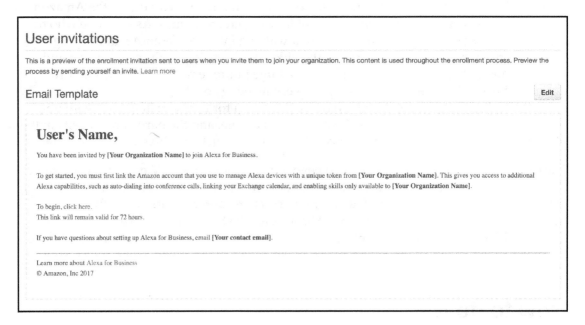

User invitations

This is a preview of the enrollment invitation sent to users when you invite them to join your organization. This content is used throughout the enrollment process. Preview the process by sending yourself an invite. Learn more

Email Template   Edit

User's Name,

You have been invited by [**Your Organization Name**] to join Alexa for Business.

To get started, you must first link the Amazon account that you use to manage Alexa devices with a unique token from [**Your Organization Name**]. This gives you access to additional Alexa capabilities, such as auto-dialing into conference calls, linking your Exchange calendar, and enabling skills only available to [**Your Organization Name**].

To begin, click here.
This link will remain valid for 72 hours.

If you have questions about setting up Alexa for Business, email [**Your contact email**].

Learn more about Alexa for Business
© Amazon, Inc 2017

Alexa User invitations

5. Choose **Users** from the left-hand menu and then click **Invite user**.
6. Send yourself an invite so that you can see the email that will be received by your users.

7. The email redirects to a web page where your users will be invited to join Alexa for Business with their personal Amazon account (or the account where they have their Echo device registered):

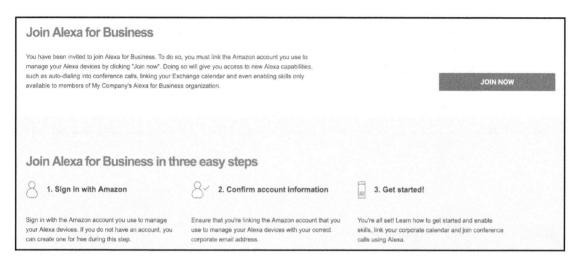

Join Alexa for Business

8. If you have an AVS device, go ahead and link your accounts.
9. Once you have finished enrollment, you can see the user **Enrolled** in the Alexa user console, as shown in the following screenshot:

Alexa Users

10. Select **Rooms** from the left-hand menu to configure rooms at your office location.

11. Click **Create room**.

12. Configure a unique conference room name, a profile name, an address, and device settings.

13. Click **Next**. If you have a device to add to a room, configure it here.

14. On the next screen, add any skill groups that you want available to this room. Skill groups are groups of Alexa skills that are either public, coming from the Marketplace, or private skills that are available for your company.

15. Click **Create room**, as shown in the following screenshot:

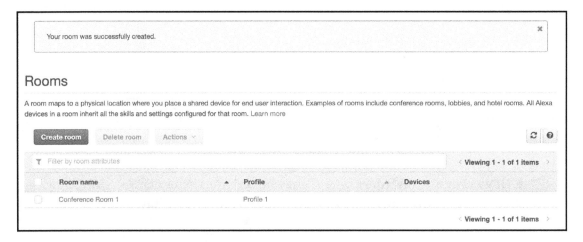

Alexa Rooms

16. Take some time to explore the other configuration options in the left-hand menu. They are very specific to your AVS devices, conference room equipment, and calendaring system, so we won't cover them in detail here.

At this point, you should have a basic understanding of how to set up Alexa for your office.

How it works...

AVS devices interact with the voice recognition services provided by Amazon in the cloud to interpret user requests and then take actions based on the settings you have configured for your office. One important thing to understand about how Alexa works is that the device itself actually has very little in the way of voice recognition and analysis capability built into it. The onboard software really only knows how to listen to the wake word—*Alexa*, *Amazon*, *Echo*, or *Computer*, depending on which word you have configured. Everything else happens in the cloud. When the device recognizes the wake word, the blue light on the top of the device starts spinning (depending on your device model), which means your voice is now being transmitted to Amazon's servers.

Amazon solved a remarkably difficult problem when it enabled reliable voice recognition from a device that may be on the other side of a room with lots of noisy distractions, and now that functionality can be used to enhance your office experience.

There's more...

Alexa for Business can integrate with the following popular conferencing systems:

- Cisco TelePresence
- Zoom Rooms
- Polycom

Alexa for Business blueprints can be used to jump-start the development of your own private skills. These skills could integrate directly with a private corporate database to provide your employees with a natural voice interaction for business-critical applications. You could build an FAQ skill that answers common questions asked by employees, or shares the latest company news, or use a skill to train new employees by quizzing them on important company knowledge.

Hosting your company's email with WorkMail

Amazon WorkMail is a full-featured host for your company's email, contacts, and calendar. It is compatible with common email clients, such as Microsoft Outlook and the iOS email app. At just $4 per user per month, it can be a very cost-effective alternative to more expensive email systems. Users also have the option of using a browser to access their WorkMail account directly.

WorkMail manages patching, security, backups, and audit logs for your company's email, without any complex configuration or manual intervention.

How to do it...

In this recipe, you will set up WorkMail for a single user to demonstrate its capabilities.

1. Log in to your AWS account and go to the WorkMail dashboard. Click the **Get started** button.
2. In this recipe, we will use the **Quick setup** option:

Set up your organization

Set up your organization using a new or existing directory, add a test mail domain (*<organization name>.awsapps.com*), and create your data encryption keys. Later, you can add custom mail domains, add users, groups and resources, and set up mobile device policies.

Learn more

Quick setup

Set up an Amazon WorkMail organization in less than 2 minutes. We'll do the following for you:

[Quick setup]

- Create a new directory
- Create a free test domain
- Use the default KMS key to encrypt mailbox contents

If you already have a directory, or want to use the WorkMail directory with WorkDocs, WorkSpaces and other applications, or use a custom KMS key, use the Standard setup instead.

Learn more

WorkMail Quick setup

3. On the next screen, give your organization a unique name:

WorkMail Organization name

4. Click **Create**. Provisioning can take a few minutes.
5. Once the organization is active, click on the alias link to go to the user provisioning screen.
6. Click **Create user** and add your own user details for testing.
7. Give the user a default password on the next screen and click **Add user**.
8. Go to the left-hand menu and click **Organization settings**:

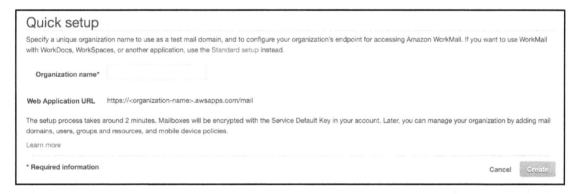

WorkMail Organization settings

9. Click the web application link to launch the browser-based email client for your domain.
10. Log in with the credentials you just created.

11. Click the letter icon to see your inbox:

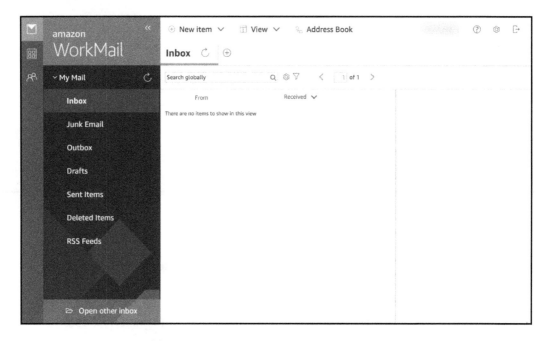

WorkMail Inbox

12. Click the calendar icon to see your calendar:

WorkMail Calendar

13. Click the contact icon to see your contacts:

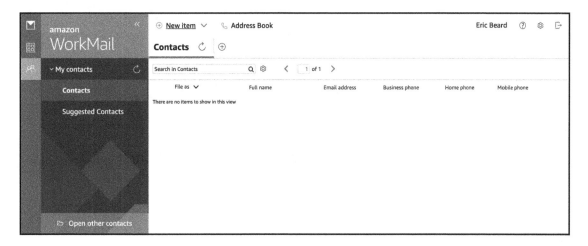

WorkMail Contacts

14. Use the interface to send yourself an email, create a calendar entry, and add a few contacts to get the feel for it. As you can see, it is a full-featured email environment.

15. Inspect the other tabs available on the **Organization settings** screen:
    - **Monitoring**: Store events in CloudWatch.
    - **Migration**: Configure Exchange migration.
    - **Journaling**: Configure an email address to receive a copy of all emails sent in your organization.
    - **Interoperability**: Set up integration between WorkMail and Exchange.
    - **SMTP Gateways**: Route outbound email through an SMTP appliance.
    - **Inbound Rules**: Set up inbound rules based on domains and addresses.
    - **Outbound Rules**: Set up outbound rules based on domains and addresses.

You now have a basic understanding of how to configure Amazon WorkMail. If you do not plan to keep using the organization you just created, remove it and delete the user directory, to avoid any future charges.

How it works...

You can create and maintain your own user directory in WorkMail, or you can leverage your on-premises directory of users so that you don't have to maintain them in two places. This is possible with both AD Connector and Microsoft AD running on AWS. It's also possible to integrate with an on-premises Exchange server.

WorkMail takes advantage of Amazon's cloud capabilities to keep storage costs low, make your data durable, secure it with services such as KMS, and save a journal of your email to meet your compliance needs.

Like every AWS service, WorkMail comes complete with an API and SDK to give you complete programmatic control and flexibility to implement custom functionality.

There's more...

Are you interested in migrating your email to Amazon WorkMail to save money and lower your administrative burden? Amazon has partnered with audriga and Transcend to offer a complete migration solution. Check out their offerings at the following links:

- `https://workmail.audriga.com/`
- `https://www.transend.com/products/transend-migrator-amazon-workmail`

AWS Partner Solutions

In this appendix, you will find a few helpful recipes that feature products that are offered by members of the **AWS Partner Network** (**APN**). Partners are a vital part of the overall AWS landscape and in many cases are a big reason to choose AWS over another cloud provider.

We will be covering the following recipes:

- Creating machine images using Hashicorp's Packer
- Monitoring and optimizing your AWS account with nOps
- Instrumenting your lambda functions with IOPipe

By diving into the AWS partner community and learning about partner products, you will be well-equipped to handle just about any task related to your cloud infrastructure.

You can learn more about the APN here: `https://aws.amazon.com/partners/`.

 Pay special attention to those partners who have achieved an AWS competency designation. These partners have passed a rigorous audit process to make sure their solutions are well-architected, and each of them features multiple public case studies that can be used as a reference to validate their capabilities. You can learn more about the AWS Competency Program here: `https://aws.amazon.com/partners/competencies/`.

Creating machine images with Hashicorp's Packer

Creating or *baking* your own **Amazon Machine Images** (**AMIs**) is a key part of systems administration in AWS. Having a prebaked image helps you provision your servers faster, easier, and more consistently than configuring them by hand.

Packer is the de facto standard tool that helps you make your own AMIs. By automating the launch, configuration, and cleanup of your instances, it makes sure you get a repeatable image every time.

In this recipe, we will create an image with the Apache web server pre-installed and configured. While this is a simple example, it is also a very common use case.

By baking in your web server, you can scale up your web serving layer to dynamically match the demands on your websites. Having the software already installed and configured means you get the fastest and most reliable startup possible.

Getting ready

For this recipe, you must have the Packer tool available on your system. Download and install Packer from the project's website at `https://www.packer.io/downloads.html`.

Packer connects to your AWS account according to your current default AWS CLI configuration. Make sure that your CLI is configured properly before attempting this recipe.

How to do it...

1. Create a new Packer template file and start by defining an `amazon-ebs` builder in the `builders` section. Note that the entire file, `13-01-Hashi.json`, is available in the GitHub repository of this book `https://github.com/PacktPublishing/AWS-SysOps-Cookbook-Second-Edition`:

```
"builders": [
  {
    "type": "amazon-ebs",
    "instance_type": "t2.micro",
    "region": "us-east-1",
    "source_ami": "ami-9be6f38c",
    "ssh_username": "ec2-user",
    "ami_name": "aws-linux-apache {{timestamp}}"
  }
],
```

 The entire template file must be a valid JSON object. Remember to enclose the sections in curly braces: { ... }.

2. Create a `provisioners` section and include the following snippet to install and activate Apache:

```
"provisioners": [
  {
    "type": "shell",
    "inline": [
      "sudo yum install -y httpd",
      "sudo chkconfig httpd on"
    ]
  }
]
```

3. Save the file with a specific name, such as `13-01-Hashi.json`.

4. Validate the configuration file you've created with the following `packer validate` command:

   `packer validate 13-01-Hashi.json`

5. When valid, build the AMI with the following command:

   `packer build13-01-Hashi.json`

6. Wait until the process is complete. While it is running, you will see an output similar to the following:

```
                       awsac — packer • packer build src/04-creating-machine-images.json — 114×31
$ packer build src/04-creating-machine-images.json
amazon-ebs output will be in this color.

==> amazon-ebs: Prevalidating AMI Name...
    amazon-ebs: Found Image ID: ami-9be6f38c
==> amazon-ebs: Creating temporary keypair: packer_587a9f63-1bcc-7e85-b9c9-eeec160cc172
==> amazon-ebs: Creating temporary security group for this instance...
==> amazon-ebs: Authorizing access to port 22 the temporary security group...
==> amazon-ebs: Launching a source AWS instance...
    amazon-ebs: Instance ID: i-0c249b526d0cabe9b
==> amazon-ebs: Waiting for instance (i-0c249b526d0cabe9b) to become ready...
==> amazon-ebs: Waiting for SSH to become available...
==> amazon-ebs: Connected to SSH!
==> amazon-ebs: Provisioning with shell script: /var/folders/vt/1kw7w5ns6h16vt8j_tk08pzm0000gn/T/packer-shell21831
1435
    amazon-ebs: Loaded plugins: priorities, update-motd, upgrade-helper
    amazon-ebs: Resolving Dependencies
    amazon-ebs: --> Running transaction check
    amazon-ebs: ---> Package httpd.x86_64 0:2.2.31-1.8.amzn1 will be installed
```

Packer build

7. Take note of the AMI ID returned by Packer so that you can use it when launching instances in the future:

```
      amazon-ebs: Verifying    : httpd-tools-2.2.31-1.8.amzn1.x86_64                    1/5
      amazon-ebs: Verifying    : apr-1.5.1-1.12.amzn1.x86_64                            2/5
      amazon-ebs: Verifying    : httpd-2.2.31-1.8.amzn1.x86_64                          3/5
      amazon-ebs: Verifying    : apr-util-ldap-1.4.1-4.17.amzn1.x86_64                  4/5
      amazon-ebs: Verifying    : apr-util-1.4.1-4.17.amzn1.x86_64                       5/5
      amazon-ebs:
      amazon-ebs: Installed:
      amazon-ebs: httpd.x86_64 0:2.2.31-1.8.amzn1
      amazon-ebs:
      amazon-ebs: Dependency Installed:
      amazon-ebs: apr.x86_64 0:1.5.1-1.12.amzn1              apr-util.x86_64 0:1.4.1-4.17.amzn1
      amazon-ebs: apr-util-ldap.x86_64 0:1.4.1-4.17.amzn1 httpd-tools.x86_64 0:2.2.31-1.8.amzn1
      amazon-ebs:
      amazon-ebs: Complete!
==> amazon-ebs: Stopping the source instance...
==> amazon-ebs: Waiting for the instance to stop...
==> amazon-ebs: Creating the AMI: aws-linux-apache 1484431202
      amazon-ebs: AMI: ami-fb816ded
==> amazon-ebs: Waiting for AMI to become ready...
==> amazon-ebs: Terminating the source AWS instance...
==> amazon-ebs: Cleaning up any extra volumes...
==> amazon-ebs: No volumes to clean up, skipping
==> amazon-ebs: Deleting temporary security group...
==> amazon-ebs: Deleting temporary keypair...
Build 'amazon-ebs' finished.

==> Builds finished. The artifacts of successful builds are:
--> amazon-ebs: AMIs were created:

us-east-1: ami-fb816ded
$
```

Packer build finished

Now, you can log in to your AWS account and go to the EC2 dashboard to verify the creation of the AMI in your default region.

How it works...

While this is a very simple recipe, there is a lot going on behind the scenes. This is why we recommend you use Packer to create your machine images.

We will go over the following items in detail in the following subsections:

- Template
- Validating the template
- Building the AMI

Template

In the `builders` section of the template, we define our build details.

We are using the most common type of AMI builder: `amazon-ebs`. There are other types of AWS builders available too, for instance, storage-backed instance types.

Next, we define the type of instance to use when baking.

 Make sure that you can decrease the time it takes to bake your instance by using a larger instance size. Remember that the minimum price paid for an instance is one hour of billable time.

The `source_ami` property in this recipe is an AWS Linux AMI ID in the `region` we have specified. `ssh_username` allows you to set the username that's used to connect and run `provisioners` on the instance. This will be determined by your operating system, which, in our case, is `ec2-user`.

Finally, the `ami_name` field includes the built-in packer variable called `{{timestamp}}`. This ensures the AMI you create will always have a unique name.

Validating the template

The `packer validate` command is a quick way to ensure your template is free of syntax errors before you launch any instances.

Building the AMI

Once you have created and validated your template, the `packer build` command does the following for you:

1. First, it creates a one-time key pair for SSH access to the instance.
2. Then, it creates a dedicated security group to control access to the instance.
3. After completing the preceding step, it launches an instance.
4. Then, it waits until SSH is ready to receive connections.
5. Afterward, it runs the provisioner steps on the instance.
6. Then, it stops the instance.
7. After this, it generates an AMI from the stopped instance.
8. Finally, it terminates the instance.

Check out the Packer documentation for more provisioners and functionality: `https://www.packer.io/docs/`.

There's more...

While Packer makes the administration of images much easier on AWS, there are still a few things to watch out for:

- Debugging
- Orphaned resources
- Deregistering AMIs
- Other platforms

Debugging

Obviously, with so many steps being automated for you, there are many things that can potentially go wrong. Packer gives you a few different ways to debug issues with your builds.

One of the most useful arguments to use with Packer is the `-debug` flag. This will force you to manually confirm each step *before* it takes place. Doing this makes it easy to work out exactly which step in the command is failing, which, in turn, usually makes it obvious what needs to be changed.

Another useful thing to do is to raise the level of logging output during a Packer command. You can do this by setting the `PACKER_LOG` variable to `true`. The easiest way to do this is by using `PACKER_LOG=1` at the beginning of your Packer command line. This will mean you get a lot more information printed to the console (for example, SSH logs, AWS API calls, and so on) during the command. You may even want to run with this level of logging normally in your builds for auditing purposes.

Orphaned resources

Packer does a great job of managing and cleaning up the resource it uses, but it can only do that while it is running.

If your Packer job aborts for any reason (most likely network issues), then there may be some resources left **orphaned**, or **unmanaged**. It is good practice to check for any Packer instances (they will have *Packer* in their name) and stop them if there are no active Packer jobs running.

You may also need to clean up any leftover key pairs and security groups, but this is less of an issue as there is no cost associated with them (unlike instances).

Deregistering AMIs

As it becomes easier to create AMIs, you may find you end up with more than you need!

AMIs are made up of EC2 snapshots, which are stored in S3. There is a cost associated with storing snapshots, so you will want to clean them up periodically. Given the size of most AMIs (usually a few GBs), it is unlikely to be one of your major costs.

An even greater cost is the administrative overhead of managing too many AMIs. As your images improve and fixes are applied (especially security fixes), you may want to prevent people from using them.

To remove an AMI, you must first *deregister* it and then remove the underlying snapshots.

 Make sure you do not deregister AMIs that are currently in use. For example, an auto-scaling group that references a deregistered AMI will fail to launch new instances!

You can easily deregister snapshots through the web console or using the AWS CLI tool.

Once an AMI is no longer registered, you can remove the associated snapshots. Packer automatically adds the AMI ID to the snapshot's description. By searching your snapshots for the deregistered AMI ID, you can find which ones need to be deleted.

You will not be able to delete snapshots if the AMI has not been deregistered, or if deregistration is still taking place (it can take a few minutes).

Other platforms

It is also worth noting that Packer can build for more platforms than just AWS. You can also build images for VMWare, Docker, and many others.

This means you could build almost exactly the same machine image (for example, using Docker) that you have in AWS locally. This makes it much more convenient when setting up local development environments, for example.

 Check the `builders` section of the Packer documentation for details.

Monitoring and optimizing your AWS account with nOps

In this book, you have learned about native AWS monitoring tools such as Trusted Advisor and CloudWatch, which are very important for an administrator to master. A partner product called nOps augments and extends this native functionality to provide user-friendly dashboards and reports to help you quickly get an overview of your account. nOps does some impressive deep analysis of the resources in your account to make recommendations around cost-saving and security improvements. If you are conducting a Well-Architected review of a workload, nOps can be a huge time-saver since it automatically gathers data from your account and answers many questions in a deterministic fashion, rather than relying on memory or documentation that might be out of date.

In this recipe, you will learn how to create a nOps trial account, connect it to your AWS account, and run reports to give you insights into everything that is happening within your infrastructure.

Getting ready

To complete this recipe, you will need to create an S3 bucket in your account that nOps will use for storing log files:

1. Log in to your AWS account and go to the S3 dashboard.
2. Create a new bucket for use by nOps and note down the name of the new bucket. Use the default settings for the bucket, taking care to make sure it is not public.

How to do it...

To complete this recipe, you will need to create a nOps trial account:

1. Go to the nOps site at `https://www.nops.io/` and click **START FREE NOPS TRIAL**.
2. Enter your email address and click **Get Started**.
3. Click **Add AWS Account** to associate your AWS account with your nOps account.
4. Use the nOps setup wizard to automate the install process.

> Go to the nOps help site if you get stuck during the install process: `https://help.nops.io/`.

5. You will be redirected to the AWS console. Review the CloudFormation summary, check the box to acknowledge that AWS CloudFormation might create IAM resources, and click **Create stack**.
6. Monitor the stack's creation until it is complete:

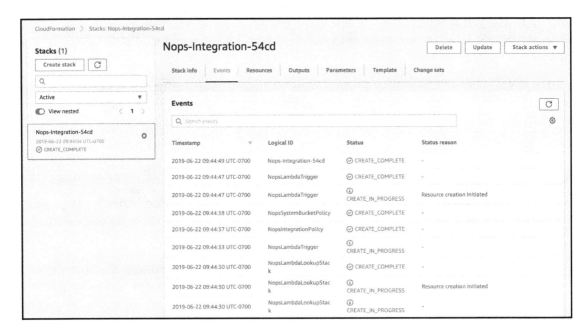

nOps CloudFormation stack

7. Log in to your nOps account. At first, much of the reporting will be blank. Wait a few hours for nOps to run its checks and populate reporting. Then, you will see a screen similar to the following:

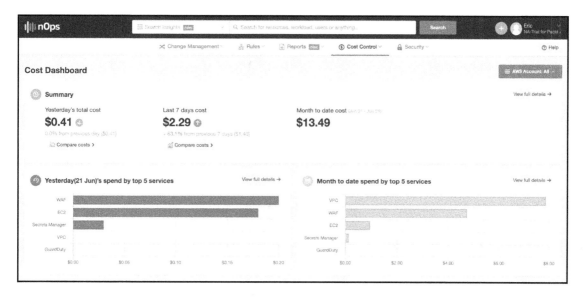

The nOps dashboard

8. Take some time to explore the dashboard. It features the following widgets:
   - A summary of your account activity
   - Yesterday's spend by the top five services
   - Month to date spend by the top five services
   - Unused resources
   - Underutilized resources
   - Month-to-date top five most expensive resources
   - Cost by user
   - Cost trend

9. Go to **Reports** from the main menu and select **WAR Report**. This report will grade your compliance with the Well-Architected Framework across a diverse set of categories:

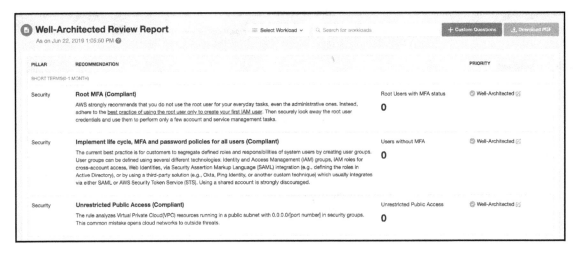

The nOps WAR report

10. Go to the **Cost Control** menu and select **AWS Resources Cost**. Select **Spend by AWS Products** to see how your costs are divided by product:

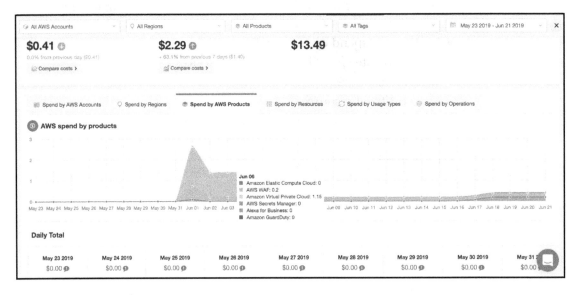

nOps spend by AWS products

Continue to explore nOps to learn about the wide variety of reports it offers.

How it works...

When you set up nOps in your AWS account, the following CloudFormation stack is created: `https://s3-us-west-2.amazonaws.com/nops-users/nOpsRole.yaml`.

This stack creates a cross-account role that allows the nOps service to get access to your resources. The S3 bucket you created for nOps is used for log data that populates the nOps reports when you log in to your account at `https://www.nops.io`.

nOps queries your resources to produce reports that are similar to the functionality of AWS Trusted Advisor, and also automates answers to many of the questions that come up during a Well-Architected review. It is common for nOps users to quickly find significant cost-saving opportunities within their accounts, and also find places in their architecture where they are not following best practices.

There's more...

We only touched on the basics of nOps in this recipe. Here are some of the additional features that it offers:

- A security compliance dashboard to point out areas where you could improve your security posture
- Reserved instance planning to help you make decisions about purchasing reserved EC2 instances
- A spot advisor that shows how much you could save by switching on-demand EC2 instances to Spot instances
- An infrastructure changes report that shows you all of the changes that have been made to your account, who made them, and the costs associated with the changes
- An inventory report that gives you a quick high-level view of common resources that have been provisioned in your account
- A rules engine that allows you to configure custom compliance rules for your account
- Readiness reports for compliance accreditation, such as SOC 2 and HIPAA

While it's possible to glean much of this information yourself by cobbling together data from AWS Trusted Advisor, AWS CloudTrail, and AWS CloudWatch, nOps is a huge time-saver that can quickly bring issues to the forefront so they can be addressed in a timely fashion.

Using IOPipe to instrument your lambda functions

IOPipe is a multi-tenant SaaS application that hooks into your Lambda functions via a function wrapper that you apply to your event handlers. It records detailed trace data from your function invocations so that you can profile your code as it runs. It helps developers while they are debugging their code, and it also helps operations spot problems quickly. Each time you make an AWS API call from within your code, the performance of that call is recorded so that you can see exactly where excess time is being spent. For example, you can see the average time it takes to execute a query of your DynamoDB table, or how long it takes to put an object into an S3 bucket.

How to do it...

In this recipe, you will create an IOPipe trial account, author a new lambda function, and observe performance information for that function as it runs. Let's get started:

1. Go to the IOPipe site at `https://www.iopipe.com/` and click **Get Started**.
2. Fill out the user profile and create your trial account.

3. On the following screen, enter a default team name and then click **New Project**. Enter a name for your project:

IOPipe setup

4. Under **Plans**, select **Lite**, which is free of charge. You don't have to enter credit card details for the lite plan. Click **Create Team**.

5. On the following screen, you will see your security token and links to tutorials for various programming languages.

6. Log in to your AWS account and go to the CodeStar dashboard. CodeStar is an AWS service that allows you to create a complete serverless application, including a code repository in CodeCommit, a lambda function, a CodeBuild project, and a CodePipeline configuration so that you can automatically deploy your code after each change. We are using CodeStar for this recipe because we need to be able to install a Node.js package, which is not currently possible via the lambda console. Also, it's good practice to avoid directly editing lambda functions in the console, and CodeStar gives us a Cloud9 web-based **Integrated Development Environment (IDE)** for this:

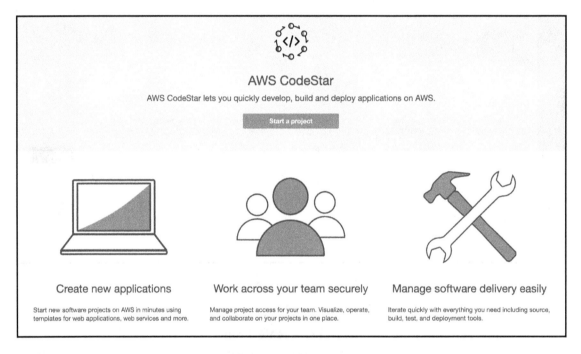

Starting a new project with AWS CodeStar

7. Click **Start a project**. You will be presented with a dialog asking you if you wish to create the CodeStar service role. Click **Yes, create role**:

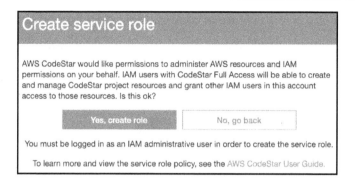

Creating the CodeStar service role

8. There are a variety of project templates to choose from with CodeStar. For this recipe, select the Node.js lambda web application:

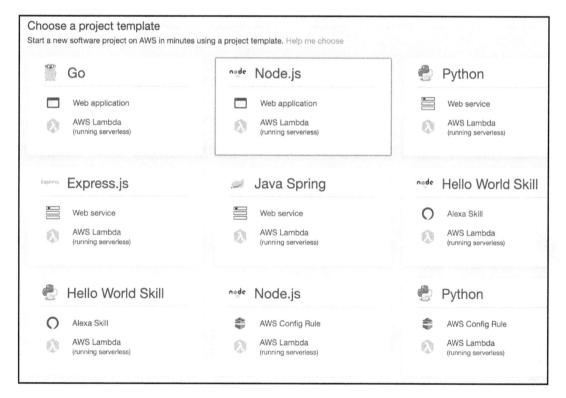

CodeStar project templates

9. Give the project a unique name and click **Next**. Then, click **Create project**.

10. When you are given a choice of code editors, select **AWS Cloud9**:

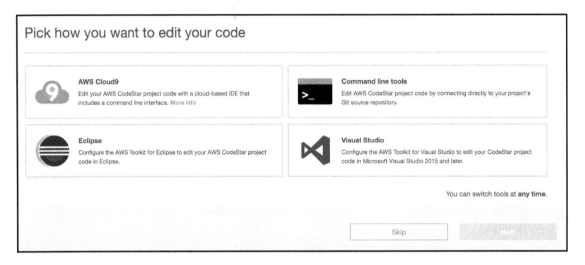

CodeStar editor selection

11. Go with the default configuration for Cloud9 and click **Next**.
12. It will take a few minutes for CodeStar to complete the setup process, but, once it's done, you'll see a screen similar to the following:

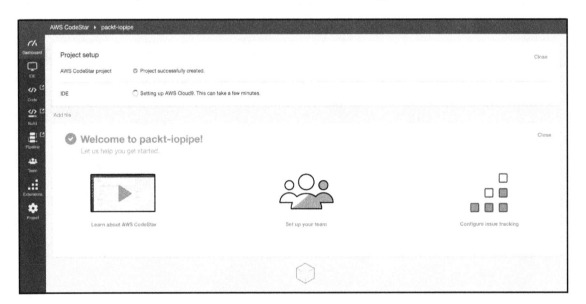

AWS CodeStar dashboard

13. Once the setup is complete, select the IDE from the left-hand side menu to open your Cloud9 environment, as follows:

AWS Cloud9

14. Expand the project folder and open both `index.js` and `template.yml`. The YAML file is your **Serverless Application Model** (**SAM**) template that defines your resources, and the JavaScript file is your lambda function.

15. In the Terminal window below the editor pane, install the `@iopipe/iopipe` NPM package using the `npm install --save` command, as follows:

```
ezb.packt.admin1:~/environment $ cd packt-iopipe/
ezb.packt.admin1:~/environment/packt-iopipe (master) $ npm install
--save @iopipe/iopipe
npm notice created a lockfile as package-lock.json. You should
commit this file.
+ @iopipe/iopipe@1.14.0
added 85 packages from 59 contributors and audited 245 packages in
7.321s
found 0 vulnerabilities
```

16. In the `template.yml` file, define an environment variable to hold your IOPipe token, as follows:

```
Resources:
  GetHelloWorld:
    Type: AWS::Serverless::Function
    Properties:
      Handler: index.get
      Runtime: nodejs8.10
      Environment:
        Variables:
          IOPIPE_TOKEN: [YOUR TOKEN HERE]
      Role:
        Fn::GetAtt:
        - LambdaExecutionRole
        - Arn
      Events: [...]
```

17. Also in the `template.yml` file, change the deployment type to be `AllAtOnce`, which will speed up the deployment for testing purposes:

```
Globals:
  Function:
    AutoPublishAlias: live
    DeploymentPreference:
      Enabled: true
      Type: AllAtOnce
      Role: !Ref CodeDeployRole
```

18. To make a change to the deployment preference, you will need to modify the policy attached to the CodeStar CloudFormation role. Go to the IAM dashboard and search for a role named `CodeStarWorker-[PROJECT NAME]-CloudFormation`.

19. Edit the inline policy in that role to include `codedeploy:UpdateDeploymentGroup`, as follows:

Editing the CodeStar CloudFormation policy to allow changes to deployment preferences

20. Modify the lambda function in `index.js` so that it uses the IOPipe wrapper:

```javascript
'use strict';

var fs = require('fs');
var path = require('path');
var iopipe = require('@iopipe/iopipe')();

exports.get = iopipe(function(event, context, callback) {
  var contents = fs.readFileSync(`public${path.sep}index.html`);
  var result = {
    statusCode: 200,
    body: contents.toString(),
    headers: {'content-type': 'text/html'}
  };
  callback(null, result);
});
```

21. Save `index.js` and `template.yml`.

22. Create a `.gitignore` file and add `node_modules` to it, since you don't want to commit all of the NPM packages that have been installed. Then, commit your changes to the CodeCommit repository, as follows:

```
ezb.packt.admin1:~/environment/packt-iopipe (master) $ git add .
ezb.packt.admin1:~/environment/packt-iopipe (master) $ git commit -
m "IOPipe"
ezb.packt.admin1:~/environment/packt-iopipe (master) $ git push
```

23. CodeStar will detect the change to the repository and kick off the CodePipeline project that was automatically set up for you. Go back to the CodeStar dashboard to watch the progress of your build:

CodeStar deployment progress

24. Once the deployment progress has completed, scroll up to application endpoints and click the URL for your application to test it:

CodeStar automatically deploys your application to a production endpoint after each push

25. Refresh that page a few times so that we have a few lambda invocations to track using IOPipe.

26. Go back to the IOPipe dashboard and look at the invocations:

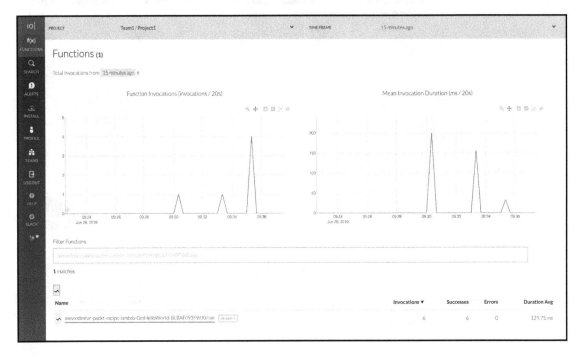

IOPipe dashboard: The text and numbers in this image are intentionally illegible

27. Click the name of the function at the bottom of the screen to see details about the function:

IOPipe function details: The text and numbers in this image are intentionally illegible

You now have experience with rapidly creating a new web application with AWS CodeStar and wiring up detailed tracing to your Lambda function with IOPipe. Take some time to explore the functionality offered by IOPipe, and then, if you no longer need this CodeStar project, be sure to delete it so that you do not incur any future charges on your AWS account.

How it works...

The wrapper you put around your Lambda event handler instruments your code so that asynchronous messages are sent to IOPipe each time your code makes an action. This data is recorded and cataloged to enable a variety of reports and alerts. With Node.js, you can review the IOPipe package located at https://www.npmjs.com/package/@iopipe/iopipe. The source code can be found in this book's GitHub repository at https://github.com/iopipe/iopipe-js.

As an Advanced AWS Technology Partner, and as a DevOps competency holder, IOPipe's architecture, which naturally runs on AWS, has been audited for best practices around security and reliability, so you can rest assured that the data being emitted by your lambda functions is safe and secure.

We will study some more functions in the following subsections:

- Metrics dashboards
- Alerting
- Profiling
- Labels and search

Metrics dashboards

A real-time view into the number of times a certain function has been invoked, along with the average duration of those function calls, can be a huge help when troubleshooting code that is misbehaving, and it can also be used by operations to quickly spot outlier behavior.

Alerting

IOPipe has a flexible alert system that allows you to configure rules and integrations with systems such as Slack and PagerDuty. You can be alerted any time a lambda function causes an error, or when the average invocation time of a function exceeds a certain threshold.

Profiling

If you are using Node.js, which is one of the most popular languages available for Lambda, you can do CPU profiling of a running function. This is a detailed profile of the performance characteristics of each individual statement in your code, which means you will spend a lot less time adding log statements to the code to see what's going on. You can compare profiles after revisions to see the effect of your latest changes.

Labels and search

If you have a large number of complex functions, which is inevitable if you have converted to a completely server-less application architecture, then you know that it can be very difficult to sort through your logs when something goes wrong. With IOPipe, it's possible to add labels to your code so that you can easily categorize various segments across different lambda functions, and a flexible search engine lets you dig through extensive log files to find exactly what you are looking for.

There's more...

IOPipe will also send you a weekly email report that details the performance of your functions. This email points out changes in behavior for your functions, common errors that are thrown by your code, and it also summarizes the alerts that were sent based on rules that you have configured.

Other Books You May Enjoy

If you enjoyed this book, you may be interested in these other books by Packt:

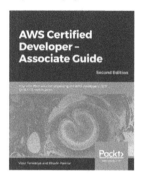

AWS Certified Developer - Associate Guide - Second Edition
Vipul Tankariya, Bhavin Parmar

ISBN: 978-1-78961-731-3

- Create and manage users, groups, and permissions using AWS IAM services
- Create a secured VPC with Public and Private Subnets, Network Access Control, and Security groups
- Launching your first EC2 instance, and working with it
- Handle application traffic with ELB and monitor AWS resources with CloudWatch
- Work with AWS storage services such as S3, Glacier, and CloudFront
- Get acquainted with AWS DynamoDB a NoSQL database service
- Use SWS to coordinate work across distributed application components

AWS for Administrators
Wayde Gilchrist

ISBN: 978-1-78646-319-7

- Get to grips with Identity and Access Management and know how to create users, groups, and roles
- Use Cloud Watch to monitor default and custom key performance metrics
- Understand how to log access and configuration changes for AWS deployments
- Deploy and update your infrastructure and applications in AWS
- Discover techniques to keep your data and applications secure using the newest services from AWS

Leave a review - let other readers know what you think

Please share your thoughts on this book with others by leaving a review on the site that you bought it from. If you purchased the book from Amazon, please leave us an honest review on this book's Amazon page. This is vital so that other potential readers can see and use your unbiased opinion to make purchasing decisions, we can understand what our customers think about our products, and our authors can see your feedback on the title that they have worked with Packt to create. It will only take a few minutes of your time, but is valuable to other potential customers, our authors, and Packt. Thank you!

Index

www.ingramcontent.com/pod-product-compliance
Lightning Source LLC
Chambersburg PA
CBHW060642060326
40690CB00020B/4489